THE SOCIAL JUSTICE
TORAH COMMENTARY

D1218444

The Social Justice Torah Commentary

Edited by
Rabbi Barry H. Block

Foreword by
Rabbi Andrea L. Weiss, PhD

Afterword by
Rabbi Jonah Dov Pesner

CCAR
Press

CENTRAL CONFERENCE OF AMERICAN RABBIS

5781 New York 2021

Published by Reform Judaism Publishing, a division of CCAR Press
355 Lexington Avenue, New York, NY 10017
(212) 972-3636 | info@ccarpress.org | www.ccarpress.org

LIBRARY OF CONGRESS CATALOGING-IN-PUBLICATION DATA
Names: Block, Barry H, Rabbi, editor.
Title: The social justice Torah commentary / Rabbi Barry H. Block, editor ;
   foreword by Rabbi Andrea Weiss, PhD ; afterword by Rabbi Jonah Dov
   Pesner.
Description: New York, NY : Central Conference of American Rabbis, CCAR
   Press, 5781 = 2021. | Summary: "Contributors write essays for week's
   Torah portion regarding social justice. Chapters address key issues such
   as racism, climate change, mass incarceration, immigration, disability,
   women's rights, voting rights"-- Provided by publisher.
Identifiers: LCCN 2021001946 (print) | LCCN 2021001947 (ebook) | ISBN
   9780881233834 (paperback) | ISBN 9780881233841 (ebook)
Subjects: LCSH: Bible. Pentateuch--Criticism, interpretation, etc. | Social
   justice--Biblical teaching.
Classification: LCC BS1225.52 .S63 2021 (print) | LCC BS1225.52 (ebook) |
   DDC 221.8/303372--dc23
LC record available at https://lccn.loc.gov/2021001946
LC ebook record available at https://lccn.loc.gov/2021001947

Text design and composition
by Scott-Martin Kosofsky
at The Philidor Company,
Rhinebeck, NY.

Cover art: Trude Guermonprez, (American, b. Germany, 1910–1976). Drawing
(detail), Design for Ark Curtain, Beth Am Synagogue, Los Altos, CA, 1968. Brush
and gouache, graphite on cream cardboard, 13 in. × 20¾ in. (330 × 527 mm).
Gift of Mr. Eric and Mrs. Sylvia Elsesser, The Trude Guermonprez Archives,
1993-121-71, Cooper Hewitt, Smithsonian Design Museum. Photo: Matt Flynn
© Smithsonian Institution. Digital image: Cooper Hewitt, Smithsonian Design
Museum/Art Resource, NY.

Printed in the United States of America
10 9 8 7 6 5 4 3 2 1 0

Contents

Leviticus

Foreword

RABBI ANDREA L. WEISS, PhD

וְיִגַּל כַּמַּיִם מִשְׁפָּט וּצְדָקָה כְּנַחַל אֵיתָן:
V'yigal kamayim mishpat utz'dakah k'nachal eitan.
Let justice well up like water,
righteousness like an unfailing stream.
—*Amos* 5:24

SOME TWENTY-SEVEN HUNDRED YEARS AGO, the prophet Amos
encapsulated an inspiring vision of justice in just six Hebrew words.
With the terseness that defines poetry and the evocative power that
marks metaphor, this ancient Israelite expressed the expectation that
individuals and the societies they inhabit will establish and execute
justice. Putting this well-known verse in context, the passage quotes
God scolding the Israelites:

> I loathe, I spurn your festivals,
> I am not appeased by your solemn assemblies.
> If you offer Me burnt offerings—or your meal offerings—
> I will not accept them;
> I will pay no heed
> To your gifts of fatlings.
> Spare Me the sound of your hymns,
> And let Me not hear the music of your lutes.
> But let justice well up like water,
> Righteousness like an unfailing stream. (Amos 5:21–24)

In the most emphatic language, God rejects religious rituals—all
means humans employ to connect to or communicate with the
Divine—if those who perform those rituals do not act in an ethical,
upstanding manner.

Other biblical prophets reiterate this message, insisting that justice and morality take precedence over the performance of religious
rites. In Isaiah 1, God spurns sacrifices, prayer, and festival gatherings
since "your hands are full of blood" (1:15). Instead, God demands:

> Cease to do evil;
> Learn to do good.
> Devote yourselves to justice;
> Aid the wronged.
> Uphold the rights of the orphan;
> Defend the cause of the widow. (Isaiah 1:16–17)[1]

The prophetic message is simple: What matters most is justice.
What God desires is a world in which humans care for one another.
According to Isaiah 58:6–7, this means a world in which we help the
oppressed to go free, we share our bread with the hungry, we clothe
the naked, we do not ignore our kin. The prophets warn us that if
there is no justice, there can be no peace:

> The way of peace they do not know,
> And there is no justice where they go . . .
> We hope for light, but, look, darkness . . .
> We hope for justice but there is none,
> for rescue—it is far from us. (Isaiah 59:8–11)[2]

The divine demand for justice repeats throughout the Bible. In
Psalm 82, God demotes the members of the divine assembly who
fail to administer justice on earth. Disappointed and exasperated by
these lesser deities, God declares:

> How long will you judge dishonestly
> and show favor to the wicked? selah
> Do justice to the poor and the orphan.
> Vindicate the lowly and the wretched.
> Free the poor and the needy,
> And from the hand of the wicked save them. (Psalm 82:2–4)

Psalm 82, like Isaiah 1 and other biblical texts, associates the administration of justice with the protection of the most vulnerable individuals, which in an ancient Israelite context meant the fatherless, the

widow, the stranger, and the poor.[3] According to Robert Alter, this psalm presents a mythological account meant to explain "the infuriating preponderance of injustice in the world."[4]

The Book of Job probes the "preponderance of injustice" that besets "a blameless and upright man who fears God and shuns evil" (Job 1:8). Job shouts and struggles, striving to make sense of a world in which bad things happen to a good person and it appears that "there is no justice" (Job 19:7). In contrast, the Book of Proverbs depicts the opposite scenario, promising that rewards will come to those who cultivate the knowledge and discipline needed to live a virtuous, just life. Like other examples of ancient wisdom literature, Proverbs distills the divine demand for justice into a series of pithy sayings. For instance, Proverbs 2:8–9 encourages the listener "to keep the paths of justice" and to "understand righteousness, justice, and uprightness," each one a "pathway of good." Proverbs 16:8 advises, "Better a pittance in righteousness, than abundant yield without justice." Proverbs 29:4 observes, "A king makes a land stand firm through justice, but a deceitful man destroys it." In this biblical book, injustice does not go unpunished, and only good things happen to good people.

Turning to the Torah, the Five Books of Moses teach us not just why, but also how, to fulfill God's demand for justice and morality. The collections of rules and case law found in the Torah turn the abstract concept of justice into concrete actions carried out in the home, in the field, and at the city gate. Take Exodus 23:2–3: "You shall neither side with the mighty to do wrong . . . nor shall you show deference to a poor person in a dispute." Or Leviticus 19:10: "You shall not pick your vineyard bare, or gather the fallen fruit of your vineyard; you shall leave them for the poor and the stranger: I the Eternal am your God." Or Deuteronomy 22:1: "If you see your fellow Israelite's ox or sheep gone astray, do not ignore it; you must take it back to your peer."[5] Adele Berlin summarizes the common thread that binds together the Torah's wide-ranging laws: "The goal is to create a balanced society in which the poor and weak are legally protected from the rich and strong, in which property and human lives are respected, and—most importantly—in which individuals are subject to the community and its laws."[6]

Outside of these legal collections, various narrative passages in the Torah explore the complexities involved in carrying out the command to pursue justice.[7] Abraham challenges God's decision to destroy the inhabitants of Sodom and Gomorrah: "Will You indeed sweep away the innocent along with the wicked? . . . Must not the Judge of all the earth do justly?" (Genesis 18:23, 25). The daughters of Zelophehad question the fairness of laws of inheritance: "Let not our father's name be lost to his clan just because he had no son! Give us a holding among our father's kinsmen!" (Numbers 27:4). After God declares, "The plea of Zelophehad's daughters is just," Moses enacts a new law to ensure that the legal system remains responsive and equitable (Numbers 27:7–11). These and other passages preserve the ways our biblical ancestors strove to "keep justice and do righteousness" (Isaiah 56:1).

In laws and stories, poems and prayers, the imperative to practice justice permeates the Torah. *The Social Justice Torah Commentary* traces this theme from *B'reishit* to *V'zot Hab'rachah*. By bringing a social justice lens to each *parashah*, the commentators in this valuable volume shed new light on the Torah and show how these ancient texts still motivate us to seek justice today. This commentary urges us to do our part to create a world in which "justice will well up like water and righteousness like an unfailing stream."

NOTES

1. Also see Isaiah 58:1–10; Jeremiah 6:19–20; Hosea 6:6, 8:13; Joel 2:12–13; Malachi 1:10, 2:13.
2. This and the translations of Psalm 82 and Proverbs from Robert Alter, *The Hebrew Bible*, vol. 3 (New York: W. W. Norton, 2019).
3. Also see Exodus 22:20, 23:5; Deuteronomy 10:18, 14:29, 24:14, and elsewhere.
4. Alter, *The Hebrew Bible*, 200.
5. The legal collections in the Torah appear in Exodus 21–23; Leviticus 19; Deuteronomy 12–26.

6. Adele Berlin, commentary on *Parashat Ki Teitzei* in *The Torah: A Women's Commentary*, ed. Tamara Cohn Eskenazi and Andrea L. Weiss (New York: Reform Judaism Publishing, an imprint of CCAR Press, 2008), 1165.

7. Deuteronomy 16:20 famously declares, "Justice, justice you shall pursue."

Introduction

Rabbi Barry H. Block

"Rabbi, we want to hear Torah, not politics, from the bimah." Every rabbi has heard this refrain, and many echo it. The plea, though, has always been discordant to my ears. No, I don't preach "politics," which I define narrowly in this context as taking to the pulpit to endorse or oppose a candidate for elective office. I understand Torah to be the Jewish people's primary teaching about how to live our lives, individually and collectively. Torah shaped our covenantal people in formation in ancient Israel and Judea, establishing fundamental norms—regarding ritual matters, yes, but even more, in legislating society's obligations toward individuals and vice versa.

The Holiness Code in Leviticus 19 offers a microcosm of the Torah's dual emphasis. Famously beginning "You shall be holy, for I, the Eternal your God, am holy" (Leviticus 19:2), the Holiness Code proceeds in the very next verse to tell us how to achieve this lofty, overarching goal of being holy. It first articulates an obligation toward other human beings, namely our parents, and then proceeds without pause to what may be viewed as a ritual commandment, the obligation to observe Shabbat. As the passage continues, injunctions to avoid idolatry and specific regulations about consumption of sacrifices are interspersed among directives about fair labor practices, care for the aged, and providing for the poor and needy. The message is clear: Israel serves God no less by pursuing social justice than through proper worship.

Even commandments that appear to regulate exclusively ritual matters often have ethical ends. For example, Professor Ruhama Weiss and Rabbi Dr. Shmuly Yanklowitz will persuasively argue in these pages that the laws of kashrut (dietary regulations) cannot be fulfilled absent fair labor practices and the ethical treatment of animals.

Thanks to Maharat Rori Picker Neiss, we will see that requiring purification for a person who has given birth, a practice out of use since Temple times and abhorrent on its surface, must inspire us to demand that our society ensure proper reproductive health care for all people. And Rabbi Craig Lewis will excavate the detailed regulations for creating the priests' bejeweled *choshen* (breastplate), marshaling *parshanut* (commentary) alongside gemology to formulate a persuasive argument for equity in education.

Three Torah passages beloved among contemporary Jews are more apparently ethical in nature: the creation of humanity *b'tzelem Elohim* (בְּצֶלֶם אֱלֹהִים), "in the image of God" (Genesis 1:27); the oft repeated injunction "You shall not wrong nor oppress a stranger, for you were strangers in the land of Egypt" (Exodus 22:20);[1] and *Tzedek, tzedek tirdof* (צֶדֶק צֶדֶק תִּרְדֹּף), "Justice, justice shall you pursue" (Deuteronomy 16:20). Still, while Rabbi Thomas M. Alpert begins his commentary with "Justice, justice . . . ," he builds his argument about the ongoing need to uproot the sin of racist lynching by turning to the next verses, a seemingly ritual commandment forbidding the Israelites from erecting "a sacred post," a form of idolatry.

Rabbis and others who articulate social justice arguments are sometimes accused—not always unfairly—of basing a complex and controversial assertion about society merely on a pithy phrase from Torah, such as one of the three aforementioned beloved passages, with little depth. This volume is both an antidote to that accusation and a refutation of it. Here, a diverse array of members of the Central Conference of American Rabbis (CCAR) and the American Conference of Cantors (ACC) and our colleagues in other movements, Hebrew Union College–Jewish Institute of Religion faculty, Union for Reform Judaism (URJ) staff, and lay leaders[2] build their social justice arguments on robust and creative employment of *parshanut haTorah* (Torah commentary), including academic biblical exegesis, classical midrash and commentary, modern midrash, and more. Rabbi Seth M. Limmer begins his chapter with the familiar verse "There shall be one law for you and for the resident stranger" (Numbers 15:15), but he does not reach his conclusion about the rights of immigrants until he has drawn on sources as diverse as the Talmud, Franklin D. Roosevelt, Dennis Prager, Ibram X. Kendi, and the *Brown-Driver-Briggs* biblical lexicon.

Much of the Torah is narrative rather than law, which is why "Law" has always been an incorrect translation of the word *Torah*, better understood as "Teaching," as it is rendered in the New JPS translation. The Sages who established Judaism as fundamentally being the study and observance of Torah also found deep meaning in the Torah's aggadah, its stories. Similarly, *The Social Justice Torah Commentary*'s authors have plumbed biblical narratives for inspiration to build a better society. Rabbi Esther L. Lederman draws fascinating parallels between Joseph's brothers selling him into slavery and America's "original sin of slavery," noting that the aftereffects of both are long-lasting. Rabbi A. Brian Stoller reinterprets the supposed "curse of Ham," turning it on its head as he personally comes to grips with his own deeply ingrained implicit racism and urges all white Jews to join him. Ilana Kaufman shares her painful experiences of not finding herself counted, demonstrating the need for our North American Jewish community to be more inclusive in its own census-taking by emphasizing the care that Moses takes in numbering the Israelites. Chris Harrison preaches against the text, insisting that the zealous Pinchas does not deserve God's *b'rit shalom* (בְּרִית שָׁלוֹם), "pact of friendship" (Numbers 25:12), for having murdered the kind of people we need to do a better job of including in our Jewish communities.

While I have cited a number of specific chapters, for each that I have mentioned, several others employ equally thoughtful and creative approaches to make important arguments, whether based on legal or narrative Torah passages.

The contemporary issues addressed in this volume are not meant to be all-inclusive of the social justice challenges facing the world today. *The Social Justice Torah Commentary* was never conceived as a book "about" social justice or an encyclopedia of the world's injustices. Instead, each author or pair of authors was asked to plumb a specific *parashah* (weekly Torah portion) and to derive a social justice argument from that process. Each *parashah* is tied to a single social justice issue—with the exception of *B'haalot'cha*, for which I received two submissions so insightful that both had to be included. Attempting to avoid duplication, I asked each author to delineate a very specific problem to be addressed. Some topics—most notably, racial justice—are explored from a variety of angles in several chapters. Other pressing problems of our day—for example, a long list of injustices outside the United States and Israel—are untouched here. While many of our authors identify as LGBTQ, only one pair of authors—Rabbis Sharon Kleinbaum and Mike Moskowitz—chose to address a topic specifically related to that community, and even that piece is as much about immigrant rights as LGBTQ rights, with Kleinbaum and Moskowitz persuasively arguing that the two are inextricably bound together.

In this context, one would be fair to ask, "What is social justice?" While each contributor to this book may have their own conception, the Center for Economic and Social Justice offers a useful definition:

> Social justice is the virtue which guides us in creating those organized human interactions we call institutions. In turn, social institutions, when justly organized, provide us with access to what is good for the person, both individually and in our associations with others. Social justice also imposes on each of us a personal responsibility to collaborate with others, at whatever level of the "Common Good" in which we participate, to design and continually perfect our institutions as tools for personal and social development.[3]

Jewish religious leaders have been advocating for social justice longer than the term "Jewish" has existed. As our contributors demonstrate throughout this volume, the Torah itself provides the guide. The Torah repeatedly argues that living as God commands includes the requirement to establish, nurture, and protect social institutions—including governments—that grant the greatest good to individuals and communities, particularly those who lack privileges and whose voices are often silenced.

Biblical prophets might not have employed the term "social justice," but they repeatedly called for it all the same. Amos, an early prophet in the Northern Kingdom,[4] excoriates the Israelites "who trample the heads of the poor into the earth's dust, and make crooked the road of the meek" (Amos 2:7). Jeremiah admonishes the king himself to "do justice and righteousness," with particular concern for foreigners residing in Judea as well as widows and orphans, the Bible's prime examples of poor people who are unable to provide for themselves (Jeremiah 22:1–3). In a passage we read on Yom Kippur morning, Deutero-Isaiah[5] castigates elite Israelites for imagining that scrupulous ritual observance will protect them from God's wrath when they oppress their workers and lash out in violence. Instead, the prophet proclaims, God will favor those who free the enslaved, feed the hungry, provide shelter to the homeless, and clothe the naked (Isaiah 58:3–8).

Gershom Gorenberg acknowledges that "Jewish religious texts celebrate diversity of opinion and multiple interpretations. And amid those many voices, neither the Bible nor the Talmud endorses a specific monetary policy, tax schedule or health plan for the twenty-first century."[6] However, Gorenberg goes on to argue for social justice as opposed to reliance on charity alone:

> To understand what's wrong with the voluntary model, I suggest reading the recent book *Justice in the City* by the scholar and activist Aryeh Cohen. Reading the Talmud and later rabbinic writing, Cohen shows that they obligate society to feed and clothe the hungry, and to provide homes for the homeless. The obligation must be carried out through political institutions, which both represent the people who live in a particular place and require, even coerce, them to pay what is needed. That is, a just society collects taxes to meet its duties to every person in its realm— which are also its duties to God.[7]

The advent of Reform Judaism brought a renewed emphasis on social justice. Rabbi Leonard J. Mervis wrote, "David Einhorn, a pioneer of Reform Judaism in Germany and later in the United States, summarized [the matter, writing,] 'We stand upon the ground of prophetic Judaism which aims at the universal worship of God by righteousness.'"[8] Mervis argues that early US Reform rabbis, even those who spoke out about slavery, did not actively advocate social justice during the period following the Civil War.[9] However, in 1885, under the influence of Rabbi Emil G. Hirsch,[10] the new Central Conference of American Rabbis (CCAR) would adopt its "Declaration of Principles"—more commonly, the Pittsburgh Platform—including as its eighth and final article: "In full accordance with the spirit of Mosaic legislation, which strives to regulate the relations between rich and poor, we deem it our duty to participate in the great task of modern times, to solve, on the basis of justice and righteousness, the problems presented by the contrasts and evils of the present organization of society."[11]

As the twentieth century began, the CCAR began to raise the collective rabbinic voice, primarily in support of fair labor practices, including child labor laws, "a more equitable distribution of the profits of industry," minimum wage, eight-hour workdays, and workers' compensation.[12] The CCAR expanded its advocacy to include women's suffrage in 1917.[13] Five years later, a half century before Sally Priesand's historic ordination at the Hebrew Union College–Jewish Institute of Religion, the CCAR sought to establish women's equality in its own ranks by calling for the ordination of women.[14]

The Religious Action Center of Reform Judaism (RAC), founded in 1961 by the Commission on Social Action of Reform Judaism (CSA)—a joint instrument of the CCAR and the Union for Reform Judaism (URJ)—was conceived at the height of the civil rights movement. According to the RAC, "The Civil Rights Act of 1964 and the Voting Rights Act of 1965 were drafted in the conference room of the Leadership Conference, which for decades was located in the RAC's building. The Jewish community has continued its support of civil rights laws addressing persistent discrimination in voting, housing and employment against not only women and people of color but also in the gay, lesbian, bisexual and transgender community and the disabled community."[15]

Like the URJ and CSA, the CCAR has, for many decades, adopted resolutions on a wide range of social justice topics. Some are focused on what all would agree are "Jewish issues," such as those related to Israel and antisemitism. Some particularly noteworthy resolutions have enshrined social justice advances in ritual practice, such as "Resolution on Same Gender Officiation,"[16] which, when adopted in 2000, officially sanctioned Reform rabbinic officiation at same-sex marriages, years after some Reform rabbis had begun officiating at them but before those unions were recognized in any US state.

I have been privileged to participate in the CCAR's process of raising the collective Jewish voice for some two decades, first as a member and later in two separate terms as chair of the CCAR Resolutions Committee. During this time, Reform rabbis have collectively taken positions on issues ranging from reproductive justice to racial justice, from Israel advocacy to demanding equality for Reform Jews in Israel and speaking out for the rights of Palestinians, from economic justice to climate justice. In 2015, which seems late, the CCAR was the first mainstream Jewish organization and very early among all religious bodies to call for equal rights for transgender and gender nonconforming individuals.[17]

A substantial majority of the social justice arguments in this volume are consistent with positions that have been taken by the Reform Movement through the CCAR, URJ, and/or CSA. However, emblematic of an effort to achieve diversity of every kind in this book, authors were explicitly welcome to depart from such positions if they wished. When I invited Rabbi Jeremy Barras to write on the social justice imperative to support Israel, I assumed that his piece would take a different viewpoint from Rabbi Jill Jacobs's on the Occupation. What I could not have imagined was that both would base their largely opposing arguments on interpretations of the same biblical notion, that the Land of Israel would "spew out" those who commit unpardonable sins upon it.[18]

Compiling this book in 2020–21 offered unique opportunities and challenges. Authors wrote during a global pandemic, at a time of surging awareness of racial injustice in the United States in the wake of the police killing of George Floyd, and in the midst of a rancorous American presidential election, with wildfires and hurricanes ravaging the West and Gulf Coasts, respectively. Inequities were brought into sharp relief by all three, offering ripe material to our authors. At the same time, wishing this book to be resonant well beyond the year of its authorship—indeed, still to be relevant at the moment of its publication—an effort was made to ensure that even as current events informed authors' arguments, they would not be quite so time-bound as a sermon for Rosh HaShanah or Yom Kippur 5781.

This book is the second I have edited for CCAR Press, following *The Mussar Torah Commentary* (2020). The two volumes appear to go in divergent directions. However, I see them as a sequence. Mussar, Jewish ethical discipline, urges us to engage in *tikkun middot*, repairing the measures of our souls. *The Mussar Torah Commentary*'s authors examined the fifty-four *parashiyot* to find lessons that would help readers train themselves to become better people. Much of that work is internal, though its success manifests in the ways we interact with the world. Too often, we who are inspired to engage in *tikkun olam*, repairing the world around us, skip a step, failing to do the internal work necessary in order to bring our best selves to *tikkun olam*.

To be sure, neither the work of *tikkun middot* nor that of *tikkun olam* is ever complete and will not be until we achieve a messianic future with God's help. Divine guidance is available to us through Torah, re-amplified in every generation. As we return to our portion in the Torah each week, let us ever find new words that inspire us to heal ourselves and this broken world.

NOTES

1. Tradition holds that this commandment is stated thirty-six times. It is stated differently in different places. Typically, though, it includes the phrase "for you were strangers in the land of Egypt."
2. Many of the authors fall in more than one of these categories.
3. "Defining Economic Justice and Social Justice," Center for Economic and Social Justice, https://www.cesj.org/learn/definitions/defining-economic-justice-and-social-justice/.
4. W. Gunther Plaut, ed., *The Torah: A Modern Commentary*, rev. ed. (New York: Union for Reform Judaism, 2005), 263.
5. "Deutero-Isaiah" is the name given to the exilic prophet whom academic Bible scholars consider to be the author of Isaiah 40–55 (or, some say, 40–66).
6. Gershom Gorenberg, "Avoiding Sodom: It's About Policy, Not Charity,"

Daily Beast, September 10, 2012, updated July 14, 2017, https://www.thedailybeast.com/avoiding-sodom-its-about-policy-not-charity.

7. Gorenberg, "Avoiding Sodom."

8. Leonard J. Mervis, "The Social Justice Movement and the American Reform Rabbi," *American Jewish Archives*, June 1955, 172, americanjewisharchives.org/publications/journal/PDF/1955_07_02_00_mervis.pdf.

9. Mervis, "Social Justice Movement," 172.

10. Mervis, "Social Justice Movement," 172.

11. Central Conference of American Rabbis, "Declaration of Principles ('The Pittsburgh Platform'—1885): 1885 Pittsburgh Conference," CCAR, https://www.ccarnet.org/rabbinic-voice/platforms/article-declaration-principles/.

12. Mervis, "Social Justice Movement," 173–79.

13. Resolution adopted by the Central Conference of American Rabbis, 1917, "Women's Suffrage," CCAR, https://www.ccarnet.org/ccar-resolutions/women-s-suffrage-1889-1972/.

14. "Ordination of Women: Resolutions and Statements: 1963," Women of Reform Judaism, https://wrj.org/ordination-women-rabbis.

15. "Jews and the Civil Rights Movement," Religious Action Center of Reform Judaism, accessed December 22, 2020, https://rac.org/jews-and-civil-rights-movement.

16. Central Conference of American Rabbis, "Resolution on Same Gender Officiation: Resolution Adopted at the 111th Convention of the Central Conference of American Rabbis, March, 2000," CCAR, https://www.ccarnet.org/ccar-resolutions/same-gender-officiation/.

17. All CCAR resolutions may be accessed at https://www.ccarnet.org/rabbinic-voice/resolution/.

18. Interestingly, the passages to which I'm referring are not in either of the *parashiyot* on which Rabbi Barras's and Rabbi Jacobs's respective commentaries are primarily based, but are found in Leviticus 18:24–28 and Numbers 35:33–34. Both Rabbi Barras and Rabbi Jacobs do, in addition, base their commentaries primarily on the designated *parashiyot*.

Acknowledgments

THE MEASURE OF A GREAT LEADER is not only in her accomplishments but also in the tradition and team she builds to continue her mission into the future. CCAR Press existed for more than a century before Rabbi Hara Person took its helm. It was and remains best known for the prayer books that were the impetus for the founding of the CCAR. However, with encouragement from Rabbi Steve Fox and others, Hara built CCAR Press into much more: the leading publishing arm of Reform Judaism, an effective vehicle for amplifying the collective voice of Reform rabbis, and a producer of thought leadership for the Jewish world.

The Social Justice Torah Commentary may be CCAR Press's first book produced entirely in the Press's "post-Hara era." To some degree, that's an exaggeration. As chief executive of the Central Conference of American Rabbis, Hara continues to provide vision and supervisory leadership to the Press. Moreover, CCAR Press remains "the Press that Hara built."

Into her shoes, Hara recruited Rafael Chaiken to succeed her as director of CCAR Press. I had the great pleasure and privilege of working with Rafael from the outset of this project to its completion. Rafael might properly be credited as coeditor of this volume. He edited every chapter of this book alongside me, and he had the arguably daunting task of editing my own words. Rafael pushed me, and emboldened me to encourage others, to achieve the highest quality in content and style. He has shared my dual commitments to excellence and to an accelerated timeline from proposal to publication. *The Social Justice Torah Commentary* is a much better book because of his significant hand in it.

Thanks are due, too, to Rafael's team: Rabbi Sonja Pilz, PhD, CCAR Press's editor, whose maternity leave ended in time for her to compose this volume's glossary; Debbie Smilow, press operations manager, who expertly brought this project to print, as she has for every CCAR Press publication for decades; Raquel Fairweather, marketing and sales manager, whose work comes after the book is in print, but who I know from experience will be central to its success; and publishing assistants Leta Cunningham and Chiara Ricisak, who expertly handled administrative matters, including countless technical tasks for this luddite editor. I'm grateful to copy editor Debra Corman, book designer Scott-Martin Kosofsky, proofreader Michelle Kwitkin, and cover designer Barbara Leff for their skilled work.

The magic of an anthology such as this one is in the diverse array of talented authors who devote their time, energy, and passion to producing the essays that jump off its pages. These contributors responded cheerfully to this often-demanding editor and my commitment to publish on the promised timeline.

Members of the Editorial Advisory Committee likely underestimate the formative role they played in the development of this anthology. Rabbis Daniel Bogard, Mari Chernow, Rachel Greengrass, Rachel Grant Meyer, Michael Namath, and Brian Stoller suggested authors whom I did not know or whom I would not have thought to invite to write for this book. While I was committed to diversity among contributors from the outset, their steadfast encouragement and repeated responsiveness helped me recruit an array of authors much broader than I could have found on my own.

I have been richly blessed to serve two congregations, each of which has, for more than a century, been led by rabbis who have understood Torah as an urgent call for social justice. I was the heir to a tradition established at Temple Beth-El in San Antonio by Rabbis Ephraim Frisch and David Jacobson, both of blessed memory, and nurtured by Rabbi Samuel M. Stahl, a contributor to this volume. My successor, Rabbi Mara Nathan, continues in their tradition.

Now, at Congregation B'nai Israel in Little Rock, Arkansas, I strive to follow the example of Rabbi Ira E. Sanders, z"l, who led the congregation from 1926 to 1963 and was a civil rights hero before his time. During his first months in Little Rock, Rabbi Sanders lent his body to the struggle against segregation, refusing to move from the back of the streetcar. Later, in Little Rock's years of infamy, congregants—women, in particular—heeded his call to organize against segregation in public schools.[1] Rabbi Sanders's predecessors—in particular, Rabbi Louis Wolsey, z"l, who would go on to lead the CCAR as its president after leaving Little Rock—and his successors before my arrival, a half century after his retirement, powerfully preached social justice from the pulpit I now have the privilege to occupy. I am deeply indebted to the members of Congregation B'nai Israel who have supported these great rabbis and now me, often heeding the rabbinic call to become social justice activists themselves.

Many thanks are due to the current leaders of Congregation B'nai Israel who support my rabbinate in and beyond the temple's walls. I am grateful for the forbearance and encouragement of Carol Parham and Amanda Ferguson, who led the congregation as presidents during the time I have worked on the project. Like their predecessors—Carmen Arick, David Bauman, and Leah Elenzweig—and their slated successor, Annabelle Imber Tuck, they have supported my engagement with the Reform Movement beyond our congregation, including CCAR leadership and publishing, and they have partnered with me to amplify Congregation B'nai Israel's social justice advocacy in Arkansas. My extraordinary professional partner, Eileen Hamilton, enables and strengthens so much of this work.

I have ancestors who immigrated before the American Revolution, and my family has been affiliated with the Reform Movement since the Reformed Society of Israelites was founded in Charleston, South Carolina, in the 1820s. With ancestors who were enslavers and Confederate soldiers, though, I cannot claim a long familial heritage of social justice.

My parents, Gay Shlenker Block and Gus Block, are members of the Silent Generation, and they were not engaged in the civil rights movement. My maternal grandmother had the same dinner bell that

A. Brian Stoller, also a Houston native, describes in his commentary on *Parashat Noach*. Nevertheless, unlike most of the Houston Jewish community in which they were raised and in turn raised my sister Alison and me, my parents opened their eyes to social injustice in the 1970s and exposed us to progressive thought and activism, rooted in Reform Jewish life at and beyond Congregation Beth Israel.

URJ Greene Family Camp, with Loui Dobin at the helm, and NFTY, under the leadership of Rabbi Dan Freelander, provided my first opportunities for social activism, which were also nurtured at Amherst College Hillel, where Hara Person and I first came to know and work with one another, inspired by Rabbi Yechiael Lander. Later, during one year as a rabbinic intern at Touro Synagogue in New Orleans, I gained a mentor and lifelong friend in Rabbi David Goldstein. With his wife Shannie, David was a hero of the struggle for Soviet Jewry, and he has continued his social activism well beyond his retirement from the pulpit.

Today, my sons, Robert and Daniel, are my social justice heroes. Both have put their bodies and souls into the struggle for racial justice—Daniel, often taking to the street and public microphones in an ongoing battle for the soul of Little Rock School District, and Robert, physically battered while peacefully protesting the extrajudicial execution of George Floyd. As I have followed both of them, we have all been led by Black community leaders—notably, our local heroes Senator Joyce Elliot and Rev./Dr. Anika Whitfield.

Toward the end of my work on this project—coincidentally, on Rev. Dr. Martin Luther King Jr.'s birthday, of all days—I received a page of the 1860 Louisiana slave census from a distant relative I did not previously know. This is the first actual proof for me that an ancestor—in this case, my great-great-great-grandmother, Magdalena Seeleman—was an enslaver. My distant relative has been working to identify the enslaved young woman, in the hope of locating descendants in order to offer at least some form of reparation. I do not know that we will ever be able to identify the twenty-nine-year-old "mulatto" woman whom my ancestor enslaved or her descendants. I dedicate this volume to her memory, in the prayer that it may serve as a tiny measure of and impetus for reparation for the grievous damage caused by my ancestors and by this nation to her and millions of others across four centuries and counting.

—*Rabbi Barry H. Block*
Erev Tu BiSh'vat 5781
Little Rock, Arkansas

NOTE
1. James Moses, *Just and Righteous Causes: Rabbi Ira Sanders and the Fight for Racial and Social Justice in Arkansas, 1926–1963* (Fayetteville: University of Arkansas Press, 2018).

GENESIS

B'REISHIT—GENESIS 1:1–6:8

Separate and Unequal: A Tale of Creation

RABBI MARLA J. FELDMAN

ON THE SIXTH DAY, God creates human beings. We are created *b'tzelem Elohim* (בְּצֶלֶם אֱלֹהִים), "in the divine image," and *zachar un'kei-vah* (זָכָר וּנְקֵבָה), "male and female" (Genesis 1:27). Alone in being formed in God's image, humans are empowered to oversee and govern all the other creatures and commanded to reproduce and multiply, filling the land. Males and females are equally reflective of the divine image, equally empowered, and equally commanded. "And it was very good" (Genesis 1:31).

A few verses later, we find a different tale of Creation in which *haadam* (הָאָדָם), "the man" (or "mankind"), is created to till and to tend the Garden all alone, with no one else to assist him (Genesis 2:15). God feels the man's loneliness and creates the animals and birds, but alas none is a proper counterpart for the man. Finally, God creates a woman, fashioned from the man's rib, to be his *ezer k'nedgo* (עֵזֶר כְּנֶגְדּוֹ), his "helpmate" (Genesis 2:18–21). We all know what happens in the next chapter of Genesis: The woman becomes curious and eats from the forbidden Tree of Knowledge of Good and Evil, leading to expulsion from the Garden. In response to Eve's transgression, God punishes all women with anguish in bearing children and by subjecting them to their husbands' rule (Genesis 3:1–17).

"No biblical story has had more influence on women's lives and identity—and none has been more often reinterpreted through later cultural biases—than the creation of woman in Genesis 2 and the expulsion from the Garden in Genesis 3," writes Dr. Tamara Cohn Eskenazi in *The Torah: A Women's Commentary*. "The version of creation of humankind in 1:26–28, which portrays equality between the sexes and their shared reflection of God's image, is typically overlooked in favor [of] the more ambiguous one in Genesis 2, which is typically read as one in which man precedes woman in time. Consequently, the first woman has been cast by later interpreters as an afterthought: second and therefore secondary in value, not essential to God's plan."[1]

In a commentary on this *parashah*, Rachel Adler notes that the Adam and Eve saga marks a fundamental change in the relationship between men and women from the idyllic oneness with Creation to a utilitarian, consumer-based "commodification" of Creation, diminishing their loving partnership:

> Genesis 1 is an account of the Creation, whereas Genesis 2–3 is an account of the creation of patriarchy—a remarkably truthful account. The world brought about by Genesis 2–3 is one in which desire is no longer joyful but oppressive. Even before the disobedience, relations between man and woman and world are commodified and function-based. *Adam* is created to till the soil. Woman is created to heal *Adam*. However lush, the garden is a workplace. Created things are good, not intrinsically as in Genesis 1, but because they are resources.[2]

The punishment for defying the divine decree is hard labor. For Eve, she, and all women after her, would suffer pain in childbirth. For Adam and all future men, the punishment would be the rigorous challenge of cultivating the land. While toil and sweat are prescribed for Adam and blamed on Eve, no work is assigned to Eve. This version of Creation establishes a divinely ordained functional separation between men and women: Adam would work the land, and Eve would provide, and presumably care for, children. Thus, the segregation of men and women in the workforce begins.

The separate spheres ascribed to men and women became embedded within our cultural norms, with a hierarchy among those roles set in place. The physical labor of men was assigned a higher value than work permitted to women such as caregiving and education.

A prime example comes in Leviticus 27:1-7, as the text outlines the work needed to build the Tabernacle. When freewill offerings are no longer sufficient, the Israelites are required to provide actual service to keep the Tabernacle operational. In lieu of service, they are permitted to make financial contributions matching the value of their labor, which varies based on age and gender: the labor of men aged twenty to sixty is worth fifty shekels, as compared to thirty shekels for women that age; the work of boys aged five to twenty is worth twenty shekels, while girls' work is worth half that amount; men over age sixty are valued at fifteen shekels, while women over age sixty are worth ten shekels. According to this text, a woman's labor is worth roughly 50 to 60 percent of a man's!

These differences are not based on intrinsic value, but rather on assessments predicated on cultural expectations and assumptions. Work that requires brawn and sweat is not inherently more valuable than work that requires fine motor skills or emotional intelligence. Yet the consumer-based labor market values women's worth and work less than that of her male counterparts. In today's workforce, we see "pink-collar" jobs such as teaching, nursing, and social services valued less than male-dominated "blue-collar" work such as construction, manufacturing, or trades. Higher paying "white-collar" professions and STEM (science, technology, engineering, math) fields continue to be hostile environments for women as they bump their heads on the glass ceiling. These salary differences across occupations and industries are the most significant factor in the current gender pay gap.[3]

Even when women and men are in the exact same field doing the same work, women are, on average, compensated at lower levels. In almost every occupation, women continue to earn less than men, with 80 percent being the average in the United States.[4] Black, Latina, and Native American women fare far worse than the national average.[5] Sadly, internal studies have shown that the gender wage gap also persists in the Reform Movement, as female professionals—rabbis, cantors, educators, and administrators—face a similar gender disparity as do other US professionals, with women earning about 85 percent of what men earn.[6]

This wage gap adds up to hundreds of billions of dollars lost by women annually, not only impacting their ability to support themselves and their families, but also harming the overall economy, businesses, and educational opportunities for the next generation. With women being the primary breadwinners in half of American families with children under eighteen, closing the wage gap could lift millions of families out of poverty.[7]

The issue of pay equity is not a woman's issue—it is a family issue. When a woman's income is suppressed, her entire family's income is diminished. Pay equity is a human rights issue, a matter of fundamental fairness and justice. When we undervalue and underpay a segment of our workforce, we are all diminished.

Fortunately, the gender wage gap is a problem that can be solved. Legislation like the Lilly Ledbetter Fair Pay Act provides remedies for employment discrimination. State and local regulations requiring employers to provide salary data and protect employees' rights to discuss salaries empower women to challenge unfair wage discrimination. Living-wage laws and salary protection for tipped workers can ameliorate the impact of low wages for pink-collar jobs.

Individuals, too, play an important role in addressing inequity in the workforce. Implicit bias and lack of salary transparency are among the causes of the wage gap that can be addressed by employers. Simple interventions such as not utilizing a job seeker's prior salary information and using gender-blind recruitment tools can help elevate women in the workforce and achieve more diversity generally.[8] Training to understand the impact of unconscious bias has proved to be beneficial.[9] Through the Reform Pay Equity Initiative's educational and training opportunities, affiliates of the Reform Movement are working collaboratively to implement these interventions and address hiring policies within Reform congregations and organizations.[10]

The gender wage gap is a manifestation of the patriarchy set in motion with the tale of Adam and Eve. Its continuing effect has corrupted the relationship between men and women and undermined the fundamental truth of their equality. The time has come to reassert the primacy of the first Creation story of *Parashat B'reishit* in which men and women are created together, of equal value, and both in the image of God.

As Rachel Adler added in her commentary, "The world of patriarchy cries out for mending. A mending world would commit itself to equality and power-sharing, to working cooperatively in order to fill needs and solve problems."[11] If we are able to see the Divine within every human being, if we share a commitment to fairness and equity, and if we work together to address the gender wage gap, this is a problem we can solve.

NOTES

1. Tamara Cohn Eskenazi, "Creation and Transformation," in *The Torah: A Women's Commentary*, ed. Tamara Cohn Eskenazi and Andrea L. Weiss (New York: Reform Judaism Publishing, an imprint of CCAR Press and Women of Reform Judaism, 2008), 2–3.

2. Rachel Adler, "Contemporary Reflection," in Eskenazi and Weiss, *The Torah: A Women's Commentary*, 30.

3. Francine D. Blau and Lawrence M. Kahn, "The Gender Wage Gap: Extent, Trends, and Explanations," Institute for the Study of Labor Discussion Paper No. 9656, January 2016, 27, http://ftp.iza.org/dp9656.pdf.

4. "What's the Wage Gap in the States?," National Partnership for Women and Families, accessed October 10, 2020, https://www.nationalpartnership.org/our-work/economic-justice/wage-gap/.

5. "Black Women and the Wage Gap," National Partnership for Women and Families, accessed November 14, 2020, https://www.nationalpartnership.org/our-work/resources/economic-justice/fair-pay/african-american-women-wage-gap.pdf; and "Beyond Wages: Effects of the Latina Wage Gap," National Partnership for Women and Families, accessed November 14, 2020, https://www.nationalpartnership.org/our-work/resources/economic-justice/fair-pay/latinas-wage-gap.pdf.

6. Marla Feldman and Mary Zamore, "Pay Equity Within the Reform Movement," *CCAR Journal*, Fall 2018, 5–97.

7. "America's Women and the Wage Gap," National Partnership for Women and Families, accessed October 10, 2020, https://www.nationalpartnership.org/our-work/resources/economic-justice/fair-pay/americas-women-and-the-wage-gap.pdf.

8. Clair Cain Miller, "Is Blind Hiring the Best Hiring?," *New York Times*,

February 25, 2016, https://www.nytimes.com/2016/02/28/magazine/is-blind-hiring-the-best-hiring.html.

9. Aaron R. Conklin, "Breaking Bias," College of Letters and Science, University of Wisconsin–Madison, posted September 17, 2020, https://ls.wisc.edu/news/breaking-bias.

10. See the Reform Pay Equity Initiative website (reformpayequity.org) to learn more about efforts of the Reform Movement to address the gender pay gap within Reform congregations and organizations.

11. Adler, "Contemporary Reflection," 31.

NOACH—GENESIS 6:9–11:32

Unconscious Racial Bias and the Curse of Japheth

RABBI A. BRIAN STOLLER

Hatred isn't something you're born with. It gets taught. In school they said segregation is what's said in the Bible. Genesis 9, verse 27. At seven years of age, you get told it enough times, you believe it. You believe the hatred. You live it. You breathe it. You marry it.
—Mrs. Pell, *Mississippi Burning*

IN THE FILM *MISSISSIPPI BURNING*, Mrs. Pell, brilliantly portrayed by Frances McDormand, tearfully bares her soul to an FBI agent investigating the murder of civil rights activists in 1964 Mississippi. Trembling and ashamed, she explains how deeply racism is ingrained in the community where she was raised and how racist attitudes are perpetuated by teaching them to children. Her heart-wrenching story about what she, as a white little girl, learned in school opens a window into how the Bible was used, tragically, to convince children—and, indeed, a whole society—of an insidious lie: that the enslavement of Black people, Jim Crow, and racial segregation were ordained by God.

The passage she quotes from Genesis 9 describes how Noah's three sons—Ham, Shem, and Japheth—react when their father is discovered one night passed out in his tent drunk and naked:

Ham—Canaan's father—saw his father's nakedness, and, outside, told his two brothers. Shem and Japheth took a cloak and put it on both their shoulders. They walked backward and covered their father's nakedness. Facing backward, they did not see their father's nakedness. Noah awakened from his wine and understood what his youngest son had done to him, so he said, "Damned be Canaan! To his brothers he shall be the basest of slaves!" And he said, "Praised be the Eternal, God of Shem; and Canaan be a slave to him. May God enlarge [*yaf't*, יַפְתְּ] Japheth; he shall dwell in the tents of Shem; and Canaan shall be a slave to him." (Genesis 9:22–27)

Noah is so outraged by Ham's disrespectful behavior toward him that he curses Ham's son Canaan, decreeing in God's name that Canaan is to be a slave to Japheth and Shem. However, according to the slanderous and ideologically driven allegorical reading of this story known as the "Curse of Ham," Noah's curse applies not only to these particular individuals, but also to their descendants for all time. On this interpretation, Ham and Canaan represent Black people, while Japheth represents white people—meaning that God has condemned Black people to be subjugated to white people forever. Scholars have thoroughly debunked this interpretation of the story, showing it to be based on an ignorant misreading of the biblical text designed to support the institution of African slavery.[1] Still, this narrative succeeded over time in its primary aim: to provide religious justification for racist oppression of Black people. The pain and terror this wicked usage of the Bible has wrought on our society and on humankind are immeasurable.

Likutei Maharil, an early twentieth-century Torah commentary by the Hungarian rabbi Yaakov Yehudah Aryeh Leib Frankel, offers insight suggesting that although Canaan is the one who is cursed, Japheth—the son regarded as the "progenitor of the Aryan races"[2]—is the true sinner. According to *Likutei Maharil*, when the Torah says that God "enlarge[d]" (*yaf't*) Japheth, it means that God's blessing led Japheth to become arrogant and filled with hubris;[3] indeed, Frankel's explanation of the Hebrew root *y-f-t* suggests that Japheth's very name (*Yefet*) means "arrogance." *Likutei Maharil*'s teaching captures the attitude of many white people throughout our country's history who arrogantly believed that God had favored them and had condemned Black people to perpetual subjugation. Over time, laws, social structures, and cultural norms were developed to enshrine this shameful ideology in daily life. As Mrs. Pell put it, the belief in white superiority "isn't something you're born with. It gets taught." It is not always taught with hateful or malicious intent, and it may not even be taught consciously. Attitudes that were taught explicitly at one time in history may later be conveyed implicitly, even unknowingly. But they are there. They are modeled by people we love and admire, people who are kind, and gentle, and do *not* hate. Tragically, these arrogant biases have become part of who we are. Call it the "Curse of Japheth."

I relate to this very personally. One of my favorite childhood memories is Friday night dinner at my great-grandmother's home. Every week, her butler Walter and her housekeeper Pearl prepared and served our meal. Both were Black. My great-grandmother kept a gold bell, shaped like a turtle, on the dining room table. Whenever she wanted something from the kitchen, which was barely three feet from where we were sitting, she would ring the bell, and Walter would come. As a little boy, I remember wanting to ring the bell for Walter, too, just like my great-grandmother, but my mom would not let me; she said it was disrespectful to Walter. I used to wonder why; after all, my great-grandmother was a respectful person, a pillar of our community. I never stopped to think about how the bell must have made Walter feel. Maybe angry, probably humiliated. In retrospect, the most embarrassing thing is that with the exception of my mother, my family and I were never embarrassed by it. We loved Walter, and we did not mean him any harm by ringing that bell. My family are good people; we would never think of ourselves as racist. But here's the thing: as a person who grew up in a wealthy, privileged white southern community, I have undeniably been shaped by—and benefited from—attitudes that are racist, as have so many of us in this country and among white members of the Jewish community.

Painful as it is, I have to admit that I grew up with the assumptions that Black people tended to work for white people and came when you rang, that their neighborhoods were scary because the people there were scary, and that many of them needed the paternalistic hand of white people to get a leg up in life. No one taught me these things explicitly; in fact, my parents raised me to treat all people equally and kindly, no matter what color they are. I guess these assumptions were just implicit—and they were all around me. Whether we are aware of it or not, the arrogance of Japheth was and still is transmitted in the very air we breathe. Children who breathe that air grow up to be business owners, attorneys, lawmakers, judges, teachers, mothers, and fathers—and we in turn contribute to the formation of *our* children and *our* society. Over time, the whole ecosystem becomes a reflection of the subtle, seemingly benign attitudes of the people who shape it. The result is systemic racism.

We in the Jewish community should be especially sensitive to the experiences of Black people because, as the scholar David Goldenberg explains, we have been closely linked together throughout history:

> From Jerome and Augustine, who saw biblical Ham as typologically the Jew while biologically the black, to the 1930s American graffito "A [n-word] is a Jew turned inside out," these two peoples have been typecast as reflections of one another, and as substitutes for one another in society's categorization of the Other. Voltaire put it succinctly: "One regards the Jews the same way as one regards the Negroes, as a species of inferior humanity."[4]

Yet many of us have forgotten this history. Perhaps because white American Jewry has, on the whole, attained unprecedented blessings and acceptance in this country, we too, like Japheth, have become arrogant.

We need to change. We need to work intently to abandon deeply held assumptions and attitudes that have been with us for generations. It will not be easy. We need to acknowledge our own unconscious biases—but acknowledgment is not enough. We need to listen to the experiences of Black people and other people of color—but listening is not enough. We need to examine our individual and collective psyches to try to understand why the "Curse of Ham" and the hubris of Japheth have remained so deeply rooted in us and our society, so that we can repudiate and uproot them completely. Indeed,

James Baldwin called on his fellow citizens to engage in precisely this kind of self-examination and self-reckoning, seeing it as essential to our eventual redemption. In Baldwin's words:

> It is entirely up to the American people whether they are going to face, and deal with, and embrace the stranger whom they've relied on so long. What white people have to do is try to find out in their own hearts why it was necessary to have a [n-word] in the first place. Because I'm not a [n-word]; I am a man. But if you think I'm a [n-word], it means *you* need it. And the question you have to ask yourself—the question the white population in this country needs to ask itself—is . . . If I'm not the [n-word] here, and you the white people invented him, then *you* have to find out *why*. And the future of the country depends on . . . whether or not it's able to ask that question.[5]

Notes

1. For a discussion of the Curse of Ham and Judaism, see David M. Goldenberg, "The Curse of Ham: A Case of Rabbinic Racism?," in *Struggles in the Promised Land*, ed. Jack Salzman and Cornel West (New York: Oxford University Press, 1997), 21–51. The medieval Jewish biblical commentator Abraham ibn Ezra also pointed out the error in the claim that Genesis 9 condemned Black people to slavery. In a comment to Genesis 9:25, Ibn Ezra writes, "There are those who say that the Black people [*hacushim*] are slaves because Noah cursed Ham, but they forgot that the first king after the Flood was Black, as it is written: 'And Cush [whose name means 'Black'] begot Nimrod; he was first among the earth's heroes. He was a mighty hunter before the Eternal; hence the saying, "Like Nimrod a mighty hunter by the grace of the Eternal." His choice domains were Babylon, . . .' (Genesis 10:8–10)."
2. Marcus Jastrow, *Dictionary of the Talmud*, Sefaria, https://www.sefaria.org/Jastrow%2C_%D7%99%D6%B6%D7%A4%D6%B6%D7%AA?lang=bi.
3. *Likutei Maharil, D'varim, Parashat Shof'tim*, s.v. *ki yakum*: "[The word] *yifteh* [in Deuteronomy 11:16; root: *y-f-t*] is the language of enlargement and arrogance, as in (Genesis 9:27): 'May God enlarge [*yaf't*] Japheth.'"
4. Goldenberg, "Curse of Ham," 21.
5. James Baldwin, as spoken on video at the conclusion of the documentary film *I Am Not Your Negro* (2017). The emphases in the quoted passage are mine. The reader is invited to compare Baldwin's comments here with the famous statement of the French philosopher (and Baldwin contemporary) Jean-Paul Sartre that "if the Jew did not exist, the anti-Semite would invent him. . . . By treating the Jew as an inferior and pernicious being, I affirm at the same

time that I belong to the elite. This elite, in contrast to those of modern times which are based on merit or labor, resembles an aristocracy of birth. There is nothing I have to do to merit my superiority, and neither can I lose it. It is given once and for all" (Sartre, *Anti-Semite and Jew: An Exploration of the Etiology of Hate* [New York: Schocken Books, 1948], 13, 27).

LECH L'CHA—GENESIS 12:1–17:27

Deserving of the Land

RABBI JEREMY BARRAS

THE INITIAL CONVERSATION between the Creator of the world and Abraham, understood to be the father of the Jewish people, began not with pleasantries but with an order that Abraham leave his homeland and move to the Land of Israel. The one-sided conversation in the opening verses of *Parashat Lech L'cha* commences with God ordering Abraham to depart for Israel and Abraham obeying without question. The move from Babylonia to Canaan represents God's desire to relocate Abraham to a land that offered greater spiritual capacity to connect with the Divine and to foresee the homeland that his people would eventually inherit. Abraham is told that moving to what will eventually be known as *Eretz Yisrael* will effectuate an actual change in Abraham's spiritual being. As the text teaches, upon moving to Canaan, Abraham's name will "be a blessing" (Genesis 12:2); those who bless him will be blessed and those who curse him will be cursed (Genesis 12:3).

Though Abraham journeys to the land that God shows him, once there he is told that his immediate descendants will not be able to inherit the land; God has not yet decided that the people then dwelling there deserve to be exiled (Genesis 15:16). The text thus suggests something unique about the land: habitation there is dependent upon moral behavior. The Israelite descendants of Abraham are not eligible to claim sovereignty over the land so long as the current inhabitants have not worn out their welcome.

Later in the Torah, we learn which crimes warrant such expulsion. While the Torah mentions a whole array of sinful behaviors that provoke God's wrath, the three cardinal sins of idolatry, murder, and sexual immorality are noted as acts that pollute the Land and cause violators to be spewed from it.[1] We can therefore infer that the Canaanites, the inhabitants referred to in Genesis 15, ultimately become eligible to be conquered and removed from the land once their idolatrous, murderous, and sexually immoral behavior exceeds the boundaries of God's tolerance; then the sanctified Land can no longer tolerate their presence.

Nevertheless, our tradition records that the Canaanites are still given the opportunity to repent from their evil ways and remain in the Land. The midrash tells us that upon entering the land, Joshua sends three letters to the current population, informing them that their sovereignty has lapsed and that if they want to stay in the Land of Israel, their behavior will have to change. Joshua offers the Canaanites three options. The first is that if they would like to leave, they could do so unharmed. The second is war—which, they are promised, would be met with war. The third would enable the Canaanites to repent from their sinful ways and remain in the Land, albeit as subjects of Israelite sovereignty. While they would not be forced to convert to Judaism, they would be required to accept the Noachide Laws and thereby discontinue the particular sins that specifically pollute the Land.[2]

Once the Israelites assume the role of sovereign nation, the clock on their sovereignty begins as well; they are held to the same standard as the previous inhabitants. The Talmud teaches that violation of the cardinal sins was ultimately what led to the destruction of the First and Second Temples and the exiles that ensued.[3] No matter the nation, performance of the three cardinal sins causes pollution of the Land. Once the threshold for sin is met, the current sovereign nation—even Israel—becomes vulnerable to attack and subject to exile.

Isaiah prophesies devastation on the Jewish nation as a result of its sinfulness during the period of the First Commonwealth, lamenting, "Alas, she has become a harlot, the faithful city, that was filled with justice, where righteousness dwelt—but now murderers" (Isaiah 1:21). Isaiah's commentary on the immoral behavior in his day suggests a recognition of sins that pollute the Land, ultimately leading to destruction and exile. We see here the repercussions that materialize in the Land of Israel when justice is absent. For Isaiah, such an atmosphere develops when murder becomes commonplace and perpetrators are not held accountable. Ibn Ezra compares the behavior of the Jewish people to a woman unfaithful to her husband. Just as she pollutes the sanctity of marriage and negates the status that exists between two spouses, so too the Jewish people, by straying, make their relationship to the Land of Israel impure and unsustainable.[4] Just as an adulterer is then removed from the spouse's home, so too Israel relinquishes its place in God's chosen home.

We can infer that unlike in other lands, exchange of authority in the Land of Israel became possible in the biblical and Rabbinic periods only when one nation reached its threshold of immorality and the Land could no longer tolerate its presence. With the return of Jewish sovereignty to *Eretz Yisrael* in our day, consideration of ancient precedent might be useful in assessing what Jewish sovereignty means today in terms of moral expectations and with respect to other nations living among the Jewish majority. In that sense, we could argue that the future of Jewish sovereignty in the State of Israel today is dependent on its own moral performance, and therefore it must take care to create a polity based on justice where immorality is not tolerated. On the other hand, that same state has the right to expect other nations living within its borders to behave in a similar fashion and to reject the three cardinal sins that pollute the Land, just as Joshua required the Canaanites who remained in the Land.

We should be very careful not to superimpose biblical and Rabbinic milieus onto present-day realities, but that does not mean we should not extract certain principles that are useful in assessing our contemporary situation. The State of Israel today implements many policies that emanate from its safety and security requirements. It is frequently argued that these policies infringe on the rights of the Palestinian people and are therefore unjust. Yet when infringements are the result of a people living within the borders of the Land who have not accepted the Noachide Laws, who have created a culture that glorifies and rewards murder of innocent Israelis, and who have not officially accepted that the State of Israel is a country like any other that deserves a permanent and secure future, we cannot indict the State of Israel for the measures it takes to defend itself. Nor can we claim that Israel has failed to establish a fair and just society that is supported by an independent judicial system.

Therefore, we Jews living in the Diaspora—who recognize in the State of Israel "the first manifestation of the approach of the redemption,"[5] who believe that Israel has a right to exist and has established a vibrant democracy in a contentious region where human rights are systematically violated by its neighboring countries—can dream of a day when Israel's adversaries inside its borders and under its rule repudiate violence, commit to peace, and accept that pollution of the Land disqualifies one's right to inhabit the Land. While we recognize that the Palestinian people have every right to continue living within the borders of Israel and in territory Israel controls and that Palestinians are in no way responsible to follow Jewish law or principles, we can nonetheless hope that they will repudiate violence in the same spirit that Joshua hoped the Canaanites would renounce the violence and murder that the Torah contends pollutes the Land.

We can be grateful that our brothers and sisters living in and defending the State of Israel, despite all the challenges they face and the constant state of war that has shadowed them since independence, have endeavored to protect themselves and their state against all odds. Surely the means that are required are sometimes disturbing, but they are necessary so long as Israel's adversaries continue to advocate violence and discord and thereby bring pollution into the Land. Our support for their efforts is well founded in our tradition, making our advocacy at every turn a social justice imperative.

Notes

1. Leviticus 18:25; Numbers 35:33; Jeremiah 16:18; Babylonian Talmud, *Shabbat* 31a.
2. *Vayikra Rabbah* 17:7.
3. Babylonian Talmud, *Gittin* 55b–58a.

4. Ibn Ezra on Isaiah 1:21.
5. From "Prayer for the State of Israel" by Rabbi Yitzchak Halevi Herzog.

VAYEIRA—GENESIS 18:1–22:24

The Abraham Bind:
The Akeidah and Religious Freedom

RABBI DAVID SEGAL

"RABBI, WHY DO WE HAVE TO READ *this* story every year?"
A distressed congregant used to ask me this question annually before the Rosh HaShanah recitation of the *Akeidah*, the Binding of Isaac (Genesis 22:1–24). As a rabbi, I find that Jews treat this story like a textual albatross around our necks. We can apologize for it or try to rationalize it, but we cannot ignore the father of our faith setting off with grim determination to slaughter his beloved son at God's command.

In everyday life, when someone claims to hear God's voice, most people respond with skepticism and—depending on what "God's voice" is telling that person to do—alarm. And yet, as Jews in America, we support the First Amendment's protection of the free exercise of religion. It is "the bulwark of religious freedom and inter-faith amity"[1] that has made America a refuge for Jews. We live in the tension of wanting limitless religious freedom for ourselves and, at the same time, limits on religious expressions that cause harm.

The *Akeidah* is the tale *par excellence* of a faith-possessed zealot embracing barbarism under the banner of piety. What kind of free exercise of faith are we defending if the *Akeidah* is our paradigm? Fortunately, studying *Parashat Vayeira* closely offers a different model. By exploring how Jewish tradition has resolved a tension within this portion, we can construct a nuanced approach to religious liberty that might inform Jewish advocacy and communal relations in twenty-first-century America.

There can be little doubt that God rewards Abraham for his willingness to carry out the ritual filicide. "For now I know," says the angel, "that you are one who fears God [*y'rei Elohim*, יְרֵא אֱלֹהִים], as you did not withhold your son, your only one, from Me" (Genesis 22:12). We may look for interpretive salves to dull the text's cruel sting,[2] but it is hard to avoid the *p'shat*, the plain meaning, of the text: God's proof that Abraham "fears God" is precisely Abraham's willingness to sacrifice "your son, your only one."

Elsewhere in *Vayeira*, there is a different way of "fearing God." After Abraham pretends Sarah is his sister, for fear of what Abimelech would do to them otherwise, Abimelech takes Sarah into his house. God reveals the truth to Abimelech in a dream and warns him to set it right. The next morning, Abimelech confronts Abraham about the deception: "What were you thinking of, that you did this?" (Genesis 20:10).

Abraham's answer shows that fearing God can look different from the horror of the *Akeidah*: "I thought, 'There is no fear of God [*yirat Elohim*, יִרְאַת אֱלֹהִים] at all in this place, and they will kill me for my wife'" (Genesis 20:11). Rabbi W. Gunther Plaut understood Abraham to mean, "Their moral standards (we would say today) are very low, and they will kill me."[3] Abraham equates fear of God with a basic commitment to ethical norms.

Abraham's understanding of *yirat Elohim* as a sense of right behavior sets a precedent within the Torah. In the beginning of the Book of Exodus, when Pharaoh orders the Hebrew midwives to kill every newborn Hebrew boy, "the midwives, *fearing God*, did not do as the king of Egypt had told them; they let the boys live" (Exodus 1:17; emphasis added). For the midwives, "fearing God" means intervening to protect innocent children. God rewards them precisely "because they feared God" (Exodus 1:21) in this way. The language echoes God's reward to Abraham after the *Akeidah*, but the contrast could not be starker: the midwives merit reward for protecting innocent children *from* a cruel decree, while Abraham merits reward for agreeing to sacrifice an innocent child *to* a cruel decree.[4]

A major thrust of Jewish tradition amplifies the humane, ethical version of *yirat Elohim*, in contrast to Abraham's fanatical devotion. Israeli scholar Avi Sagi summarizes this view: "The *Akedah* is no longer a paradigm of religious life but a one-time event at the dawn of history, a plea to God for compassion and mercy. Religious life is not cruelty, but pity and compassion, and these are required, above all, from God."[5] The *Akeidah* should be compartmentalized as a unique, liminal moment, not treated as an exemplar to emulate.

One need not be a liberal Jew to embrace the idea that Torah is broadly compatible with ethics. Ancient Rabbinic sources suggested that the mitzvot (commandments) are not arbitrary, but rational and good.[6] Maimonides expounded on that view: "Every one of the 613 precepts serves to inculcate some truth, to remove some erroneous opinion, to establish proper relations in society, to diminish evil, to train in good manners, or to warn against bad habits."[7] The commandments are not the capricious whims of an irrational deity, but a set of tools with a higher purpose that is discernible by the human mind, independent of a direct experience of God's voice.

Nachmanides advanced this notion when he argued that the Torah *expects* us to use our ethical reasoning because it does not and cannot address every possible scenario: "Even regarding what God did not command, you should set your mind to do what is good and just in God's eyes, because God loves the good and the just."[8] God has given us the ability to distinguish right from wrong and the responsibility to use it.

Another concept from Jewish tradition that we can deploy to neutralize the *Akeidah* is the sunsetting of prophecy. As the Rabbis taught, "After the last prophets Haggai, Zechariah, and Malachi died, the holy spirit [*ruach hakodesh*; i.e., prophetic revelation] departed from the Jewish people."[9] The Rabbis understood that you cannot maintain a social contract or justice system if everyone has a "God told me so" escape clause. In place of direct revelation, the Rabbis centered the practice of robust debate, through which conflicts could be negotiated and resolved. Prophecy had to give way to deliberative community.

This legacy should inform our nuanced support of religious

freedom today. In our advocacy efforts, we should continue to speak truth to power, not only in the prophetic voice of justice, but also in broadly accessible moral terms. We must articulate not only our principled opposition to discrimination under the guise of religious freedom, but also the real harms caused to human beings by religiously motivated behaviors.[10] When a religious business owner refuses service to LGBTQ individuals on a claim of sincerely held belief,[11] we should affirm publicly the principle of LGBTQ equality as well as the verifiable reality that anti-LGBTQ sentiment sustains a social climate in which rates of self-harm and suicide are markedly higher among LGBTQ individuals, especially teens.[12] It is not simply a matter of hurt feelings. Professor Aaron Koller captures the connection between this notion of harm and our text: "And so this is the ethical teaching of the *Akedah*: . . . one person's religious fulfillment cannot come through harm to another."[13]

At the same time, Rabbinic tradition calls us to check our own prophetic certainty, even on our most passionately fought social justice battlefronts. I am not suggesting that we weaken our commitment to protect the most vulnerable members of society. But we should acknowledge that if prophecy has ended, it has ended for us, too. We should be careful about claiming the mantle of "God told me so"; even when it is right, it is unlikely to persuade. We can instead be defenders of good-faith claims of sincerely held belief as well as defenders of the vulnerable, the Isaacs of the world at risk of being sacrificed at the altar of another's blind religious zeal.

Finally, we must double down as practitioners of deliberative community. For many of us in Reform Judaism, advocacy in the legislative or judicial process is our social justice inheritance and comfort zone. But change comes in other forms, and spiritual activists can exercise power in realms beyond the legislative and jurisprudential. Douglas Laycock, an expert in religious liberty and the law, writes, "Government must treat [all constitutionally protected religious beliefs] with neutrality and tolerance"—even unpopular ones— but "other Americans can disapprove and try to persuade."[14] Our influence—and, therefore, our responsibility—does not start and end with the judge's gavel or lawmaker's vote.

Sincerely held religious beliefs and common ethical norms are both fluid categories. More recently than is comfortable to admit, American enslavement of Black Africans was considered biblically approved by Christian and Jewish voices alike.[15] Even within our lifetime, LGBTQ individuals were denied the equal right to marry, an exclusion defended by many on religious grounds.[16] When Congress enacts laws, when the Supreme Court issues landmark rulings, when religious denominations pass resolutions to correct what we believe in retrospect are obvious injustices, the human agents making those decisions do so because their moral imaginations have expanded beyond those of their forebears. Sincerely held beliefs and moral commitments evolve, especially when our eyes are opened to the faces and stories of those suffering harm.

Let us continue our advocacy efforts for policy outcomes to protect the most vulnerable from discrimination disguised as fidelity to religious conviction. But let us also reaffirm the importance of the grassroots relational work, across lines of difference, that cultivates a cultural and social context in which our vision of justice can take root and bloom.[17]

God has shown us what we need: Torah, our own moral intuition, a deliberative tradition across time, and a deliberative community across lines of difference. To be a Jew committed to social justice is to leverage all these tools. Then we will fulfill our destiny as descendants of Abraham, the one whom God chose in *Parashat Vayeira* to "teach his children and those who come after him to keep the way[18] of the Eternal, doing what is right and just" (Genesis 18:19).

NOTES

1. Union of American Hebrew Congregations, "Separation of Church and State," resolution adopted 1965, Union for Reform Judaism, https://urj.org/what-we-believe/resolutions/separation-church-and-state.
2. A midrash in *B'reishit Rabbah* (56:12) even suggests that God only wanted Abraham to "take Isaac up" on the mountain and then take him down, playing on an ambiguous reading of *haaleihu* (Genesis 22:2), which can also

mean "offer as a burnt offering." See also Aaron Koller, *Unbinding Isaac: The Significance of the Akedah for Modern Jewish Thought* (Philadelphia: Jewish Publication Society, 2020), 113–26, especially his treatment of Jeremiah, Amos, and Ezekiel's rejection of child sacrifice. See also Avi Sagi, "The Meaning of the 'Akedah' in Israeli Culture and Jewish Tradition," *Israel Studies* 3, no. 1 (Spring 1998): 55–56, http://www.jstor.com/stable/30246795, on the tradition of "protest midrashim" against the Akedah. See also Wendy Zierler, "In Search of a Feminist Reading of the Akedah," *Nashim: A Journal of Jewish Women's Studies & Gender Issues* 9 (Spring 5765/2009), for a feminist approach to redeeming the *Akeidah*.

3. W. Gunther Plaut, ed., *The Torah: A Modern Commentary*, rev. ed. (New York: Reform Judaism Publishing, an imprint of CCAR Press, 2005), 131, note on Genesis 20:11.

4. See also the end of Genesis, where Joseph devises a test to determine his brothers' worthiness before revealing his identity. He offers to let them take food to their starving families, as long as one of the brothers remains behind. "Do this," Joseph says, "and live—I am a *god-fearing* man!" (Genesis 42:18; emphasis added). Joseph's self-description is meant to reassure: to fear God is to be decent, trustworthy, even merciful. Since he fears God, the brothers have no reason to fear him—quite unlike a father who would sacrifice his own son.

5. Sagi, "Meaning of the 'Akedah' in Israeli Culture and Jewish Tradition," 56.

6. For example, *Midrash Tanchuma* 15b says the purpose of mitzvot is the refinement of God's creatures; *D'varim Rabbah* 8:5 says the purpose of mitzvot is preserving the world.

7. Maimonides, *Guide for the Perplexed* 3:31.

8. Nachmanides, commentary on Deuteronomy 6:18; see also his comments on Genesis 6:2 and 6:13 and Leviticus 19:2. See also Koller, *Unbinding Isaac*, 71–72, whose translation is adapted here.

9. Babylonian Talmud, parallel texts at *Yoma* 9b, *Sanhedrin* 11a, and *Sotah* 48b. Although a *bat kol* (divine voice) was thought to remain, even that was said to be reserved for only the rare worthy soul in a generation (Babylonian Talmud, *Sanhedrin* 11a). And even when a rabbi could invoke the *bat kol* to bolster his argument, as in the Oven of Achnai story (Babylonian Talmud, *Bava M'tzia* 59a–b), the majority of the Rabbinic council overruled the divine voice!

10. The Reform Jewish Movement has a history of doing this, as in Union of American Hebrew Congregations, "Appointing Committee to Present to State Legislatures Petition for Enactment of Sabbath Observance Laws," resolution adopted 1876 (Union for Reform Judaism, https://urj.org/what-we-believe/resolutions/appointing-committee-present-state-legislatures-petition-enactment), which defends "the dictates of . . . conscience" alongside "legitimate business" concerns. See also Rabbi Jonah Pesner, "Reform Jewish Movement Condemns Decision to Allow Discrimination in Foster Care System," press release, January 23, 2019, Religious Action Center, https://

rac.org/press-room/reform-jewish-movement-condemns-decision-allow-discrimination-foster-care-system; and Barbara Weinstein, "Reform Movement Condemns Proposal Expanding Religious Exemptions for Federal Contractors," press release August 14, 2019, Religious Action Center, https://rac.org/press-room/reform-movement-condemns-proposal-expanding-religious-exemptions-federal-contractors.

11. See, e.g., Masterpiece Cakeshop, Ltd., et al. v. Colorado Civil Rights Commission et al., June 4, 2018, https://www.supremecourt.gov/opinions/17pdf/16-111_j4el.pdf.

12. "Facts About Suicide," The Trevor Project, accessed December 24, 2020, https://www.thetrevorproject.org/resources/preventing-suicide/facts-about-suicide/. Note: "Each episode of LGBT victimization, such as physical or verbal harassment or abuse, increases the likelihood of self-harming behavior by 2.5 times on average."

13. Koller, *Unbinding Isaac*, 147; see also 154.

14. Douglas Laycock, "The Broader Implications of Masterpiece Cakeshop," *BYU Law Review* 2019, no. 1 (Summer 2019): 195.

15. Howard B. Rock, "New York's Pro-Slavery Rabbi," *Tablet*, September 19, 2012, https://www.tabletmag.com/sections/news/articles/new-yorks-pro-slavery-rabbi; Noel Rae, "How Christian Slaveholders Used the Bible to Justify Slavery," *Time*, February 23, 2018, https://time.com/5171819/christianity-slavery-book-excerpt/.

16. In *Obergefell v. Hodges*, the Supreme Court ruled in favor of a constitutional right to same-sex marriage, June 26, 2015, https://www.supremecourt.gov/opinions/14pdf/14-556_3204.pdf. See Sarah Zylstra and Morgan Lee, "'Outrage and Panic' Are Off-Limits, Say Evangelical Leaders on Same-Sex Marriage," *Christianity Today*, June 26, 2015, https://www.christianitytoday.com/ct/2015/june-web-only/evangelical-leaders-react-supreme-court-same-sex-marriage.html, for a roundup of Christian voices opposing the Supreme Court decision based on their long-standing defense of "traditional" and "biblical" marriage. Franklin Graham's opinion is emblematic of this view: Franklin Graham, "God Defines Marriage, Not the Supreme Court," Billy Graham Evangelical Association, June 26, 2015, https://billygraham.org/story/franklin-graham-god-defines-marriage-not-the-supreme-court/.

17. Note in these Reform Jewish Movement resolutions the evolution from a 1965 non-negotiable commitment to separation of church and state, to a 1987 call to work with other faiths to develop community sensitivity to minority faiths: Union of American Hebrew Congregations, "Separation of Church and State," resolution passed 1965, Union for Reform Judaism, https://urj.org/what-we-believe/resolutions/separation-church-and-state; Union of American Hebrew Congregations, "Sectarian Prayer in Public Settings," resolution passed 1987, Union for Reform Judaism, https://urj.org/what-we-believe/resolutions/sectarian-prayer-public-settings.

18. See Nehama Leibowitz, *Studies in Bereshit* (Israel: Maor Wallach Press, n.d.),

169–70, where she cites Jeremiah to show that "the doing of righteousness and justice is synonymous with knowing the Lord."

Marriage Justice in
Our Biblical Stories

RABBI NAAMAH KELMAN

AT THE HEART of the *Parashat Chayei Sarah*, we discover a sixty-five-*pasuk* (verse) novella, Genesis 24, one of the longest chapters in our *Tanach*. It is a fully developed story, with a beginning, middle, and end. And unlike many other biblical tales of strife, jealousy, and rebellion, this one has a happy conclusion. In the story, Abraham's unnamed servant seeks to find a wife for his master's son (Genesis 24:2–4). After the dramatic Binding of Isaac, told in only nineteen *p'sukim* (verses), Abraham seeks to secure his future. The opening of the story tells us, "And the Eternal had blessed Abraham in all ways [*bakol*, בַּכֹּל]" (Genesis 24:1). The biblical narrator is saying we can relax and enjoy the tale because it will end happily.

This narrative can be read on many levels. It can be read literally, by following the tension, character development, and more. It can also be read as an epic, a story that might hint to other stories, future stories. Is it a love story? Is it a story, like much of *B'reishit* (Genesis), of legacy and succession? Is it all the above?

In this narrative, we learn about the Torah's first arranged marriage. In the ancient world, a woman went from her father's household to her husband's, with or without her consent. What is striking here, however, is that Rebekah *is* asked for her consent (Genesis 24:57–58), although the arrangement is already signed and sealed (Genesis 24:50–51). Not only is she asked for, and gives, consent, she "falls off her camel" at the sight of Isaac (Genesis 24:64), as if smitten by "love at first sight." More importantly, we learn that Isaac brings her into his tent, where he loves her and is comforted by her (Genesis 24:67). One might think that Rebekah and Isaac have agency by the end of the story, though certainly not at the onset.

Only in the modern era do women have autonomy to choose their marriage partner, but even now this agency in matters of marriage is not universal. In the State of Israel and in Orthodox circles around the world, women have a subordinate status in rituals surrounding marriage and are bound to their husband's will in matters of divorce.

According to the Mishnah in Tractate *Kiddushin*, a woman could be taken in marriage/union in three ways: *kesef* (כֶּסֶף), *sh'tar* (שְׁטָר), or *biah* (בִּיאָה)—through a monetary gift, with a *ketubah* or document of engagement, or through sexual relations.[1] Thankfully, even during the Rabbinic period, the tradition changed dramatically. While the Rabbis forbade sexual relations as a way of "acquiring" a wife, the other two arrangements hold until today. Every marriage needed a *ketubah*. The *ketubah* was the basis for future divorce, guaranteeing women release and some financial compensation so long as their husband consented to a divorce. Today, the *ketubah* has only symbolic significance in traditional marriages.

In the Diaspora, where civil marriage and divorce exist, Jewish women have full autonomy to enter and exit marriages, although Orthodox and Conservative women would need a *get*, a halachic divorce, to remarry in a Jewish ceremony. In Israel, marriage and divorce are under the complete control of the Orthodox Chief Rabbinate. Women do not have full autonomy in marriage procedures and have no freedom in divorce. Jewish women in Israel must use the *mikveh* (ritual bath) in order to prepare for their marriage ceremony. They do not have any role in the *ketubah* writing or signing. They say nothing during the wedding ceremony. These requirements and restrictions apply to any Israeli woman who goes through the Chief Rabbinate, as the majority of non-Orthodox Israelis do. Most are willing to tolerate this ancient, patriarchal system for a host of reasons—not least because Israel has no civil marriage, and the Israeli government does not recognize any Jewish marriages conducted outside the authority of the Chief Rabbinate. Sadly, if a secular, non-Orthodox couple gets divorced, they have no recourse except to go back to the Chief Rabbinate, where women discover their subordinate status.

The contrast with the loving couple in our *parashah* is stark. Even if it is symbolic, Rebekah agrees, Isaac loves, and they find comfort in one another. What the story does not mention is that Rebekah will be the one to determine the future of *B'nei Yisrael*, the Children of Israel. She will hold the fate of our people in her control, choosing Jacob over Esau to inherit the patrimony (Genesis 27:6–17). If the decision were left to Isaac, we would be *B'nei* Esau (Genesis 27:1–4). Rebekah plays a double role—even a transformative one. It is Rebekah who understands the destiny of her people, and she will use her love, for Isaac and for Jacob, as a means of redemption, securing the lineage.

There are clues in the story itself alluding, not so subtly, to another biblical narrative in which the fate of the Jewish people is changed by redemptive, transformative love that will set the legacy and lineage straight—the story of Ruth. In *Chayei Sarah*, the strange verb *hakreih* (הַקְרֵה) is found in the speech of Abraham's servant, asking God to *"bring me luck* today" (Genesis 24:12) by identifying the woman to be Isaac's wife. The same verb is repeated in Ruth, where we are told that *"vayiker* [וַיִּקֶר, as luck would have it], Ruth *mikreha* [מִקְרֶהָ, stumbled upon] the piece of land belonging to Boaz" (Ruth 2:3). The events in these two stories do not happen by chance; they are God's work. Abraham's servant discovers a certain well only to discover Rebekah, and Ruth "stumbles" upon Boaz's field.

Ruth, the embodiment of love and *chesed* (loving-kindness), will give birth to the messianic, redemptive lineage (Ruth 4:13–22). Her kindness is recognized (Ruth 2:11), just like Rebekah's (Genesis 24:42–48). Abraham's servant meeting Rebekah at the well is not a coincidence;[2] it will become the catalyst for choosing her, just as Boaz will reveal Ruth's devotion and compassion. Both are brought into Israelite households so they can be healed. They "choose" their destinies and the destinies of the Children of Israel. Once the connections are made, it is clear to the servant and later to Naomi that

God has not abandoned them, but rather that God's *chesed* has guided them to these circumstances (Genesis 24:27; Ruth 2:20).

As inspiring and hopeful as these stories are, centuries will pass before women gain freedom and agency in marriage and divorce. These biblical women have to act in order to guarantee the heir who will assume his rightful place in the ongoing story of the Children of Israel. Jacob is Rebekah's choice for receiving the birthright, and Ruth will make the line of David possible. Jacob is David's ancestor as well, and David's line will, according to prophecy, bring forth the Messiah. Ruth is cast as a vessel of loving-kindness throughout her story. For Rebekah, a more devious and difficult journey ensues, pitting her own twin sons against one another.

And yet, unlike our other patriarchs and matriarchs, Isaac and Rebekah share a lifelong, monogamous marriage—as do Ruth and Boaz, from the time they meet—with no additional wives or maidservants. We cannot call these marriages equal, but they are partnerships based on love and commitment, not economic or status gain. For much of Jewish history, marriages were of the latter type: arrangements between families, often based on status and class, with neither partner having much choice.

With the rise of Jewish feminism, the marriage ceremony outside Orthodoxy—and, in some quarters, even within it—has changed in remarkable ways. Couples now write their own egalitarian *ketubot* together. *Mikveh* has been reimagined for marriage partners of all genders, in heterosexual as well as queer marriages. The ceremony includes a double ring exchange. Even the Blessing of Engagement, *Birkat Eirusin*, and the Seven Blessings, *Sheva B'rachot*, are rewritten to reflect our current sensitivities. Women have full agency in these ceremonies.

Divorce is another story. The Reform Movement eliminated the tradition of the writ of divorce and simply replaced it with civil divorce.[3] While the CCAR's rabbi's manual[4] offers an egalitarian divorce ritual, it is not widely used, at least not yet. For Jewish couples in Israel, only Orthodox divorce under the supervision of the

Chief Rabbinate is legally recognized, even for couples who have a civil marriage abroad.

Many Israelis now choose common law arrangements for registry purposes, but a growing percentage, including the modern Orthodox, have created their own ceremonies.[5] While not recognized by the authorities, these marriages are embraced by a growing community. Today, civil courts determine child custody, alimony, division of property, and similar matters in Israel. MARAM, our Israeli Reform rabbinical association, requires Israeli Reform rabbis to utilize prenuptial agreements issued by the Israel Religious Action Center to make divorce more equitable in court. This is largely intended to protect women. The prenup is their protection from the rabbinic courts and the basis for agreements in the civil courts.

We learn much about the importance of women's agency in marriage from the stories of Rebekah and Isaac, Ruth and Boaz. These moving narratives show that marriages in which women remain objects or vessels are not based on loving-kindness or fairness. Marriages work best when love and equality are the foundation.

Notes

1. *Mishnah Kiddushin* 1:1.
2. Malbim, Genesis 24:15, *inter alia*.
3. Central Conference of American Rabbis, "162. Reform Judaism and Divorce," *American Reform Responsa*, vol. 90 (New York: CCAR Press, 1980), 84–86; available online: https://www.ccarnet.org/ccar-responsa/arr-511-514/.
4. *L'chol Z'man V'Eit: For Sacred Moments; The CCAR Life-Cycle Guide* (New York: CCAR Press, 2015).
5. Phil M. Cohen, "Israel's Undemocratic Marriage Laws," *Tablet*, August 19, 2019, https://www.tabletmag.com/sections/israel-middle-east/articles/israels-undemocratic-marriage-laws.

TOL'DOT—GENESIS 25:19–28:9

Digging Isaac's Third Well: Water and Systemic Racism

RABBI DAVID SPINRAD

WHEN I WAKE UP in the morning, the amount of water I will use in the coming day is never on my mind. The #4Liters Challenge from DigDeep, a nonprofit that brings running water to underserved American communities, seeks to change that. The organization challenges people to stretch four liters of water—about a gallon, the minimum amount to satisfy an individual's needs—across twenty-four hours.[1] As I began the #4Liters Challenge, I had to strategize how I was going to do so. In a time of COVID-19, how would I wash for the recommended twenty seconds? If I did this under running water, it would immediately exhaust my four liters.[2] I need three to four liters of water per day to feel hydrated. If I consumed that much, how would I meet my hygiene needs?

When I started the #4Liters Challenge, two things were certain: (1) my water *needs* were about to become *wants*, and (2) half a liter of water would be devoted to coffee. Two hours into the challenge, I added a third certainty: the #4Liters Challenge is an exercise in privilege. My hardship was self-induced and temporary. Other than mentioning the inverse relationship between how much water I had and how often I thought about it, it would be fruitless to recount the details of my day because the experience was false. I could have stopped the challenge at any time and returned to easy and endless access to clean, affordable water. Unlike the two million Americans living without basic access to safe drinking water and sanitation[3] or the more than forty-four million Americans served by water systems with recent Safe Drinking Water Act violations,[4] I had the privilege to forget about the preciousness of safe water access. I am counted among the ranks of ordinary American citizens, who typically use eighty-eight gallons (about 333 liters)[5] of water per day.

In contrast to the freedom I have to suspend my privilege, systemic racism in the United States—the policies and structures that create and maintain racial inequity in nearly every facet of life for people of color—underpins the opposite experience of those who could never dream of turning off access and equity like a faucet. According to African American civil rights leader Benjamin Chavis, systemic environmental racism manifests in policy making, the enforcement of regulations and laws, the deliberate targeting of communities of color for toxic waste facilities, the official sanctioning of life-threatening poisons and pollutants in communities of color, and the history of excluding people of color from leadership in ecology movements.[6] Further, systemic racism underlies the reality that race is the leading predictor of water and sanitation access and affordability.[7]

Nationwide, African American and Latino households are nearly twice as likely to lack complete plumbing than white households. Indigenous households are nineteen times more likely. The proportion of Native American, African American, Latino, or Pacific Islander residents in a census tract is correlated with the percentage of homes that lack complete plumbing.[8] Race, ethnicity, and language spoken have the strongest relationships to slow and inadequate enforcement of the Safe Drinking Water Act of any sociodemographic characteristics.[9] Sadly, though, unless we experience these impacts of systemic racism directly, we can more easily ignore them than commit ourselves to the task of dismantling them.

For many, the mass lead poisoning in Flint, Michigan, marked a moment of awakening. Fifty-seven percent of Flint residents are African American, and 40 percent live below the poverty line.[10] Nearly one hundred thousand people, including nine thousand children,[11] were exposed to dangerous amounts of lead when the water source was switched from the Detroit Water Authority to the Flint Water

System. This crisis is the paradigmatic example of how systemic racism affects water supply.

Flint fell under state control in 2011 because of its desperate economic conditions, leading to a 2014 decision by then-governor Rick Snyder to appoint an unelected emergency manager, Michael Brown. Both are white. In a cost-cutting move, Brown switched the city's water supply from Detroit's treated water to the untreated water of the Flint River. In treating the river water, the city failed to add a corrosion inhibitor, causing lead to leach from the city's pipes. For eighteen months, polluted, discolored, foul-smelling, and foul-tasting water that had traveled through aging, lead-leaching pipes was continuously directed into predominantly African American homes. Residents suffered rashes, hair loss, illness, and death from Legionnaire's disease, and the number of Flint's children with dangerously elevated blood lead levels doubled, even tripling in some neighborhoods.[12]

Further, the persistent US rejection of its obligation to the human right to water entrenches systemic racism. In 2020, We the People of Detroit, an organization committed to community research and water rights, released a report that identified a correlation between water shutoffs and increased cases of COVID-19.[13] Discontinuing water service for inability to pay is incompatible with human rights, never more so than at a time when personal hygiene is necessary to avoiding contracting and spreading a deadly virus.

What do the Torah and its commentaries teach us about the struggle for water? In *Parashat Tol'dot*, Isaac follows Abraham's path during a time of famine. Lacking water, he and his household journey and sojourn in Gerar, where Isaac contends with Abimelech, king of the Philistines. Isaac prospers, enjoying enough access to water that his crops return a hundredfold and his livestock increase exponentially. In response to his prosperity, the Philistines stop up the wells Abraham's servants had dug. Abimelech, fearful and envious of Isaac's success, drives him away (Genesis 26:12–16).

Departing, Isaac encamps at the Wadi of Gerar, where he reopens another well that had been dug by Abraham's servants. The herdsmen

of Gerar quarrel with Isaac's herdsmen over access to this well, leading Isaac to name the place Esek, which according to Nachmanides
means "contention."[14] Later, Isaac's herdsmen dig a second well, his
right to which the herdsmen of Gerar dispute. Convinced that their
arguments are malicious and illegitimate, Isaac responds by naming
the place Sitnah, which Chizkuni teaches means "hatred"[15] (Genesis
26:20–21).

Isaac then digs a third and final well, and no quarreling ensues.
Relieved, Isaac names the place Rehoboth, meaning "open spaces."
He exclaims, "Now the Eternal has granted us *ample room* and will
make us fruitful in the land" (Genesis 26:22).

While citing the Torah for examples of systemic racism would
be retrojective overreach, we are grounded in a foundational Jewish
identity as migrants. As Jews, we see ourselves as the perpetual other
and respond accordingly. While Jews of Color represent at least 12
to 15 percent of American Jews,[16] our responsibility to ensure equal
access to safe water extends beyond our Jewish community to all who
lack this basic human right.

Nachmanides questions why the Torah goes to such lengths when
discussing the wells. The story appears to serve no purpose. However,
from a verse in Jeremiah in which God is likened to the "source of
living water" (Jeremiah 17:13), Nachmanides suggests that the story
hints at the first, second, and eventual third Jerusalem Temples—the
last being central to the traditional messianic dream. He teaches
that—in contrast to the first two wells, whose names testify to their
destruction and that of the first two Temples—the name of the third
well, Rehoboth, alludes to the future, messianic era Temple that
will one day be built without conflict or hatred.[17] Concluding with
"[the Eternal] will make us fruitful in the land" (Genesis 26:22), the
verse portends a time in which all nations will serve the Eternal with
singular resolve. The name Rehoboth invites us to imagine a world
perfected and to endeavor to hasten it.

Today, affordable access to water seems like a messianic dream,
but working toward this fundamental human right is within our
capacity. Senator Kamala Harris and Dolores Huerta, cofounder

with Cesar Chavez of the United Farm Workers, offered concrete solutions to this problem:

> We must [establish] safe water . . . [as] an engine of equitable economic growth. The United States needs a $1 trillion investment to meet our collective water infrastructure needs over the next 25 years, which would create millions of family-sustaining jobs. We should guarantee that front-line communities receive their fair share of investment, including those served by very small water systems and household drinking wells, as well as in our urban cities. We must pass the Water Justice Act, which will invest in communities that have burdened environmental injustices for generations. It would establish a new $10 billion water affordability program and make a $220 billion investment in clean and safe drinking water initiatives. . . . Make no mistake, this fight for water justice is a fight for environmental justice. It is a fight for climate justice. It is a fight for racial justice.[18]

While passage of legislation like the Water Justice Act would positively contribute to the fight for racial justice, we should go further—all Americans must embrace safe and affordable water access as a basic human right. This will bring us closer to the prophetic vision foreseen by Isaiah, an age when water will flow unceasingly for all and "joyfully shall [we] draw water from the fountains of salvation" (Isaiah 12:3).

Notes

1. "The #4Liters Challenge," DigDeep, accessed December 24, 2020, https://www.digdeep.org/4liters.
2. "Per Capita Water Use: How Much Water Do You Use in Your Home?," United States Geological Survey, accessed December 24, 2020, https://water.usgs.gov/edu/activity-percapita.php.
3. *Closing the Water Access Gap in the United States: A National Action Plan* (DigDeep Right to Water Project and US Water Alliance, 2019), 12, http://uswateralliance.org/sites/uswateralliance.org/files/Closing%20the%20Water%20Access%20Gap%20in%20the%20United%20States_DIGITAL.pdf.
4. *Closing the Water Access Gap in the United States*, 13.
5. WaterSense, "Statistics and Facts," United States Environmental Protection Agency, November 7, 2018, https://www.epa.gov/watersense/statistics-and-facts.

6. Peter Beech, "What Is Environmental Racism?," *Global Policy*, August 4, 2020, https://www.globalpolicyjournal.com/blog/04/08/2020/what-environmental-racism.

7. *Closing the Water Access Gap in the United States*, 20.

8. *Closing the Water Access Gap in the United States*, 22.

9. Kristi Pullen Fedinick, Steve Taylor, and Michele Roberts, *Watered Down Justice* (National Resources Defense Council, September 2019), 4, https://www.nrdc.org/sites/default/files/watered-down-justice-report.pdf.

10. "Quick Facts: Flint City, Michigan," United States Census Bureau, accessed December 24, 2020, https://www.census.gov/quickfacts/flintcitymichigan.

11. "Flint Lead Exposure Registry," Centers for Disease Control and Prevention, July 30, 2019, https://www.cdc.gov/nceh/lead/programs/flint-registry.htm.

12. "Transition to a New Water Source," in "Flint Water Crisis," Wikipedia, updated December 24, 2020, https://en.wikipedia.org/wiki/Flint_water_crisis#Transition_to_a_new_water_source.

13. "Detroit Water Shutoffs Led to More COVID-19 Cases," WLNS.com, July 9, 2020, https://www.wlns.com/news/michigan/detroit-water-shutoffs-led-to-more-covid-19-cases/.

14. Ramban to Genesis 26:20.

15. Chizkuni to Genesis 26:21.

16. Dr. Ari Y. Kelman, Dr. Aaron Hahn Tapper, Isabel Fonseca, and Dr. Aliya Saperstein, *Counting Inconsistencies: An Analysis of American Jewish Population Studies, with a Focus on Color* (Jews of Color Field Building Initiative, Concentration in Education and Jewish Studies at the Stanford Graduate School of Education, and Swig Program in Jewish Studies and Social Justice at the University of San Francisco, May 2019), 2, https://jewsofcolorfieldbuilding.org/wp-content/uploads/2019/05/Counting-Inconsistencies-052119.pdf.

17. Ramban to Genesis 26:20.

18. Kamala D. Harris and Doris Huerta, "Opinion: Racism Is Fueling Disparities in Access to Safe Water," *Mercury News*, July 16, 2020, https://www.mercurynews.com/2020/07/16/7301162/.

VAYEITZEI—GENESIS 28:10–32:3
Waking Up to Climate Change

RABBI JULIE SAXE-TALLER

And Jacob left Beersheba and set out for Haran. Coming upon a [certain] place, he passed the night there, for the sun was setting; taking one of the stones of the place, he made it his head-rest as he lay down in that place. He dreamed, and lo—a ladder was set on the ground, with its top reaching to heaven, and lo—angels of God going up and coming down on it. And lo—the Eternal stood above it, and said, "I, the Eternal, am the God of your father Abraham and God of Isaac: the land on which you are lying I will give to you and to your descendants. And your descendants shall be like the dust of the earth, and you shall spread out to the west and the east and the north and the south. Through you and your descendants all the families of the earth shall find blessing. And here I am, with you: I will watch over you wherever you go, and will bring you back to this soil. I will not let go of you as I have yet to do what I have promised you." Waking from his sleep, Jacob said, "Truly the Eternal is in this place, and I did not know it!" He was awestruck, and said, "How awe-inspiring is this place! This is none other than the house of God, and this is the gate of heaven!"
—*Genesis 28:10–17*

JACOB WILL SOON BE RENAMED ISRAEL, not only the ancestor but the namesake of the Jewish people. Inheritors and readers of the text can thus see this pivotal scene in Jacob's spiritual development as an instructive source for our own growth. It is a text about spiritual awakening, change, realizing one is not alone, and accessing courage in a time of intense fear and real danger. In other words, it is a text for all time and for our time.

In our context, multiple crises threaten the present and future of the earth. Ignoring what we know about the trajectory of atmospheric warming, despairing that it is too late to change it, or resigning ourselves to feelings of powerlessness all have practical implications that we cannot afford. And yet avoidance, despair, and resignation are understandable responses to the fearsome enormity of the situation. For a long time, climate change was spoken of in North America as something dangerous but far off in both time and place. But to continue to think this way is to delude ourselves. Since the late 2010s, the fire season in the western region of the continent has become an annual period marked by devastating losses and hazardous air quality. Among the losses in 2017 was URJ Camp Newman, beloved site to generations of campers and staff. Other parts of the continent are being hit by increasingly destructive hurricanes and floods, among a variety of unprecedented disasters. Yet when the smoke clears and the floodwaters recede, we talk about things "heading back to normal." What will it take for us to engage with the problems of rising temperatures and sea levels, threats to our food and water supplies, and not turn away? As we struggle to move from avoidance into action, like Jacob, we arrive at this scene in need of spiritual resources to build our strength.

Jacob has left home to fulfill his destiny as heir to his parents and grandparents. We begin with his specific points of departure and destination—Beersheba and Haran—but quickly zoom into an unnamed place in between. The Hebrew word *bamakom* (בַּמָּקוֹם), "upon a [certain] place" (Genesis 28:11), is vocalized to indicate that is a particular site. The word *makom* (מָקוֹם), "place," is repeated three times in this single verse. Before lying down to sleep, Jacob prepares deliberately; details in the text indicate that something significant is coming. One midrash enhances the drama by explaining that "the sun set suddenly for him, not at its regular time, so that he would spend the night there."[1]

Indeed, Rabbinic sources identify the "certain place" where Jacob has arrived as Mount Moriah, the same location where Jacob's father Isaac was nearly sacrificed by Abraham and also the future site of the Jerusalem Temple.[2] This place is the most revered site in all of Jewish tradition! More importantly, like the humble bush through which God speaks to Moses, Jacob has discovered that an unnamed place can become a portal of revelation, and therefore perhaps *every* place on earth has this sacred potential. This insight shines painful light on the damage we have done to the planet, as well as on the disparities in which lands bear the brunt of that damage. In general, while wealthier countries have produced the vast majority of the climate-warming emissions, lower-income countries are encountering negative impacts such as sea level rise and more extreme hurricanes and cyclones. Higher-income countries also have more resources both to prepare for and to recover from such events and changes. The Netherlands, for example, has built walls against rising sea levels, and the United States was able to spend more money on recovery from Hurricane Sandy than the entire GDP of most low-income countries.[3] These examples and many more illustrate that the climate crisis is both a threat to all forms of life and an ongoing travesty of social justice.

Contemporary Bible scholar Aviva Zornberg calls Jacob's sleep in this scene a paradox, pointing out that other Jewish sources admonish against sleeping in a holy place. Zornberg also notes that Rashi speaks of Jacob's *lacking* sleep before he leaves home[4] and that Jacob himself describes the years following this scene as a time when "sleep fled from my eyes" (Genesis 31:40). Zornberg contrasts this sleeplessness with the surprising fact that "all God wants of Jacob is that he *sleep* there. . . . 'Shall he get off without a night's sleep there?' God asks, as though such sleep is the ultimate religious duty." For us, who spend our nights looking at screens that deny darkness and find it hard to prioritize stillness and rest, making time for sleep may be exactly that, a vital mitzvah. Rashi imagines that upon awakening, Jacob is afraid that he has done something wrong by sleeping: "If I had known [that God was here], I would not have slept."[5] "But," Zornberg continues, "the paradox is clear: if Jacob had not slept, he would not have dreamed of God and angels, would not have received his first message from God, and would not know that this is a holy place."[6]

Sleep, which requires relaxation, respect for natural biological rhythms, and cessation from work, represents the opposite of the current conditions of life under advanced capitalism. People are working more, achieving less financial security, and sleeping less than in previous times.[7] New York City, a center of the world economy, is aptly known as "the city that never sleeps." The forces working against sleep are the same ones that fuel the quest for endless production and market expansion without regard for environmental impacts. Journalist and climate activist Naomi Klein writes, "While it is true that climate change is a crisis produced by an excess of greenhouse gases in the atmosphere, it is also, in a more profound sense, a crisis produced by an extractive mind-set, by a way of viewing both the natural world and the majority of its inhabitants as resources to use up and then discard."[8]

While Jacob sleeps, God comes to him in a dream with a twofold message. First is the promise of blessing and success that entails a thorough transformation of Jacob, from the "homespun man, keeping to the tents" (Genesis 25:27) to the father of a people who will spread out in all directions. Second is the promise that God will accompany Jacob throughout the trials this transformation will entail. What about us? As frightening climate events unfold, we cannot claim to know that blessing and success await us. Can we keep faith in the second part of the promise, that God is with Jacob and therefore with us?

"Truly, the Eternal is in this place, and I did not know it!" (Genesis 28:16). Upon awakening, Jacob knows something that he did not know the night before, and not merely a newfound fact about God. Jacob is changed by his dream, and the change will lift him into action. We too seek this kind of transformation. Can we learn from Jacob how to prepare ourselves? "Taking one of the stones of the place, he made it his head-rest as he lay down in that place" (Genesis 28:11). Resting his head on a stone from the land, Jacob connects himself with the place. The Hebrew enables some to say instead that he collected a number of stones and set them *around* his head, as if enacting a ritual.[9] With this simple description, the text reminds us of the power of connecting with nature and of ritual to help us slow down, increase our awareness, and become receptive to the Presence we so often ignore.

Ritual and slowing down can connect us not only to nature and its Source, but also to each other. God tells Jacob, "Through you and your descendants all the families of the earth shall find blessing" (Genesis 28:14). Indeed, facing that climate change is here and now will itself help us to connect with communities in other places, facing other impacts. And as we grow our strength, we must use it not only to rebuild a camp or repair a flooded synagogue, but also to organize for long-term policy changes, ultimately making the transition from a society that is always running, never stopping to rest, to one that minimizes harm to the planet.

Notes

1. Rashi on 28:11, "because the sun had set."
2. Rashi on 28:17, "This is none other than the house of God."
3. S. Nazrul Islam and John Winkel, "Climate Change and Social Inequality" (working paper, United Nations Department of Economic and Social Affairs, October 2017), 22–23, https://www.un.org/esa/desa/papers/2017/wp152_2017.pdf.
4. Rashi on 28:11, "and lay down in that place."
5. Rashi on 28:16, "and I did not know it."
6. Aviva Gottlieb Zornberg, The Beginning of Desire: Reflections on Genesis (Philadelphia: Jewish Publication Society, 1995), 189.
7. "Sightlines Financial Security Special Report: Seeing Our Way to Financial Security in the Age of Increasing Longevity," Stanford Center on Longevity, 2018, https://longevity.stanford.edu/sightlines-financial-security-special-report-mobile/#educators (decreasing financial security); Jagdish Khubchandani and James H. Price, "Short Sleep Duration in Working American Adults, 2010–2018," Journal of Community Health 45 (September 5, 2019) : 219–27, https://link.springer.com/article/10.1007/s10900-019-00731-9 (decreased sleep); John Cline, PhD, "Are We Really Getting Less Sleep than We Did in 1975?" Psychology Today, January 18, 2010, https://www.psychologytoday.com/us/blog/sleepless-in-america/201001/are-we-really-getting-less-sleep-we-did-in-1975 (decreased sleep); Patti Neighmond, "Working Americans Are Getting Less Sleep, Especially Those Who Save Our Lives, Morning Edition, NPR, October 28, 2019, https://www.npr.org/

sections/health-shots/2019/10/28/773622789/working-americans-are-getting-less-sleep-especially-those-who-save-our-lives (decreased sleep, connected with stress); Derek Thompson, "Workism Is Making Americans Miserable," *The Atlantic*, February 24, 2019, https://www.theatlantic.com/ideas/archive/2019/02/religion-workism-making-americans-miserable/583441/ (working more).

8. Naomi Klein, *On Fire* (New York: Simon & Schuster, 2019), 270.

9. *B'reishit Rabbah* 68:13.

Vayishlach—Genesis 32:4–36:43

Dismantling the Patriarchy from All Sides

Evan Traylor

A POWERFUL MAN, sweet talking and lustful, rapes a woman. Other men become involved and ignore the feelings and reactions of the woman. Ultimately, deadly revenge is enacted upon the rapist. The woman is never heard from again, and we do not know if she feels justice has been achieved.

Tragically, components of this story from *Parashat Vayishlach* exist throughout our society today. For far too many people, especially women, trans, and gender nonconforming people, sexual violence is pervasive. Men—especially cisgender, heterosexual men—are the perpetrators; not all the time, but we disproportionately commit these vicious, brutal crimes. The events surrounding the rape of Dinah in *Parashat Vayishlach* epitomize a patriarchal system that persists today. According to feminist author bell hooks, "Patriarchy is a political-social system that insists that males are inherently dominating, superior to everything and everyone deemed weak, especially females, and endowed with the right to dominate and rule over the weak and to maintain that dominance through various forms of psychological terrorism and violence."[1] This patriarchal system features physical violence against women as a cultural norm of toxic masculinity that both forces and empowers men to uphold the patriarchy. This *parashah* demonstrates the harm of patriarchy and toxic masculinity on all genders, calling on us, especially men, to create new forms of positive masculinity and smash this patriarchal system from all sides.

"Shechem son of Hamor the Hivite, the local prince, saw her; he took her and lay her down and raped her. He was then captivated by Jacob's daughter Dinah and, falling in love with the young woman, spoke tenderly to the young woman" (Genesis 34:2–3). In these two short verses, Shechem, a powerful government official, violently rapes Dinah, Jacob's daughter. Lacking details, this brutal section of Torah raises many questions: Why does Shechem rape Dinah? Is Dinah the first woman that he raped? Why does no one stop him? All of the answers are bound together through patriarchal ideas and actions that have harmed, silenced, and destroyed women throughout history, both in the days of the Torah and today. Shechem, with a powerful position in the community, believes and upholds the patriarchal idea that he must continue to dominate others in order to retain his power and succeed in life. Therefore, it is likely that Dinah is not the first woman that Shechem assaulted or raped, but one of his many victims. However, in the case of Dinah, Shechem pursued his victim because "his soul felt a strong attachment to her on account of her beauty as well as on account of the fact that she was the daughter of an outstanding personality, Jacob."[2]

Enacting immense harm through physically violent patriarchal behavior, Shechem targets and pursues Dinah because she is a beautiful woman with an influential father, hoping to demonstrate to other men, especially those in leadership positions, that he is domineering and powerful. Shechem's position in the community "was the reason that no one came to Dinah's assistance when she cried for help against being raped."[3] Although related in only two short verses, Shechem's rape of Dinah explains much about how men cultivate, hoard, and protect power through sexual violence—and how so many people, especially men, refuse to speak out against other powerful men. In the era of the #MeToo movement, this story has played out multiple times: President Donald Trump, Michael Steinhardt, Harvey Weinstein, and so many more.

Vicious societal judgments stemming from the smog of patriarchy silence many victims of sexual assault and rape. Too often, their stories are untold, their names unrevealed. Our Torah seems to validate this tendency, silencing Dinah throughout this story. Patriarchal ideas and actions continue to harm the most vulnerable in our society. To combat the patriarchy, men, especially cisgender and heterosexual men, must change the forces that perpetuate it.

The harm that men enact upon ourselves to uphold the patriarchy and toxic masculinity also deserves our attention and analysis. Surrounding Shechem's rape of Dinah, *Parashat Vayishlach* provides important commentary on the power of patriarchy to harm men throughout our lives. In the beginning of the *parashah*, Jacob is fearful when he learns that Esau is coming to meet him for the first time since Jacob stole his birthright and left home. However, according to Rashi, Jacob "was afraid lest he be killed, and he was distressed that he might have to kill someone," namely Esau.[4] Patriarchal ideas tell men that they must "kill or be killed," that to survive and thrive in life requires being aggressive toward others in order to dominate them through all spheres of life. In this instance, Jacob is sadly forced to contend with this harmful idea. Without the rigid protocols of patriarchy, there would always be an opportunity for true reconciliation and peace.

The night before meeting Esau, Jacob famously wrestles with an angel (Genesis 32:25–27). Much has been written about Jacob's transformation, including the angel's changing his name from Jacob to Israel, or one who "struggled with God" (Genesis 32:29). This transformation bears fruit the next day: When they meet, both Jacob and Esau lay down their aggressive, patriarchal mindsets and lovingly embrace one another (Genesis 33:1–17). However, throughout the rest of the *parashah*, Jacob is identified by both "Jacob" and "Israel," marking an incomplete name change and therefore an incomplete transformation. Following Shechem's rape of Dinah, we see that Jacob has not fully shed his mask of toxic masculinity, and the patriarchy has not disappeared from society.

After his son rapes Dinah, Shechem's father, Hamor, comes to Jacob to bargain for their children to be married (Genesis 34:8). If Jacob answers, the Torah does not record his response. Instead, Jacob's sons agree to Hamor's proposal, but only if the men of his tribe circumcise themselves to join Jacob's family (Genesis 34:13–17). Then, with Shechem, Hamor, and all their tribe debilitated by their recent circumcisions, two of Jacob's sons, Simeon and Levi, kill all of the men in the tribe (Genesis 34:25), and the other sons take many of their possessions (Genesis 34:27–29). Jacob is clearly distraught about the vengeful, murderous actions of his sons; but he is only concerned about how others will think of him and their family. He remains completely silent about how Dinah feels after this traumatic event and takes no recorded action to comfort or support her (Genesis 34:30). In response to Jacob's rebuke of their actions, his sons reply patriarchally, "Should he then have been allowed to treat our sister like a whore?" (Genesis 34:31). Throughout these components of the story, we see that Jacob's transformation does not extend to washing away his patriarchal ideas and actions. Although they do not perpetrate Shechem-like sexual violence, Jacob and his sons reveal internalized patriarchal ideas emphasizing domination over healing justice as they silence their own daughter and sister, bargain with the father of Dinah's attacker, and lead a murderous rampage in revenge.

To this day, patriarchy unleashes its violent influence and wrath throughout all aspects of society. Patriarchal systems keep women from being paid the same as men, create sexist expectations for women's actions, scrutinize and restrict women's reproductive rights, and create violent home, school, and work environments. Men, especially cisgender and heterosexual men, are the main perpetrators of this violent system, inflicting harm on others through sexual assault, rape, domestic abuse, and mass shootings. Yet patriarchy and toxic masculinity also create insecure, emotionally detached men who inflict harm upon themselves through alcoholism, drug abuse, and suicide. A multitude of policy changes are necessary to combat patriarchy throughout society, including gender pay equity, reproductive health access and freedom, sexual violence prevention, and equal rights and freedom for LGBTQ individuals. In addition to policy, there are numerous ways in which all of us—but especially men—can take responsibility for creating positive, loving forms of masculinity that validate our worth and the value of all people.

Knowing the destructive impact of patriarchy and witnessing its brutality in our Torah and throughout society, men must work forcefully to destroy the current structures of toxic masculinity. We must imagine a world in which we do not seek to dominate others physically, sexually, or emotionally—a world in which we are no longer insecure, feel as if we must fight, or imagine that we must know all of the answers. That world is possible, but it will require more than individual transformations. As we witness with Jacob, individual transformation is not enough. Only systemic change will ensure that each and every person feels safe, valued, and loved.

NOTES

1. bell hooks, *The Will to Change: Men, Masculinity, and Love* (New York: Atria Books, 2004), 18.
2. Or HaChayim on Genesis 34:2.
3. Radak on Genesis 34:3.
4. Rashi on *B'reishit Rabbah* 26:2.

VAYEISHEV—GENESIS 37:1–40:23

The "Original Sin" of Slavery

RABBI ESTHER L. LEDERMAN

THE TORAH'S FIRST SIBLING RIVALRY ends in fratricide. Who can forget the slaughter of Abel at the hands of his brother Cain, who replies to God's call with another question: "Am I my brother's keeper" (Genesis 4:9)?

By the time we reach the final narrative arc of Genesis, our Jewish ancestors are still grappling with family dysfunction, brotherly jealousy, and competition for a father's affections. The narrative of *Parashat Vayeishev* proceeds as follows: Jacob favors Joseph, his firstborn from his beloved Rachel. He showers his son with affection, most notably with a coat of multiple hues and colors. The brothers become jealous and one day hatch a plan to kill Joseph. Tempered by Reuben's caution, they throw him instead into an empty pit and then sell him into slavery through a wandering group of Ishmaelite traders. Upon arrival in Egypt, Joseph is sold as a slave into the house of Potiphar.

Avivah Gottlieb Zornberg argues, "The brothers' crime remains throughout Jewish history as a kind of ineradicable original sin, with proliferating effects. . . . Rambam refers to this original sin of our forefathers; in constant self-reminder of this evil, we sacrifice a goat for all communal sin-offerings; the goat that was substituted for Joseph's remains a symbol of hatred and violence in the consciousness of the whole people."[1] Calling Joseph's sale into slavery our "original sin," Zornberg suggests that the act leaves a permanent stain with ongoing consequences for Jewish history.

The same has been said about American slavery. The Reverend Jim Wallis authored a book called *American's Original Sin: Racism, White*

Privilege, and the Bridge to a New America.[2] In June of 2020, former secretary of state Condoleezza Rice argued that "our country has a birth defect: Africans and Europeans came to this country together—but one group was in chains."[3]

What can one learn by plumbing the depths of *Parashat Vayeishev* that might illuminate the very situation in which we Americans find ourselves—still living with slavery's legacy while many white citizens of this country believe it to be an issue of our past and not our present?

Let us take a look at the motive. What leads a band of brothers to sell their own kin? At the beginning of Genesis 37, the text reads, "Yet Israel loved Joseph better than his other sons. . . . When his brothers saw that he was the one their father loved, more than any of his brothers, they hated him and could not bear to speak peaceably to him" (Genesis 37:3–4).

In a commentary on the phrase *v'lo yachlu dabro l'shalom* (וְלֹא יָכְלוּ דַּבְּרוֹ לְשָׁלֹם), "could not bear to speak peaceably to him," the medieval commentator Sforno says, "Even though the brothers had to speak to Joseph pertaining to their business dealings, both concerning household problems and problems with the herds and flocks, something imposed upon them by their father's command to see in him their manager, they did not speak to him concerning any private matters, brotherly concerns."[4]

In other words, the relationship between Joseph and his brothers is purely transactional, built on maintaining the family business and ensuring household efficiency. They have no real relationship to speak of, no emotional intimacy, no sense of kinship and love. To borrow the phrase coined by Martin Buber, Joseph and his brothers lack an I-Thou relationship.[5]

Radak took a different direction with this same verse: "Any conversation with Joseph did not revolve around peacefully discussed matters of common interest, but concerned only matters of dispute between them."[6] In this telling, there are only matters of conflict between the brothers. There is nothing of shared interest, concern, and commonality, at least as the brothers can see.

A commentary by Rabbi Jacob ben Asher, the *Tur HaAroch*, states, "You will note that the Torah did not write that the brothers did not speak to him altogether. Rather, whenever they spoke, even to strangers, and Joseph became part of their conversation, they referred to him negatively."[7] This interpretation raises the possibility that the words of peace the brothers could not speak to Joseph were not conversations with him but rather conversations with others, even complete strangers. This reading leads one to imagine that the brothers engaged in smear tactics against their brother, fueled by jealous rage.

These three commentaries highlight a trajectory that begins with isolation and continues through to hate. There is no relationship to speak of between the brothers and Joseph. Joseph is a tool for the brothers, just part of the family business. These interpretations present a collective image of Joseph, in the eyes of the brothers, as less than human. In a commentary to *Parashat Mikeitz*, Rabbi Jonathan Sacks concludes, "As far as [the brothers] are concerned, there is no Joseph. They don't recognize him. . . . They never did. They never recognized him as one of them, as their father's child, as their brother with an identity of his own and a right to be himself."[8]

The enslavement of people of color was predicated on seeing Black and Brown individuals as property, by definition the opposite of human. The United States Constitution counted people of color as three-fifths of a person. Enslaved people became a tool for economic growth—indeed, much of the accumulated wealth of the United States could be said to be have been built through the work of Black bodies.[9]

Returning to the text, by the time Jacob sends Joseph to go looking for his brothers in Dothan, the brothers are ready for something sinister: "They saw him in the distance, and before he neared them, they wickedly plotted against him, to bring about his death. They said to one another, 'Here comes the master of dreams! Now then, let us kill him and throw him to one of [these] pits and say, 'A wild animal devoured him.' Then we'll see what becomes of his dreams!" (Genesis 37:18–20).

The midrash in *B'reishit Rabbah* even goes on to imagine the brothers unleashing their dogs on Joseph.[10] The commentary by Rabbi Chayim ibn Attar, the *Or HaChayim*, states, "We could say further that 'and they saw him from afar off' refers to the distance of their hearts, because they did not see him as brothers see their brothers, rather, they saw him like a man distant from them."[11]

The *Or HaChayim* is commenting on the lack of intimacy between Joseph and his brothers. The word *meirachok* (מֵרָחֹק), "in the distance," is no longer just a reference to physical distance but also to an emotional chasm.

Bryan Stevenson, the founder of the Equal Justice Initiative in Montgomery, Alabama, and the author of *Just Mercy*, is fond of saying that our challenge is to "get proximate." In a 2018 commencement speech, he told graduates, "You have to find ways . . . to get proximate to people who are suffering, to get closer to people who are excluded, to go into the parts of the community that other people say you shouldn't go to."[12] The brothers were far from proximate to Joseph. We in the United States, particularly those of us who are white Jews, need to become more proximate to people of color and understand the unique legacy slavery has wrought. We must not see this problem *meirachok*, but from close up.

In his commentary on Genesis 37:18, Sforno writes, "They did not think that he had come to make peace with them but that he was spying on them, to cause them to commit a sin either that would bring their father's curses on them or that would cause God to punish them."[13] The brothers are afraid of Joseph's purpose in arriving at Dothan. They project sinister motives onto him. In this telling, the brothers jump at the chance to kill Joseph, assuming he is seeking to further hurt their standing with their father and with God.

A mindset of scarcity sets these brothers upon Joseph. A similar mindset of scarcity holds this country back in addressing the terrible devastation that slavery, convict leasing, and lynching have brought to people of color. We have not yet been able to pass a bill that would allow Congress to *explore* reparations, let alone implement them. What do we in the white community project onto the descendants of slaves? What are we so afraid of?

When Cain says to God, "Am I my brother's keeper?" God replies, "Your brother's blood is shrieking to Me from the ground!" (Genesis 4:10). The blood of Joseph, as symbolized by the blood of the goat used by the brothers to cover up their crime,[14] called out to Jacob as well. So too does the blood of sold, tortured, and lynched Black bodies call out to us from the soil of this country. Are we ready to get proximate, in the language of Bryan Stevenson? Or, asked another way, are we ready to respond to Cain's eternal question, "Am I my brother's keeper?" Yes. We are. We must be.

Notes

1. Avivah Gottlieb Zornberg, *The Beginning of Desire: Reflections on Genesis* (New York: Schocken Books, 1995), 271. The Rambam is taken from *Guide for the Perplexed* 3:46.
2. Jim Wallis, *America's Original Sin: Racism, White Privilege, and the Bridge to a New America* (Grand Rapids, MI: Brazos Press, 2017).
3. Condoleezza Rice, "This Moment Cries Out for Us to Confront Race in America," *Washington Post*, June 4, 2020, https://www.washingtonpost.com/opinions/2020/06/04/condoleezza-rice-moment-confront-race-america/.
4. Sforno on Genesis 37:4.
5. Martin Buber, *I and Thou*, trans. Ronald Gregor Smith (Edinburgh: T. & T. Clark, 1937).
6. Radak (Rabbi David Kimchi) on Genesis 37:4.
7. Rabbi Jacob ben Asher, *Tur HaAroch* to Genesis 37:4.
8. Rabbi Jonathan Sacks, "*Mikketz* (5771)—Sibling Rivalry," Office of Rabbi Sacks, December 4, 2010, https://rabbisacks.org/covenant-conversation-5771-mikketz-sibling-rivalry/.
9. P. R. Lockhart, "How Slavery Became America's First Big Business," *Vox*, August 16, 2019, https://www.vox.com/identities/2019/8/16/20806069/slavery-economy-capitalism-violence-cotton-edward-baptist.
10. *B'reishit Rabbah* 84:14.
11. Rabbi Chayim ibn Attar, *Or HaChayim* to Genesis 37:18.
12. Bryan Stevenson, 2018 Commencement address, Johns Hopkins University, https://hub.jhu.edu/2018/05/24/commencement-2018-stevenson/#:~:text=1.,go%20to%2C%22%20Stevenson%20said.
13. Sforno to Genesis 37:18.
14. See Zornberg, *Beginning of Desire*, 269.

MIKEITZ—GENESIS 41:1–44:17

Emerging to Govern:
Reentry after Incarceration

RABBI REUBEN ZELLMAN

AFTER TWO YEARS IN OFFICE, the governor of California faced disaster. The warming climate had dried out the land and had begun to deliver—most unusual for California—storms of dry lightning, which ignited wildfires worse than any seen before. Desperate for innovative approaches to save lives, the governor was discussing the fires with various members of the State Assembly when one of his top aides spoke up: "You know, I have an idea that might help. When I was serving time at Folsom Prison, my cellmate Andy was an inmate firefighter. He was promoted fast to leadership of the prison squad; he just had an incredible head for logistics and was really good at strategy for containment and prevention. We used to call him the 'Fire Whisperer.' The warden had him working on Folsom's safety and evacuation plans. Maybe you should talk to him." That same day, the governor's chief of staff put a call in to Folsom Prison. Andy the Fire Whisperer was granted parole in order to achieve compelling government objectives. He went to work for CalFire and eventually had a successful career in the US Department of the Interior.

Is the story above true? You may be thinking how unlikely Andy's trajectory sounds. Would a man serving prison time really be recognized for his talents, entrusted with important responsibilities, and eventually become a leader in his nation? Indeed, "Andy" is not a real person, and this chain of events is nearly unthinkable in our present world.

And then comes the Torah, to remind us of other worlds and other ways we could think. "Andy the Fire Whisperer" is a thought experiment, but his story is not. It is the tale of our ancestor Joseph.

Parashat Mikeitz begins:

> At the end of two years' time, Pharaoh had a dream: there he was, standing by the Nile, when seven cows came up out of the Nile, handsome and fat. They grazed among the reeds. And now seven other cows came up after them from the Nile—repulsive and gaunt. They stood beside the [other] cows at the bank of the Nile. The cows that were repulsive and gaunt then ate the cows that were handsome and fat, and Pharaoh woke up.
>
> ... In the morning his spirit was troubled; he put out a call for all the soothsayer-priests and sages of Egypt; Pharaoh related his dream to them, but no one could interpret them for Pharaoh. The chief cupbearer then spoke to Pharaoh, saying, "This day I [must] acknowledge my sins! Pharaoh had grown angry at his servants, so he put me under guard in the house of the Captain of the Guard—me and the chief baker. We dreamt a dream on a single night, he and I, each dream of ours with its own meaning. Now, there with us was a Hebrew lad, a slave of the Captain of the Guard; when we related our dreams to him, he interpreted for us, interpreting each one's dream according to its own meaning. And as he interpreted for us, so it came to be—[Pharaoh] restored me to my position, and him [Pharaoh] hanged." So Pharaoh sent to summon Joseph; they hurried him from the pit: he shaved, changed his clothing, and came to Pharaoh. (Genesis 41:1-4, 8-14)

Thus begins Joseph's life as a formerly incarcerated man.

The story has much to teach us about incarceration. Joseph's profile is all too familiar today: a man of marginalized socioeconomic status, belonging to an ethnic group long treated as suspicious,[1] condemned due to ambiguous or false accusations, sent to a prison meant to be temporary[2]—and then forgotten for years. Joseph is a victim of severe sexual harassment, but his is not the version of events that counts. He goes to prison because he angered someone more powerful than he.[3] There he meets other men imprisoned under wildly unclear circumstances; both the cupbearer and the baker "offended against their master" (Genesis 40:1). This system of justice is sadly familiar in many countries today. Statistically, as with Joseph, whether an individual experiences incarceration has much to do with our race, income, health, and other life circumstances, and less to do with our actions.[4]

But for now, let us set aside the question—so critically important—of how people become incarcerated. Regardless of whether a person ought to be in prison in the first place, most people who are incarcerated eventually get out, and the Torah offers some pointed guidance about what reentry can and should be. When we examine Joseph's life during and after prison, we find an understanding of human nature and of justice that challenges, profoundly, the way that reentry works today.

Let's begin with Pharaoh, who, after releasing the cupbearer from prison, restored him to his prestigious career. When the cupbearer tells Pharaoh that his cellmate, still imprisoned, has a proven ability to interpret dreams, Pharaoh listens and then acts on his input. Apparently, in this pharaoh's court, a former inmate may return not only to freedom and livelihood, but to credibility and authority. Furthermore, acting on the word of this formerly incarcerated man, Pharaoh then entrusts an even more important job to Joseph, still locked up in the pit.

Then there is the *sar hamashkim* (שַׂר הַמַּשְׁקִים), the "chief cupbearer." He says: *Et chata-ai ani mazkir hayom* (אֶת־חֲטָאַי אֲנִי מַזְכִּיר הַיּוֹם), "This day I [must] acknowledge my sins" (Genesis 41:9). *B'chor Shor*, following the plain meaning of Genesis 40:23, suggests that one of the cupbearer's sins is simply forgetting about Joseph's plight, and therefore failing to help Joseph sooner.[5] According to Gersonides, the cupbearer realizes that in order to tell Pharaoh (belatedly) what he knows about Joseph's abilities, he would have to mention his past offense.[6] We can understand the cupbearer's story in any number of ways, but the important point is this: the cupbearer is able to refer to his incarceration in the past while continuing to be treated as a valuable, credible human being in the present. This is the simple and profound opportunity that suddenly seems so improbable when the cupbearer is placed in California as the fictional aide to the governor. It is also worth noting that the cupbearer is an example of *t'shuvah g'murah*,[7] "complete repentance." He acknowledges his mistakes openly, drawing on his own experience to secure for a fellow inmate a second chance like the one he received himself.

Rabbi Avahu taught that "in the place where *baalei t'shuvah* [penitents] stand, even the completely righteous are not able to stand."[8] That is, a person who has done something wrong and then made repair has grown in a way more profound than had they not sinned in the first place. The tradition affirms: People make mistakes, and some make serious ones. But we can learn, and we can change, and when we do damage, we can try to repair the harm. When we examine Joseph's incarceration and its aftermath, we are invited into a Jewish understanding of punishment, redemption, and human potential. No criminal record follows Joseph. He and the cupbearer are offered meaningful, respected work in areas where they have talent and training. They can be honest about their incarceration experience, but it is far from the totality of who they are, and it does not determine the rest of their lives. They are able not only to reenter their society; they become part of its leadership.

Could our present system ever allow a Joseph? Incarceration today marks a person with a heavy stigma for the rest of their life, whether or not it was just, and no matter how great their *t'shuvah* (repentance). As a result, even after an incarcerated person is released, inestimable human potential often remains locked away. Joseph's story teaches what people can do if given a real chance at reentry, the opportunity to nourish the best in themselves. We see that development most clearly when Joseph, now prime minister of Egypt, encounters his brothers. In his youth, Joseph dreamed of having power over his family. As an adult, he receives job training and responsibility while incarcerated (Genesis 39:22), and by the time his brothers appear before him, he has slowly learned to direct his power for good.[9] Joseph is not some exceptional prisoner who proves the rule. He is just a person like all of us, with many struggles and great gifts, who matures, as we all can, in response to opportunity, trust, and time.

As I write, my home state of California is engulfed in flames and smoke. Of the firefighters who are working in terrible conditions to protect us, thousands are currently incarcerated, serving on trained inmate fire crews.[10] When they are released from prison, they have long been ineligible to pursue work in the regular firefighting force; because they have a criminal record, the state has denied them the required certifications. But just this month, California has finally begun to remove some of the laws barring inmate firefighters from using their skills when they get out.[11] Millions of inmates could develop their own abilities while in prison, as Joseph did, preparing for meaningful contributions and a good life after incarceration. But these opportunities are rare in our current system. American prisons offer very little either to nourish potential or to treat underlying struggles while people are inside.[12] And when people get out, the path to reentry often remains blocked at every turn—even though we need their contributions as urgently as Egypt needed Joseph's. Restrictions keep formerly incarcerated people away from many occupations, as well as voting, education, and housing. The California Department of Corrections and Rehabilitation reports that 65 percent of people released from prison return within three years.[13] This recidivism rate should be no surprise. It is a natural consequence of denying people the opportunity to meet their basic needs and to find purpose, of dismissing their potential and their dignity.

Amid the richness of Joseph's story, we should not lose sight of one more truth it reveals. The Torah reminds us several times that "the Eternal was with Joseph" (Genesis 39:21, 39:23), that God's spirit was in him (Genesis 41:38), that he was noticed and cared for (Genesis 41:42)—inside prison and outside. How might our system change if we were reminded so consistently and forcefully of *every* person's multifaceted role in God's unfolding plan? Joseph's incarceration is only one part of his story. First, we learn that he had a cool rainbow coat, a bad teenage attitude, a talent with dreams, and a God who cared what happened to him. In other words, Joseph is pretty much like everyone else—like any of us could be, if we had the opportunities he had, if potential were allowed to flourish, if we lived in a society where it is possible to rebuild after making mistakes: "For he can, indeed, emerge from a dungeon to govern" (Ecclesiastes 4:14).

Notes

1. The racialized language of Madam Potiphar's report can be seen in, for example, Genesis 39:17.
2. Confinement in Torah is limited to holding someone temporarily, to prevent them from escaping until their punishment is decided. See, for example, Ibn Ezra on Genesis 40:3.
3. Althalya Brenner, in *The Torah: A Women's Commentary*, ed. Tamara Cohn Eskenazi and Andrea L. Weiss (New York: Reform Judaism Publishing, an imprint of CCAR Press and Women of Reform Judaism, 2008), 223.
4. Adam Looney, "5 Facts about Prisoners and Work before and after Incarceration," Brookings, March 14, 2018, https://www.brookings.edu/blog/up-front/2018/03/14/5-facts-about-prisoners-and-work-before-and-after-incarceration/.
5. *B'chor Shor* on Genesis 41:9.
6. Rabbi Levi ben Gershon (Gersonides), *P'rushei Ralbag al haTorah, Parashat Mikeitz, hatoalot, hash'mini.*
7. Maimonides, *Mishneh Torah, Hilchot T'shuvah* 2:1.
8. Babylonian Talmud, *B'rachot* 34b.
9. See, for example, Brenner, in *The Torah: A Women's Commentary*, 225.
10. Their pay is one to five dollars per day.
11. Audrey McNamara, "California Bill Allows Inmate Firefighters to Pursue Career after Incarceration," *CBS News*, September 12, 2020, https://www.cbsnews.com/news/california-bill-allows-inmate-firefighters-pursue-career-after-incarceration/.
12. Ram Subramanian and Alison Shames, *Sentencing and Prison Practices in Germany and the Netherlands: Implications for the United States* (New York: Vera Institute of Justice, 2013), https://www.vera.org/downloads/Publications/sentencing-and-prison-practices-in-germany-and-the-netherlands-implications-for-the-united-states/legacy_downloads/european-american-prison-report-v3.pdf.
13. "Recidivism Rates," California Innocence Project, accessed December 25, 2020, https://californiainnocenceproject.org/issues-we-face/recidivism-rates/.

Joseph's Journey from Forced Migration to Redemption: A Model for Immigration Justice

RABBI SHARON KLEINBAUM
and RABBI MIKE MOSKOWITZ

HE WAS NOT LIKE the other boys. While they went out to the fields he stayed behind, curling his hair and kohling his eyes.[1] He walked with a lilt[2] and wore a colorful coat that caught everyone's attention (Genesis 37:3). He was a dreamer. The other boys hated him and could not even bring themselves to utter a friendly word in his direction (37:4). One day their hatred grew so intense that they tore off his clothes and sold him into slavery, at just seventeen years old (37:2). This began Joseph's forced migration down to Egypt (37:23–28), and it ultimately led to our national enslavement.[3]

In our contemporary world of social justice, we often place different struggles in separate silos, imagining that somehow they exist in isolation. We assume that the struggle for the full equality of LGBTQ people is separate from the struggle for immigrant rights and protections. The Torah never makes this mistake. And in *Parashat Vayigash*, the interweaving is powerful. LGBTQ people are among the immigrants who struggle for asylum and refugee status and are also among the refugees who flee from violence and persecution. Economic collapse is a truth for all, regardless of sexual orientation and/or gender identity. And those who are LGBTQ and/or gender nonconforming face an even greater burden as immigrants.

At Congregation Beit Simchat Torah, the largest LGBTQ synagogue in the world, we collaborate with the New Sanctuary Coalition
of NYC, SAFE, and RUSA LGBT to offer a *pro se* legal clinic for
immigrants. Our clinic supports immigrants from all over the world,
75 percent of whom are LGBTQ and/or HIV-positve, making ours
the only clinic with this special focus. We welcome and work with
immigrants for any reason. Dozens of synagogue volunteers and a
small staff have dedicated their resources to supporting and expanding these efforts.

Our Rabbis understand Joseph as a person who stood out from
his brothers and suffered greatly from their unwillingness to accept
him as he was. His experience resonates with many LGBTQ folks
who are forced from their homes and made to travel to foreign places
in dangerous conditions, reflecting the complicity of a society that
enables these atrocities.

Joseph's position upon arrival in Egypt is precarious. The midrash
teaches that both his master, Potiphar, and his master's wife desire
Joseph and plot to sexually abuse him.[4] He is alone, vulnerable, and
eventually imprisoned for trying to defend himself. Yet despite his
hardships and suffering, Joseph perseveres, becomes the viceroy of
Egypt, and reinvests in healing and advancing the relationships with
his brothers.

Although Joseph is dehumanized and expelled, he rallies, exceed-
ing all expectations to navigate climate change and the subsequent
food insecurities, while saving Egypt and his family of origin (Genesis
41:54). His Hebrew name, *Yosef*, alludes to these two roles: to add on
and to gather together.

It is perhaps because he is born into cycles of displacement[5] and
humiliation (Genesis 30:23) that he is so committed to ending it.
Joseph's ability to prioritize human dignity, unity, and forgiveness
over hate, division, and fear produces the first set of biblical siblings
who are able to get along with each other.[6] It is one of the reasons
that we have a custom to bless our children as Joseph's children were
blessed.[7]

In chapter 45 of Genesis, Joseph finally comes out to his brothers,

revealing his identity while modeling restorative justice and rehabilitation of society. Because the brothers have never been open to
seeing Joseph as an equal, they're unable to recognize him when he is
talking to them from a position of power.

Only when the pain of staying silent outweighs the pain of screaming out does Joseph finally give voice to his internal turmoil. With
tremendous sensitivity and deep empathy, he removes everyone else
from the room and communicates his humanity to them in the universal language of crying (Genesis 45:1–2).

In one of the most intense moments in the Bible, Joseph simultaneously reveals, rebukes, and rebuffs the brothers' false claims of
innocence and equality by saying, "I am Joseph—is my father [really]
alive?" (Genesis 45:3). The brothers have claimed to be preoccupied
with the well-being of their father and how Jacob couldn't possibly
survive being separated from his son Benjamin, so here they are
reminded that they didn't seem to care at all about their father when
they sold Joseph and then crassly asked Jacob to identify Joseph's
unique outfit (Genesis 37:32).

Ani Yosef haod avi chai (אֲנִי יוֹסֵף הַעוֹד אָבִי חָי), "I am Joseph—is my
father [really] alive?" (Genesis 45:3). The Rabbis see these five words
as challenging our confidence in our own choices. If Joseph, among
the youngest of the brothers, leaves them with no way to respond for
their actions,[8] how are we going to answer those who will introduce
themselves to us as "one of the children you put in cages"?

It is not the responsibility of people we have separated from their
children, denied asylum, or kept captive in exploitative conditions
to educate, support, or forgive us. But that is the role Joseph takes
with his oppressors. As a corrective reaction to their "[seeing] him in
the distance and . . . wickedly plotting against him to bring about his
death" (Genesis 37:18), Joseph invites them to "come, draw near to
me" (45:4), engaging them in a way that makes it easiest for them to
be receptive.[9]

Joseph then reviews with them the fact-based history of what
happened—and, with excessive encouragement, he actually helps
them process it (Genesis 45:5). Unfortunately, this absurdity is often

observed when privileged people feel encumbered by their own entitlements and need to be reassured of their own self-worth.

None of this, however, absolves the brothers of their actions nor the need to make amends for the communal impact. There is a curious moment in the brothers' reunion when Joseph gives each one a change of clothing, but he gives Benjamin four additional sets of clothing plus three hundred silver pieces (Genesis 45:22). The Vilna Gaon explains that the three hundred silver pieces are a form of reparations for Benjamin—who, due to Joseph's absence, had to work harder.[10] Even though this was by no means Joseph's fault, he teaches his brothers the importance of trying to make the community whole.

Many commentators are surprised that Joseph seems to favor Benjamin with extra clothing in the same way that Jacob earlier favors Joseph with a splendid coat.[11] They explain that Joseph is demonstrating his confidence in his brothers' rehabilitation. Judaism defines repentance as being in the same circumstances but responding differently. Although the brothers had initially been jealous of Joseph's special clothing, Joseph knows that they have changed and will not resent Benjamin's extra garments.

As Joseph sends the brothers home to retrieve their father, he warns them not to fight during the journey (Genesis 45:24). The midrash explains that Joseph is worried that the brothers will spend time arguing about who was to blame for Joseph's sale and, in so doing, lose sight of the larger goal of family reunification. Today as well, we must take care not to allow factional infighting to distract us from achieving our dream of a just society.

Like Joseph, many LGBTQ immigrants seeking asylum in the United States make their journey alone. Today, Joseph is a young gay man from Russia whose parents and siblings have disowned him, with a plane ticket and $100 in his pocket, thanks to a tiny organization that helped him leave behind the daily fear that he might be beaten or killed. Today, Joseph is a transgender woman from Chechnya whose cisgender partner managed to scrape together money for a plane ticket to get her to safety; however, because they are not legally related, they have no path to living together safely in either country.

Today, Joseph is a gay woman from a small village in Nigeria who has never heard the acronym LGBTQ+, but who spent years trying to understand why she was constantly being attacked and beaten for wanting to live with her best friend instead of marrying a man.

Like our ancestor, today's Josephs are fleeing violence and rejection by families of origin, traveling and navigating new systems, often in a new language. They may have families of choice but very rarely have access to any legal documentation of those relationships from the countries they leave behind; they are much more likely to go through the months or years of applying for asylum alone.[12]

Everyone loses when we deny people the ability to be and to contribute. We, like the brothers, must atone for our actions and inactions by following Joseph's model, coming together to create the opportunities for all people to have their dignity restored and preserved.

NOTES

1. *B'reishit Rabbah* 84:7.
2. *B'reishit Rabbah* 84:7.
3. The intergenerational trauma from the sale of Joseph is attributed as the cause of the ten martyrs.
4. Babylonian Talmud, *Sotah* 13b.
5. Rashi 37:2: "Everything that happened to Jacob happened to Joseph."
6. Their mother, Asenath, also had a traumatic background; she was born through the rape of Dina (*Pirkei D'Rabbi Eliezer* 48).
7. Traditionally, boys are blessed in accordance with words that Jacob speaks to Joseph's sons, Ephraim and Manasseh: "By you shall [the people of] Israel give [their] blessing, saying, 'May God make you like Ephraim and Manasseh'" (first found in the siddur of Rabbi Jacob Emden).
8. See Genesis 45:3, "But his brothers were unable to answer him."
9. Rashi on Genesis 45:4.
10. Meir Yechiel Halevi Halstock, *Or Torah haShalem*, *Vayigash*, 257, based on Rashi.
11. Babylonian Talmud, *M'gillah* 16a.
12. For more on the unique challenges facing LGBTQ immigrants, see "Covering LGBTQ Immigration Issues," GLAAD, accessed December 25, 2020, https://www.glaad.org/vote/topics/immigration.

VA-Y'CHI—GENESIS 47:28–50:26

Living in the Face of Death

RABBI SUSAN TALVE

"VA-Y'CHI (וַיְחִי), And Jacob lived" (Genesis 47:28). We know from previous use of this language (Genesis 23:1) that there is a reason that Torah does not say, "And Jacob died." Living in the face of death takes courage; it takes believing that we are part of something greater than ourselves, and it takes the hope that our legacy will live on through the blessings that we leave for the next generations. Rashi's first comment on the *parashah* asks why it is a closed portion,[1] that is, why does it begin without the usual space in the Torah scroll separating it from the last portion? He tells us that space represents the pause needed for contemplation and preparation for what is to come. Jacob's death and the four hundred years of slavery arrive so quickly that there is no time for preparation, and "the *eyes and hearts of Israel were closed.*"[2] *Midrash Rabbah* suggests that the portion is closed because Jacob wished to give his children a glimpse of the end of all exile, but that was hidden from him.[3] He wanted somehow to let his descendants know that no matter how devastating enslavement would be, there would be an end to it. Jacob may not be able to see the end of exile himself, but with the blessings he gives to his children, he manages to reach into the future with the promise that there is a way through the suffering that will lead to peace.

This closed portion pushes us to discover truths about living together as human beings, sharing a planet that will let us live, even in the face of death. It pushes us to ask what it means to live with the tension of knowing that disaster may come at any moment and threaten to close our eyes and hearts, and yet still maintaining the hope that we can survive even our worst nightmares. The narrative of the end of both Jacob's and Joseph's lives helps to prepare us to live intentionally as individuals and as a people, even in the face of death.

The last chapters of Genesis prepare us for the transition from being a family to being a people with a purpose. Jacob has been living in Egypt under the protection of his son Joseph, who has a seat at the current table of political power. Joseph learned at an early age that unshared privilege could be dangerous. His father's favoritism earned him the ire of his brothers and set off the journey that would take us to Egypt, where the injustice of slavery would imprint on our collective soul. We would remember the bitterness and vow never to do to others what was done to us. Joseph heard the words spoken by his brother Judah suggesting that if something were to happen to their brother Benjamin, Jacob would surely die, because *nafsho k'shurah v'nafsho* (נַפְשׁוֹ קְשׁוּרָה בְנַפְשׁוֹ), "one soul was bound up with the other" (Genesis 44:30).[4] Hearing these words, Joseph's heart opens to forgiveness; he embraces his brothers, he gives them what they need to feed their families and all the families of the region, and a time of peace prevails.

By the end of this portion, both Jacob and Joseph have died. In the next, a pharaoh arises who knows not Joseph (Exodus 1:8), and our fleeting place of privilege is lost. But even with eyes and hearts closed, the S'fat Emet reminds us that the spark of godliness may be hidden but is always there. He tells us in a commentary on this portion that the text does not say that Jacob *va-y'hi* (וַיְהִי), "was," in the land of Egypt; rather that, *va-y'chi* (וַיְחִי), "he lived" in the land of Egypt (Genesis 47:28), teaching that he was truly alive, even in that narrow place. According to the S'fat Emet, "'Life' here means being attached to the root and source from which the life-force ever flows."[5] To reveal the end means to let his children know that even in the depths of despair, it is possible to be awakened by our desire to bless the generations that are yet to come, to reject self-interest and work for the common good, and to embrace that vision of harmony, unity, and a more just world even in the worst of times.

The years of slavery deepened the understanding in our bones that until all are free, none can be completely free; thus, our purpose as a people is to level the playing field for the citizen and the stranger alike. The journey through our exodus unfolds a theology of liberation that we will carry with us. We will take the lessons of our story into our journey through many lands—setting up settlement houses for the immigrant, aid societies for the poor, and hospitals to make sure that no one is excluded from access to health care. When we would have our own nation, we would try to create a system in which health care is a right for all and not a privilege for some. As challenging as our political positions in other nations would be, we would champion public health systems, while at the same time recognizing that no amount of privilege can protect people from the effects of pollution or pandemics. Knowing what it meant to be blamed for plagues, we worked to understand the scientific causes of illness. We understood the importance of addressing the social, economic, and racial disparities that affect mortality rates and health outcomes. We knew that education was among the strongest indicators of health and life expectancy,[6] so we valued, invested in, and sacrificed for learning above all else.

Many times in our story, our eyes and hearts have been closed by our own suffering. At other times, we have been part of systems of oppression running so deep that we cannot see or feel the pain of others, losing sight of the very values that define us. When suffering has hardened our hearts, we have forgotten that our lives are all connected, one soul bound up with the other; and we have become part of the problem, rather than part of the repair.

Our third child was born with congenital heart disease. For years, as she received care, I would sit by her bedside in a state-of-the-art hospital where no expense was spared to save lives. Just outside, however, in the same zip code, children went to bed hungry. These disparities, especially along racial lines, cause mortality rates 40 percent higher than in the general population. The stress of racism, the hopelessness of poverty, and growing gun violence threaten our collective health. Seeing this up close pushed me to found Missouri Health Care for All, a statewide grassroots organization that fights for equity in health care and the adoption of a public health approach to protect us all. Much of our work has been to cross the many divides and work for unity across urban and rural, religious, racial, gender, and economic differences. We seek to show how our personal health is connected to our community's health and how none can be safe and healthy until all are safe and healthy. The relationships we have made across divisions have helped us become a force for the common good, even as so many still hold onto the illusion of separateness and self-interest. Without a national, perhaps even a global, commitment to the principles of public health—living by the values we have learned through our years as a people—pandemics will continue to threaten our lives, and the disparities that cause the most vulnerable to suffer will continue to divide and devastate our dreams of peace.

Just before Jacob dies, the midrash tells us that he gathers his children and grandchildren around his bed to give them a glimpse of redemption—but the *Shechinah*, the Holy Presence, departs from him. He worries that this has occurred because one of his sons is not worthy of this knowledge, but they assure him that they understand his lessons of unity and the connectedness of all.[7] The Talmud has his sons respond to his fears with the words *Sh'ma Yisrael Adonai Eloheinu Adonai Echad*, "Hear, O Israel, *Adonai* is our God, *Adonai* is One" [Deuteronomy 6:4]. Just as in your heart there is only oneness, so in our hearts there is only oneness." Relieved that this essential lesson has been passed on, Jacob gives us his blessing with this response: *Baruch shem k'vod malchuto l'olam va-ed*, "Blessed is the Name whose glorious Presence is forever and ever."[8] In that moment the *Shechinah* is restored. The love expressed between the generations awakened the possibility of unity and harmony, because we found it with each other. We put aside our self-interest and were willing to sacrifice for the common good. This is why the portion begins with the word *va-y'chi*. Jacob *lived* with purpose in the face of death to teach us that no matter how stuck or sad or broken we might be, no one can take from us the inner spark that promises that equity, justice, and peace are possible.

And at the end of every book of Torah we say *Chazak, chazak, v'nit'chazeik*, "Be strong, be strong," each of us making sure that everyone is cared for, and we will be stronger and healthier together.

NOTES

1. Rashi on Genesis 47:28.
2. Rashi on Genesis 47:28.
3. *B'reishit Rabbah* 96:1.
4. Author's translation.
5. Rabbi Yehudah Leib Alter of Ger, *The Language of Truth: The Torah Commentary of the Sefat Emet*, translated and interpreted by Arthur Green (Philadephia: Jewish Publication Society, 1998), 73.
6. "Adolescent and School Health," Centers for Disease Control and Prevention, August 13, 2019, www.cdc.gov/healthyyouth/health_and_academics.
7. *B'reishit Rabbah* 98:3.
8. Babylonian Talmud, *P'sachim* 56a.

EXODUS

SH'MOT—EXODUS 1:1–6:1

Victims of Injustice: Saying Their Names

RABBI MARI CHERNOW

PARASHAT SH'MOT is bursting with social justice themes. Its story is a foundational narrative for the Western world, one that champions freedom and universal human dignity. It introduces the paradigmatic civil rights leader, Moses—and conversely, the archetypal tyrannical despot, Pharaoh. Perhaps as a warning, it models the very few steps required to transform the relationship between a minority culture and the majority from peaceful coexistence to generations of degradation and abuse.[1] The oppression ends when a small society of women works in quiet cooperation to set off a revolution.

At the center of Sh'mot is courageous human action that changes the world for good.[2] It has inspired countless individuals and societies to rise up against evil. It is nothing if not a story of empowerment and change. However, it also contains a critical lesson about how a measure of justice can be achieved when empowerment is impossible and when change comes too late.

Sh'mot means "names." In English, we call the second book of the Torah "Exodus," based on the primary story told in the book. In Hebrew, the book takes its name from this parashah. The parashah and the Book of Sh'mot begin by listing the names of Jacob's sons who came down to Egypt with him (Exodus 1:1–5). Rashi elaborates:

> Although Scripture has already enumerated them by name while they were living, when they went down into Egypt (Genesis 46:8–27), it again enumerates them when it tells us of their

deaths (Exodus 1:6), thus showing how dear they were to God—
that they are compared to the stars, which also God brings out
and brings in by number and name when they cease to shine,
as it is said, "[God] brings out their host by number [and] calls
them all by name" (Isaiah 40:26).[3]

Rashi, always looking out for language that appears to be extraneous,
observes that readers of the Torah already know who the sons of Jacob
are. We have read their stories in great detail in the Book of Genesis.
Therefore, there must be a critical reason to name them again now.
That reason, explains Rashi, is to show us "how dear they were to
God." In other words, knowing their names highlights the unique
and sacred nature of their lives to God and to us. Saying their names
is a means of validating and valuing their very existence.

Rashi's notion that the stating of names confers dignity resonates through to contemporary struggles for social justice. The Say
Her Name movement[4] began in 2014 with a report by the African
American Policy Forum documenting the stories of Black female
victims of police brutality.[5] The report's central assertion is that the
stories of Black women, girls, and transgender and gender nonconforming individuals who are targeted by racism and state violence are
excluded and marginalized. It names many such people and tells their
stories, seeking to ensure that violence against all Black victims elicits
"equal outrage and commitment." It demands accountability for all
Black lives that have been altered and lost.

Our names are closely associated with our identity and our individuality. To exclude the names of those who suffer from injustice is to
participate in the oppression. It robs the innocent of dignity, denies
the uniqueness of their stories, and belittles their place in history.

Consider the relationship between cruelty and dehumanization.
As Moshe Halbertal points out, prior to our *parashah* the Israelites
were integrated into Egyptian society. How does it happen, he asks,
that the Egyptians, once friends and neighbors of the Israelites,
shift dramatically so that they can embitter their lives with terrible
cruelty? Halbertal's answer is a process he calls "verminization."[6] It
begins with the loss of historical memory and the erosion of personal

relationships. The text brings this change to our attention in noting that the new Pharaoh "did not know Joseph" (Exodus 1:8). It continues as Pharaoh generates fear, characterizing the Israelites as a threat (1:10), and culminates in verses 12–13: "But the more [the Israelites] were oppressed, the more they increased and spread out, so that [the Egyptians] came to dread the Israelites." The Egyptians ruthlessly forced work upon the Israelites.

Once the Egyptians view the Israelites more akin to bugs than to fellow human beings—increasing, spreading out, worthy of dread—they are fully poised to treat them with callousness and brutality. There is no call to have compassion for a large mass of dangerous creatures who have no individuality, no stories, no names.

Consider also the words of Kate Bowler, author of *Everything Happens for a Reason: And Other Lies I've Loved*. Bowler was unexpectedly diagnosed with stage IV cancer at age thirty-five. Upon hearing her news, many readers of her work sent her pithy reassurances. In her book she acknowledges their good intentions but responds:

> This is the problem, I suppose, with formulas. They are generic. But there is nothing generic about a human life. . . . I am excellent in the stern of a canoe, but I never got the hang of riding a bike with no hands. . . . I spent weeks of my childhood riding around on my bike saving drowning worms after a heavy rain. My hair is my favorite feature even though it's too heavy for most ponytails, and I still can't parallel park. There is no life *in general*. Each day has been a collection of trivial details—little intimacies and jokes and screw-ups and realizations. My problems can't be solved by those formulas—when my life was never generic to begin with.

As Bowler stares directly at her own mortality, the unique peculiarities of her particular life take on greater importance. Without saying the names of victims of injustice, we ignore these vital individualities.

The Jewish tradition teaches that every human being is both wholly unique and of infinite value.[7] There is no replacing a life lost; that truth deepens every tragedy—all the more so when the tragedy is born of injustice.

Saying the names of victims of violence, brutality, oppression, racism, sexism, and the many deadly evils that plague our society will not bring them back. It will not send the daughters of Pharaoh to buck the system and save the lives of their infants. It will not invoke through a burning bush the voice of God, who has heard their cries of suffering and will spare no miracle to ease their pain. It will not lead them to the shores of the sea where, just behind Moses and Miriam, they will step foot into a new life full of endless possibilities.

Yet saying their names will elevate their stories. It will bear witness to their truths and to the unique lives that they led. It will restore their dignity and remind us all how very dear they were to God.

Notes

1. This occurs in merely four verses. I learned this insight from a course at the Shalom Hartman Institute, Jerusalem, taught by Moshe Halbertal.
2. Assisted by some miracles here and there.
3. Based on *Sh'mot Rabbah* 1:3; *Tanchuma Yashan* 1:1:2.
4. Often cited as the origin of the Say Their Names movement.
5. Kimberlé Williams Crenshaw and Andrea J. Ritchie, *Say Her Name: Resisting Police Brutality against Black Women* (New York: African American Policy Forum; Center for Instersectionality and Social Policy Studies, July 2015 update), https://static1.squarespace.com/static/53f20d90e4b0b80451158d8c/t/5edc95fba357687217b08fb8/1591514635487/SHNReportJuly2015.pdf. The origin of the movement is described in Mary Louise Kelly and Heidi Glenn, "Say Her Name: How the Fight for Racial Justice Can Be More Inclusive of Black Women," *All Things Considered*, NPR, July 7, 2020, https://www.npr.org/sections/live-updates-protests-for-racial-justice/2020/07/07/888498009/say-her-name-how-the-fight-for-racial-justice-can-be-more-inclusive-of-black-wom.
6. Moshe Halbertal, oral lecture, Shalom Hartman Institute, Jerusalem.
7. Shalom Freedman, *Living in the Image of God: Jewish Teachings to Perfect the World: Conversations with Rabbi Irving Greenberg as Conducted by Shalom Freedman* (New York: Jason Aronson, Inc., 1998), 31.

VA-EIRA—EXODUS 6:2-9:35

Moses, Internalized Oppression, and Disability

RABBI LAUREN TUCHMAN

IN SOCIAL JUSTICE DISCOURSE, the concept of internalized oppression is gaining widespread acknowledgment. This is the notion that marginalized individuals tend to internalize many of society's most degrading or negative ideas about them, including some of the most pernicious stereotypes about aptitude, ability, and feelings of belonging. Internalized oppression can lead to chronically low self-esteem. Understanding the role internalized oppression plays on the individual and collective level is important, because if we are unable to name the internal impact marginalization has upon us, we cannot do the external societal work for social justice.

Parashat Va-eira describes poignantly the impact of internalized oppression on both the individual and collective levels. The *parashah* simultaneously describes our people's crying out for justice and their inability to hear and internalize the redemptive promise God delivers through Moses:

> "I have now heard the moaning of the Israelites because the Egyptians are holding them in bondage, and I have remembered My covenant. Say, therefore, to the Israelite people: I am the Eternal. I will free you from the labors of the Egyptians and deliver you from their bondage. I will redeem you with an out-stretched arm and through extraordinary chastisements. And I will take you to be My people, and I will be your God. And you shall know that I, the Eternal, am your God who freed you from the labors of the Egyptians. I will bring you into the land which

I swore to give to Abraham, Isaac, and Jacob, and I will give it to
you for a possession, I the Eternal." But when Moses told this
to the Israelites, they would not listen to Moses, their spirits
crushed by cruel bondage. (Exodus 6:5–9)

Commenting on the impact of having a spirit crushed by the cruelties of slavery, Rashi, the preeminent medieval Torah commentator,
observes that when people are beaten down, their breath comes in
short bursts.[1] For those who have internalized their oppression, a full,
relaxed, and calming breath is impossible. Our environmental reality
shapes our imaginative possibility, as do the beliefs we have about
ourselves, internalized from our families, communities, and educational institutions. If one believes oneself to be inherently inferior,
dispensable, and unimportant, redemption feels like a fantasy at best.
How then do we make progress given the systemic impact internalized oppression has on us as individuals and as marginalized groups?

With its examination of the impact of limiting beliefs upon Moshe
Rabbeinu himself, *Parashat Va-eira* provides us with a way forward.
Thrice in the Book of Exodus, Moses makes reference to being a
man of slow speech and few words (Exodus 4:10, 6:12, 6:30). Many
have understood this to mean that Moses has a speech impediment.
Indeed, this read has been adopted in large measure by people with
disabilities as illustrative of God's unfailing belief in all of God's children to lead in their own way.

Moshe Rabbeinu, like so many of us, experiences significant self-
doubt, what we might call internalized oppression, as he approaches
God's charge to speak to Pharaoh. "How then should Pharaoh heed
me, a man of impeded speech!" (Exodus 6:12). Nearly the same scene
repeats itself in Exodus 6:30. In both cases, God's response is to
provide Moses with a reasonable accommodation: Aaron, his elder
brother, is his spokesperson.[2] Significantly, this accommodation
does not diminish Moses's role but instead allows Moses to bring his
full self to his holy work.

Our *sidrah* comes on the heels of *Parashat Sh'mot*, with its famous
dialogue between God and Moses regarding his speech impediment.[3]
God reminds Moses and all of us that we are each created *b'tzelem*

Elohim, in the divine image: Who made you as you are, whether you are blind, deaf, have a mobility impairment, a speech impediment, or perhaps an intellectual disability? Maybe you are neurodiverse. You are part of My creation, God says emphatically.[4] And to Moses specifically, after providing the aforementioned accommodation, God demands: Now go and do this holy work.[5]

Nevertheless, Moses still struggles with feelings of inadequacy. How can a person who cannot be easily understood lead? Moses, raised in luxury, likely never met anyone who spoke like him. It is not difficult to imagine Moses being bullied and ridiculed for how he spoke. He might have concluded that it would be better to be silent than to absorb the emotional blows from those around him. Without the love and support of others who experience the world as he does, Moses's self-deprecating stance is understandable, if also deeply tragic. Perhaps this is why God must reassure Moses twice that he is truly fit to lead and that a reasonable accommodation is not a burden but simply what is needed.

I am the only blind woman ordained to the rabbinate. That is, to put it simply, a complexly layered experience. It means coming to terms with the reality that I am a trailblazer, whether I want to be or not. It means entering a field without a road map for success. It means not having anyone who went before me to turn to for the practical and the existential questions. It means relying upon a village of incredible rabbinic mentors with disabilities, upon whose shoulders I metaphorically stand. With very few peers with disabilities in Jewish leadership, it also means turning to our ancient forebears for *chizuk* (strength).

Moses's journey serves as a signpost for my own. God's unflinching *emunah* (faith) in Moses's indispensability and potential made it such that I could not forget our tradition's core teaching—that we are all created *b'tzelem Elohim*, all of us carrying within us a pure spark of holiness that cannot be sullied, no matter what human-made oppressive structures and systems tell us. Indeed, God's message and reminder to Moses in Exodus 4 that God created Moses as he is, just as God creates all of us as we are, is not merely a repetition of

Genesis 1:27. The specificity matters. I have been told by educators too numerous to name that my blindness was an inherent limitation to my ability to learn their material and that teaching me was simply not worth it or impossible. Most stinging and long-lasting of all was when, while I was a rabbinical student, a Hebrew teacher of mine told me that I was just going to have to try harder to be a visual person, as if the mere fact of my blindness translated into a profound, irreparable flaw in my very humanity.

Too many of us, living with compounding oppressions—race, class, sexual orientation, health status, gender identity, and more—internalize this imposed inferiority. The structural barriers to our ability to flourish and thrive are tangible, real, and without end, or so it seems. All of these daily interpersonal and systemic inequities and indignities chip away at our essence, our *n'shamot*, our very souls. We can never be reminded too often that we carry a spark of holiness within, in a world that seeks to deny this about us. We may not walk, speak, read, or communicate in the same way. But how boring the world would be, God reminds us, if all of humankind operated in the same manner. It is our job to dismantle the notion of normality, and we can start by providing a redemptive microcosm of the world we dream and breathe into being in our own circles and spheres of influence. The field of diversity, equity, and inclusion is becoming more prominent in social justice organizations and other communities who want to build the world as it should be, not accept the world as it is.

If you do not self-identify as a person with a disability, ask yourself: To whom do you turn for leadership, and how many of them have disabilities, invisible or visible? Take some time in quiet contemplation to examine your own beliefs about disability, people with disabilities, and the realities of living with one or multiple disabilities. That *cheshbon hanefesh*—deep, introspective soul-work—is not going to be easy or pretty, but it is deeply necessary if we want to make this world a true dwelling place for the *Shechinah*, the Divine Presence.

If you live with one or multiple disabilities, what have you internalized about yourself over time? Take some time to journal, meditate, or talk with a trusted spiritual mentor, friend, therapist, or clergyperson. My own uncovering has been painful at times and deeply discomfiting. Being able to name what I have internalized has allowed me to begin the slow, painstaking work of dismantling and relearning. That process can open up possibilities for personal *tikkun* (repair) that we may never have dreamed were available.

The opening verses of *Va-eira* tell us that our people's breath contracted and their spirits sank because of the cruelty of enslavement. We also know that Moshe Rabbeinu, our greatest prophet, felt the weight of internalized oppression and inadequacy. These are deeply human emotional responses and impulses. But God does not despair. Though our spirits are crushed, God knows redemption and freedom are at hand. And we know from *B'nei Yisrael* (the Children of Israel) that becoming a free people is a forty-year process. So, too, we witness in *Va-eira* just how hard it is for individuals to free ourselves from the self-limiting beliefs we internalize. Knowing the arc of our people's national history, may we be encouraged to move forward and not give into despair. As Moses comes more fully into himself, flaws and all, may his journey serve as inspiration for so many of ours.

NOTES
1. Rashi to Exodus 6:9.
2. See, for example, Exodus 4:14–17.
3. Exodus 4:10ff.
4. Paraphrase of and expansion on Exodus 4:11.
5. Paraphrase of Exodus 4:12.

Bo—Exodus 10:1–13:16

The Exodus, Freedom, and Welcoming the Stranger

Rabbi Sandra Lawson

BEFORE ENTERING RABBINICAL SCHOOL, I did not spend a lot of time thinking much about God, spirituality, or religion. Instead, I was focused on social justice, *tikkun olam*, and exploring how my Jewish values fit into a larger society. My experiences are shaped by my identity as a queer, Black Jew, with parents who grew up dirt-poor in the Jim Crow segregated south. My identity allows me to see our society through the eyes of marginalized people. I also sit on the margins of Jewish life. I am often seen as an outsider in the Jewish world and not authentically Jewish, which gives me an interesting perspective on Judaism and our society.

One of the things I love about Judaism is that we are all connected by the Torah portion of the week. We are simultaneously reading the same text, and our reading gets filtered through the experiences of the times we are currently living in. Throughout the Book of *Sh'mot*, Exodus, we follow the Israelites from slavery to freedom and then redemption. *Sh'mot*, one could argue, is an entire book about a slave uprising. Much of how I view myself as a Jew, an activist, and a rabbi comes from this book.

In *Parashat Bo*, we are at the climax of Israel's struggle for freedom. Plague after disgusting plague has struck Egypt, and Pharaoh is now willing to let some of the Israelites go free, but not all of them (Exodus 10:10–11). Moses insists that none of the Israelites will go unless all of them can. Moses wants freedom for all, not just a few. He says, "We will go, regardless of social status; we will go with our sons and our daughters . . ." (Exodus 10:9). In other words, "We ain't leavin' anybody behind!"

We all know the song "Let My People Go," an African American spiritual based on the text from Exodus, but the next phrase of Scripture is missing from the song. God says, "Let My people go to worship Me" (Exodus 9:13). Our liberation is connected to God. The Torah is a fascinating story of enslaved people struggling for their freedom. The slaves gain their freedom because God sides with the Israelites over their oppressor, Pharaoh. Then, once the Israelites are free, rules of behavior and laws are created for a new society and social system that underlies freedom for all people. You may be thinking that the Torah does not abolish slavery, and you are right, a fact that has always concerned me. Instead, the Torah lists a series of laws in *Parashat Mishpatim* on how to protect the slave. Slavery existed during biblical times and still exists today. The Torah gives us laws to protect slaves from abuse and mistreatment; it appears to try to correct some of the pitfalls of slavery. It's as if the Torah cannot imagine a world without slavery. Even though the Torah does not abolish slavery, it sets in motion a series of fundamental laws that will lead people to abolish slavery of their own accord.

In the Torah, liberation begins with and emphasizes a concern for the poor, the oppressed, and the marginalized. God sides with the oppressed and marginalized and against the oppressors.

We need to be free in order to worship God. The founders of the United States created a society based on freedom of religion. The freedom to worship as one wants is built into the fabric of our nation's founding documents. As Jews, we are keenly aware of the need to worship freely. Many Jews fled from pogroms in Europe, and America's open doors offered shelter and opportunity. And when America kept its doors tightly shut as the Nazi regime grew more deadly, we suffered the agony of those who were left to die. Burned in our minds are images like those of the hundreds of refugees on the *St. Louis*, seeking to escape Hitler and Nazi Germany. The United States and Cuba refused them entrance. Instead of being given a safe haven, they were sent back to Europe, and many perished in the Holocaust.

The Torah repeatedly emphasizes a positive, welcoming approach to the stranger, the immigrant, and the person in need. This attitude is one of the foremost lessons of our exile in Egypt. No less than thirty-six times, the Torah reminds us not to oppress the stranger, often with a companion explanation to remember that we know the heart of the stranger because we were once strangers in the land of Egypt— for example, "You shall not oppress a stranger, for you know the feelings of the stranger, having yourselves been strangers in the land of Egypt" (Exodus 23:9).

After World War II, many in the Jewish community witnessed the African American community's civil rights struggles. They realized that not all of us are free in our society, and they worked with the Black community to make life better for all. They wanted America to hold true to its promise of freedom for everyone. Today, too, many Jews are waking up to racism experienced by Black and Brown people in America. And, as many of us watch police or vigilantes murder unarmed Black people time and time again, we realize that not all of us are yet free.

Many Jews are protesting racism and doing whatever they can to end racism in our society. However, the Jewish community also needs to do some internal work to focus on the racism within. Many Jews who are white treat Black and Brown Jews as if we do not belong and are not a real part of the community. Upon entering Jewish spaces or when I meet white Jews for the first time, I am often asked a myriad of question: When did you convert? Were you born Jewish? Once, when I was introduced to the parent of a potential Elon University student who was also Jewish, I was introduced as the rabbi. The parent repeatedly asked if I was an ordained rabbi, as if a nationally ranked university would hire a non-ordained rabbi.

Diversity within the Jewish people is not new. In *Parashat Bo*, we read, "Moreover [*v'gam*], a mixed multitude [*eirev rav*] went up with them, and very much livestock, both flocks and herds" (Exodus 12:38). I want to highlight the Hebrew word *v'gam* (וְגַם), which we can just as accurately translate as "and also." The Torah doesn't want us to forget that the people who escaped slavery so long ago in search of freedom were not monolithic. The focus on the livestock and herds reminds us that some in the community were well off enough to own property and others may have been poor, indicating that those who fled came from diverse socioeconomic backgrounds. I often tell the college students I work with to imagine the budding relationships that were happening. Perhaps an Israelite fell in love with an Egyptian. When the Israelites were leaving, some Egyptians threw their lot in with the ones they loved and followed Moses into the wilderness. This text is a reminder that we were and always have been a diverse group. A few lines later, the Torah tells us, "There shall be one law for the citizen and for the stranger who dwells among you" (Exodus 12:49). When one who has previously been a stranger joins us, that person must be treated as one who is born in the Land. We are to treat everyone equally.

Each of us is a dynamic and awesome being who, when we live up to our potential, can do amazing things—maybe even become the Moses of our generation. Let us remember that our freedom is connected to God. When we treat others in our community as if they don't belong, we prevent others from worshiping God, and we are not living up to our Jewish values.

B'SHALACH—EXODUS 13:17–17:16

Our Obligations to DREAMers and Ourselves

Cantor Seth Warner

PARASHAT B'SHALACH tells of the Israelites' newfound freedom from Egypt, some 430 years after Jacob's arrival. The Israelites initially prosper there, but eventually "a new king arose over Egypt who did not know Joseph," and he enslaves them (Exodus 1:7–11). Ultimately, God's intervention in the form of the plagues softens Pharaoh's heart just enough for a momentary declaration of freedom (Exodus 12:31–32). Soon enough, though, Pharaoh's court has "a change of heart," and Pharaoh and his armies begin to pursue the Israelites in hopes of recapturing them (Exodus 14:5–8). Arriving at the shore of the Sea of Reeds, with Pharaoh's army approaching, the Israelites are trapped. In one of the Torah's paramount miracles, with Moses's outstretched arms, God splits the sea in two, allowing the Israelites to cross on dry land (Exodus 14:21–22). When the Egyptians approach, even though they try to escape, "the Eternal hurled [them] into the sea" (Exodus 14:27).

In celebration of their freedom, Moses and the Israelites sing to the Eternal *Shirat HaYam*, the "Song at the Sea"—or more simply, the *Shirah*, the "Song." Exodus 15:1–18 is uniquely laid out in the Torah scroll, with the words written in a bricklike pattern with large spaces in the center of the column on alternating lines. The song tells of God's saving power, including the text of *Mi Chamochah* (Exodus 15:11). The message of *Mi Chamochah* is so powerful that it is sung in nearly every service in our tradition, reminding us of this heroic celebration of freedom.

The *Shirah* describes a pivotal point in our people's existence—the transition from captivity to freedom. The text and cantillation paint a picture of hope and change. The cantillation uses a different melody for the *Shirah*, different from any other in the *Tanach*, as a way to draw attention to this pivotal point in the relationship between God and the Israelites. Moses is said to have sung the *Shirah* in a special voice to glorify God's saving power, and the melody reflects that shift from biblical narrative to Moses's words. This change in melody further emphasizes that God is saving and claiming the Israelite people—the two now have an unbreakable bond.[1]

Once freed from danger at the Sea of Reeds, the Israelites become refugees. They have escaped their captors and are alone. But they are not as alone as they might think, as the Torah tells us: they have a unique guardian, God. "And when Israel saw the wondrous power which the Eternal had wielded against the Egyptians, the people feared the Eternal; they had faith in the Eternal" (Exodus 14:31). They seem to understand in this moment that God has used extraordinary forces to guarantee their freedom, including the decimation of the Egyptians who sought their recapture. They realize right now that their freedom is the result of miraculous divine intervention.

As they begin their wanderings in the desert, perhaps the most important message of their freedom emerges: how God expects the Israelites to treat the stranger. "You shall not wrong nor oppress a stranger, for you were strangers in the land of Egypt" (Exodus 22:20). This text, while not in *Parashat B'shalach*, refers to the freedom that the Israelites inherited in it. It is repeated more than any commandment in the Torah, thirty-six times, which we understand as "double *chai*," or two lives. The message: Consider both lives, yours and the stranger's, as equally important in the eyes of God. As our Sages explicate, "The fact that we were slaves awakens our sensitivity and consideration for strangers and for the unfortunate who suffer and need help, as it is stated: 'Do not oppress the stranger, for you know how it feels to be a stranger, since you were strangers in the land of Egypt.'"[2]

The commandment is not as simple to fulfill as it is easy on the ears. Rabbi David Jaffe notes, "The commandment is directed at a people that was once vulnerable but now is in a position of power in relation to vulnerable people in our society. . . . Absent a process of dealing with the transition from vulnerability to power, [contemporary Jewish communities] are at risk of mistreating the vulnerable in their own societies."[3] By repeating the injunction so many times, the Torah hopes to habituate even the powerful Israelite or contemporary Jew to break the inclination to become an oppressor.

The laws of treating the stranger with respect do not simply suggest a stance of tolerance or even affability: "The strangers who reside with you shall be to you as your citizens; *you shall love each one as yourself*, for you were strangers in the land of Egypt: I the Eternal am your God" (Leviticus 19:34; emphasis added). To love the stranger as you love yourself presents a conundrum. Ideally, when saying you love yourself, you are inherently acknowledging your imperfections; you are trying to appreciate what they have taught you and are striving to fold those teachings into the values of your life. When we understand our propensity to become the oppressor, as Rabbi Jaffe suggests we must, we can acknowledge our own trauma of oppression and therefore be inclined to feel more naturally loving, embracing, and truly interested in the stranger we encounter.[4] When accepting responsibility for the stranger, we are affirming a love for that person. We are linking our own well-being to theirs.

Sadly, our American government often treats immigrants with an attitude similar to that of the Pharaoh who didn't know Joseph. The stated reason for Pharaoh's hatred of the Israelites is that they are growing too numerous and could become a potential enemy of the Egyptians (Exodus 1:9–10). This ideology is shared thousands of years later in our country, as xenophobia veiled as security concerns about those seeking a secure home in our country.[5]

Since we don't expect that a biblical God to intervene and protect those oppressed in our world today, the responsibility for their safety and well-being falls to us. We mortals may not be able to part rivers or bring about biblical plagues, but we can employ appropriate measures to assist others toward freedom. Throughout history, humanity has been called upon to help refugees in need. And throughout history, since the parting of the Red Sea, we Jews have been called upon to help those in need by loving and caring for them as if they were our own.

Americans overwhelmingly support DREAMers, immigrants who were brought to this country as children without legal documentation.[6] DREAMers take their name from the bipartisan Development, Relief and Education for Alien Minors Act, first proposed in 2001 but never adopted by Congress. Instead, President Barack Obama's Deferred Action for Childhood Arrivals (DACA) executive order in 2012 serves as a stopgap but provides no long-term security to DREAMers. People who have every right to expect that they are safe in the United States are used in a political tug-of-war by those who oppose immigration. In 2017, the Trump administration sought to dismantle parts of the plan but was ordered to reinstate core parts by the Supreme Court. Then, in July 2020, Trump officials announced they would restrict legal protections of DACA recipients, limit their renewals to one year instead of two, and reject new applications.[7] The disparate treatment of DREAMers reflects different values, specifically the value of human life. Our tradition commands us to embrace the stranger, not reject them, and to treat every human being with the dignity that God helped us see in ourselves. Even as we continue to struggle to love ourselves, we are no better than the stranger in our midst. In fact, we are both equally worthy of acceptance and love.

When the Israelites cross the Red Sea, the *Shirah* proclaims their unabashed glorification of God and the joy of their freedom. Guided by God, they are shown to the Promised Land. Our freedom comes with the enduring responsibility to see to it that all people can sing their own *Shirah*, their own song of the God-given right to freedom.

NOTES

1. More in-depth discussion of nuances of the Song at the Sea cantillation can be found in Marshall Portnoy and Josée Wolff, *The Art of Torah Cantillation* (New York: URJ Press, 2000); and Joshua R. Jacobson, *Chanting the Hebrew Bible* (Philadelphia: Jewish Publication Society, 2017).

2. *Peninei Halachah, Pesach* 15:7:6, Commentary on *Sh'mot* 23:9.

3. David Jaffe, "Standing with the Stranger: A Spiritual Practice for Personal and Communal Healing," undated blog, accessed December 28, 2020, https://www.rabbidavidjaffe.com/standing-with-the-stranger.

4. Jaffe, "Standing with the Stranger."

5. Julia Tallmeister, "Is Immigration a Threat to Security?," E-International Relations, August 24, 2013, https://www.e-ir.info/2013/08/24/is-immigration-a-threat-to-security/.

6. Chantal Da Silva, "74 Percent of Americans Support Full Legal Status for DACA Dreamers, Poll Finds," *Newsweek*, June 18, 2020, https://www.newsweek.com/nearly-74-americans-support-legal-status-daca-dreamers-poll-finds-1511670.

7. Francesco Rodella and María Peña, "'Very Alarmed': Dreamers Slam Trump's New Limits on DACA Program," *NBC News*, July 29, 2020, https://www.nbcnews.com/news/latino/very-alarmed-dreamers-slam-trump-s-new-limits-daca-program-n1235184.

Yitro—Exodus 18:1–20:23

Systems of Justice:
The Model and the Reality

Rabbi Rachel Greengrass

Judges take on a sacred call to uphold the law and seek justice. *Yitro* is the name of not only of our Torah portion, but also of Moses's father-in-law—in English, Jethro—the man who gifts the court system to ancient Israelite society. Jethro instructs Moses that true justice cannot be achieved by one man alone, saying, "The thing you are doing is not right" (Exodus 18:17). Only after Moses establishes the judicial system that Jethro recommends does he receive the Ten Commandments. Courts may therefore be understood as prerequisite for a just society. Our tradition insists that judicial systems are not only for the Children of Israel. Even the Noachide Laws, the seven laws our tradition established to determine the righteousness of a non-Jewish society, include courts as a requirement.[1]

Parashat Yitro reminds us that society cannot function without systems of justice. It models for us a justice system that shows no partiality toward the rich, the poor, the resident, or the alien. It asks the judges to see each defendant as a kinsman. Yet, we still have a long way to go in the United States to achieve this vision of justice.

Black and Brown people are more likely to be defendants in court. Many are charged with nonviolent drug crimes.[2] Even though studies have shown that drug use is roughly the same between Blacks and whites,[3] our courtrooms are still disproportionately filled with Black and Brown defendants. Even with respect to violent crimes, which constitute the minority of cases, when income is held steady, there is no difference between the rates of offenses committed by whites and people of color.[4] Can justice really be achieved when such bias is shown in who is "brought to justice" in the first place?

Early in *Parashat Yitro*, we learn that Moses, in naming his children, emphasizes foreignness. He names his firstborn Gershom, because "I have been a stranger [*ger*] in a foreign land" (Exodus 18:3). *Ger* means "stranger," "alien," or "immigrant," someone who is seen as outside of the system. We are to have "one law for the citizen and for the stranger [*ger*] who dwells among you" (Exodus 12:49). Ibn Ezra writes that the Torah particularly warns about situations in which a judge errs in judgment regarding the widow, orphan, or stranger living among us. These people lack the same ability as the powerful and well-connected to be heard when they try to explain that they have been wrongfully judged.[5] In our society, though, the most vulnerable fall victim to the flaws of the justice system.[6] They cannot afford top lawyers,[7] lack connections within the system itself, and yes, have the "wrong" skin color.[8] Too often justice is not for all, but for those whom the system favors. We are taught: "You shall not judge unfairly: you shall show no partiality; you shall not take bribes, for bribes blind the eyes of the discerning and upset the plea of the just" (Deuteronomy 16:19). Tragically, we have yet to realize that ideal in our American justice system.

In Deuteronomy, when Moses reiterates our *parashah*'s establishment of the judicial system, he adds, "Fear no one, for judgment is God's" (Deuteronomy 1:17). Moses recognizes that people may easily be biased. Humans naturally favor people who are most like themselves.[9] We are easily intimidated by the wealthy, powerful, and politically influential. But if "judgment is God's," biblical scholar Jeffrey H. Tigay suggests, one "ought to fear offending God more than [they] fear offending any human."[10] In the Book of Chronicles, King Jehoshaphat advises the judges, "Consider what you are doing, for you judge not on behalf of human beings, but on behalf of the Eternal, who is with you when you pass judgment. Now let the fear of the Eternal be upon you; act with care, for there is no injustice or favoritism or bribery with the Eternal our God" (II Chronicles 19:6–7).

Judges are our conduits to justice. They are to be above bribery and politics and to serve justice above themselves or their office. And yet, many have to run in elections to acquire and keep their seats on the bench, opening them up to the influence of politics and political contributions.[11]

Even if the majority of our judges reflect Jethro's suggestion to "to seek out, from among all the people, capable individuals who fear God—trustworthy ones who spurn ill-gotten gain" (Exodus 18:21), we have failed to live up to the rest of his advice: "Set these over them as chiefs of thousands, hundreds, fifties, and tens." Jethro's system is designed to afford judges of first recourse a small caseload that allows for a deep understanding of the case and even an intimacy for all parties involved. When a person was initially brought to trial, their case would be heard by a judge of "tens," someone who knows them and their situation—who sees them as a human, as part of their community, and who is invested in their success.

Instead, we have created a cold, bureaucratic system that fails to see the individual, only the alleged crime. True justice happens when we acknowledge the full humanity of the person who stands before us. Perhaps this is why our Rabbis ruled that if defendants have no one brought to speak on their behalf, we must acquit them, for surely injustice is being done.[12]

We have a great deal of work to do. The task of justice is too much for one person to bear. It's up to all of us to help bring about a just society, one in which we all rise, we all bear part of the load. If all members of society work together, we can achieve the kind of justice the Torah imagines—where we are able to look beyond the accusation of offense and see people as people. This point is beautifully illustrated in a Chasidic tale that has been repeated in many iterations:

> Many women came to a Hasidic rabbi on the eve of Yom Kippur with questions relating to *kashrut*. He replied to each one, without exception, but the food was kosher and could be eaten. When approached by a rabbi colleague who suggested that it might be more proper to be stricter in rendering decisions on the eve of the Day of Atonement, the Hasidic rabbi responded: "On the

contrary. If I should declare a chicken of doubtful *kashrut* unfit for eating, I may be guilty of sitting against my brother-in-law who may not have anything else to eat before the fast, and a sin against man will not be expiated on Yom Kippur. However, if I declare the chicken to be kosher even though there may be some doubt, I am sinning only against God, and as you know, the Day of Atonement brings pardon for sins against God.[13]

NOTES

1. The Noachide Laws are found in the Babylonian Talmud, *Sanhedrin* 56a; cf. *Tosefta Avodah Zarah* 8:4 and *B'reishit Rabbah* 34:8. Commenting on Genesis 34:13, Nachmanides broadens the requirements of courts: "In my opinion, the laws that the Noachides were to establish according to their seven commandments is not only to establish courts in each town, but that they were also commanded concerning theft, abuse, usury, labor relations, damages, loans, business, and the like, just as Israel was commanded to set up laws in these matters."

2. Three-fourths of all people imprisoned for drug offenses have been Black or Latino, despite the fact that the majority of illegal drug users and dealers nationwide are white. Marc Mauer and Ryan S. King, *Schools and Prisons: Fifty Years After* Brown v. Board of Education (Washington, DC: Sentencing Project, 2004), 28.

3. US Department of Health and Human Services, Substance Abuse and Mental Health Services Administration, *Summary of Findings from the 2000 National Household Survey on Drug Abuse*, NHSDA series H-13, DHHS pub. no. SMA 01-3549 (Rockville, MD: US Department of Health and Human Services, 2001).

4. In his book *How to Be an AntiRacist*, Ibram X. Kendi references a study that found that Black males committed violent crime at a higher rate than white males. However, when the researchers only compared employed males of both groups, any discrepancy disappeared. Another study found that a 2.5 percent decrease in unemployment resulted in a 4.3 percent decrease in robberies, 2.5 percent decrease in auto theft, 5 percent for burglary, and 3.7 percent for larceny. Ibram X. Kendi, *How To Be AntiRacist* (New York: One World, 2019), 79.

5. Ibn Ezra on Exodus 22:22–23.

6. *McKlesky v. Kemp*, 482 U.S. 279,327 (1989), Brennan, J., dissenting, notes that Georgia prosecutors sought the death penalty in 19 percent of cases involving white defendants, while when the defendant was Black, they sought the death penalty in 70 percent of cases.

7. John Mathews II and Felipe Curiel, "Criminal Justice Debt Problems,"

Human Rights 44, no. 3 (November 30, 2019), https://www.americanbar. org/groups/crsj/publications/human_rights_magazine_home/economic-justice/criminal-justice-debt-problems/.

8. See Ojmarrh Mitchell and Doris L. MacKenzie, "The Relationship between Race, Ethnicity, and Sentencing Outcomes: A Meta-Analysis of Sentencing Research," document no. 208129 (research report submitted to the US Department of Justice, December 2004); and Christopher Schmitt, "Plea Bargaining Favors Whites, as Blacks, Hispanics Pay Price," *Mercury News* (San Jose, CA), December 8, 1991, which show that, at virtually every stage of pretrial investigation, whites are more successful than Blacks.

9. Jeffrey J. Rachlinski, Sheri Johnson, Andrew J. Wistrich, and Chris Guthrie, "Does Unconscious Racial Bias Affect Trial Judges?," *Cornell Law Faculty Publications* 786 (2009), http://scholarship.law.cornell.edu/facpub/786.

10. Jeffrey H. Tigay, *JPS Torah Commentary: Deuteronomy* (Philadelphia: Jewish Publication Society, 1996), 13.

11. "Today, about 90 percent of state judges must run for office, and the elections have become increasingly expensive and nasty" (Jeri Zeder, "Elected vs. Appointed?," *Harvard Law Today*, July 1, 2012, https://today.law.harvard. edu/book-review/in-new-book-shugerman-explores-the-history-of-judicial-selection-in-the-u-s/).

12. Babylonian Talmud, *Sanhedrin* 17a, translated in *The Talmud Vol. 15: The Steinsaltz Edition: Tractate Sanhedrin, Part 1* (New York: Random House, 1996), supra note 22, at 179–87: "Rav Kahana said: A Sanhedrin where each one saw fit to convict, acquits him. Why? Because Gemara teaches us the rule to delay [the sentence overnight] to find [arguments for] his innocence, and these are not looking for it."

13. Philip Goodman, *The Yom Kippur Anthology* (Philadelphia: Jewish Publication Society of America, 1971), 114–15.

MISHPATIM—EXODUS 21:1–24:18

Stricken from the Text: Sacred Stories of Reproductive Justice

RABBI JOSHUA R. S. FIXLER

and RABBI EMILY LANGOWITZ

In 1952, my grandmother Audrey would have been about twenty years old. Recently married, she and her husband were planning to begin having children in a few years, after he graduated from college in Connecticut. But as the Yiddish proverb says, "People plan and God laughs"; Audrey quickly became pregnant. A few weeks later, however, the joyous laughter was drained from this pregnancy when she contracted the German measles. Her doctor warned that the fetus was at great risk for congenital rubella syndrome and that, even if it survived to term, it would likely suffer severe birth defects. The doctor and all of his colleagues urged her to seek an abortion, though such a procedure was illegal. Audrey and her husband were young, scared, and far away from their family and support system as they struggled with what to do.

And yet, they were also lucky to have means and connections. Someone recommended they travel to see a friendly doctor in Boston, who helped them find certainty. Even almost seventy years later, Audrey can still hear him saying, "If you were my daughter, I would not let you carry this pregnancy to term." He admitted her to the hospital and wrote on her chart that she had come for a D&C after a miscarriage, to hide their illegal act. Audrey remembers at the time being terrified—of the procedure itself, of the illegality of it, and mostly of the thought that she might never be able to have children afterward. Yet now, looking back, she remarks that she has never once regretted her decision.

> She did what she knew was right for her. She consulted her doc-
> tor, her husband, her God, and made a responsible choice.
> —*Rabbi Joshua R. S. Fixler*

A STUDY BY THE PEW RESEARCH CENTER found that 83 percent of
American Jews say that abortion should be legal in all or most cases.[1]
American Jews' widespread support for permissive abortion laws
finds grounding in Jewish tradition's approach to pregnancy and its
end. Though the Torah makes no specific reference to any process
resembling a modern abortion, the following passage from *Parashat
Mishpatim* provides our tradition's earliest guidance on the termination of a pregnancy:

> When individuals fight, and one of them pushes a pregnant
> woman and a miscarriage results, but no other damage ensues,
> the one responsible shall be fined according as the woman's
> husband may exact, the payment to be based on reckoning. But
> if other damage ensues, the penalty shall be life for life, eye for
> eye, tooth for tooth, hand for hand, foot for foot, burn for burn,
> wound for wound, bruise for bruise. (Exodus 21:22–25)

The passage contrasts two scenarios in which two men are fighting
and accidentally strike a nearby pregnant woman. The permutations
differ only in who or what is harmed. In the first, only the fetus is lost,
and the punishment is a monetary fine, paid to the woman's husband.
In the second, the woman herself is harmed or killed. There, the punishment is retributive: an eye for an eye and a *nefesh*—literally, "soul,"
but in this case meaning a human life possessing personhood—for a
nefesh. From this, we may derive the principle that a woman has the
full status of a person, *nefesh*, while the fetus—though valued—has a
lesser status.

The Mishnah expands this understanding of differential value
by stating that if a woman's life is threatened in childbirth, the fetus
inside her can be destroyed, even to the point of "taking it out limb
from limb, for her life comes before the fetus's life."[2] Through the
graphic language of this text, the Mishnaic author leaves no ambiguity as to whose life takes precedence. This text sets the standard

from which all other halachah (Jewish law) on abortion flows. Later commentators debate in great detail the implications of this text, particularly the breadth or narrowness of the definition of a threat to the life of the woman.[3] Some are more permissive of a range of emotional as well as physical impacts that could justify an abortion, while others understand the instances of permissibility with excruciating parsimony. Still, from the outset, Judaism can imagine some instances when an abortion would be permitted and even required.[4]

Furthermore, the Gemara concludes that prior to forty days, a fetus is not a person but rather is considered "mere water."[5] The debate about abortion in America hinges on questions related to what constitutes personhood and when life begins. But these are religious and spiritual questions, about which people of faith and conviction can disagree. The Supreme Court held in *Roe v. Wade* that abortion is protected under the Constitution's Fourth Amendment, which guarantees a right to privacy, including a right to private medical procedures. For American Jews, the protection of access to abortion could also be understood under the First Amendment's free exercise of religion clause. Because Jewish law permits abortion under certain circumstances as a morally acceptable choice, or even in some cases a halachic requirement, any law that limits a woman's right to choose might limit a Jewish woman's ability to make a decision in accordance with her religious beliefs. When people of faith seek to adopt laws asserting when life begins, they endeavor to enshrine their own religious understanding in law. In civic discourse, the fact that Judaism understands these issues differently can be a powerful antidote to the pervasive sense that religious voices are only to be found on one side of this debate. Judaism is unequivocally "pro-life" in that it values life in all its forms, both actualized and potential. But where that term has come to mean "anti-abortion," then it is clear that Judaism allows for abortion under at least some circumstances and therefore calls us to advocate for civil laws that protect a woman's right to access abortion services.

These texts and their subsequent interpretations are a vital resource for all of us who seek to affirm Jewish support for the choice to terminate a pregnancy and to advocate from a Jewish perspective for laws that protect reproductive choice. And we are called to go further; the law is only one facet of a full and holistic justice. Even as *Parashat Mishpatim* guides us to a choice-oriented understanding of abortion law, it also leaves us with the injustice of a silenced story.

The text in Exodus 21 begins with an act of violence perpetrated against a pregnant woman, and yet this woman is all but absent from subsequent conversation about this passage. Across the centuries, almost all of the voices of Jewish interpretation, and even many modern commentators, fail to acknowledge her story. The interpreters miss the opportunity to see her as subject, rather than object. To see the woman in this text as merely a hypothetical in a legal case study is to deny that cases such as these were very real to the people who experienced them. To reach a full sense of justice in our understanding of abortion, we must pair *mishpatim* (laws) with *sipurim* (stories).

We cannot go back in time to ask this woman how *she* experienced the day her pregnancy ended so abruptly. But Judaism gives us plenty of precedent to offer this woman—and all those who live through challenging or stigmatized reproductive experiences—the power of our curiosity and our questions. How might we ask this text something new? What might we gain by looking to it not just for legal precedent but for narrative as well? Discussions of abortion so often center on the personhood of the fetus. This approach allows us to elevate the personhood of the one carrying the pregnancy.

To achieve the justice owed this woman, hearing the truth of her story, we might ask her: Who are you? What was your name and your life story? What circumstances brought you into such close proximity with this fight? If you survive, what will you tell your other children about the day you lost your pregnancy? What was your relationship to the pregnancy you carried, and what value did you assign to its loss?

Our tradition offers techniques we can employ to reveal answers. First, we can look for parallel texts within the Torah to give this woman's story greater context. There is a nearly identical case of two men fighting near a woman in Deuteronomy 25:11–12. In that episode, a woman attempts to break up a fight between her husband and another man. In the process, she accidentally touches the other man's genitals and is sentenced to have the offending hand cut off. The woman of our verses in *Mishpatim* might have known of such a punishment. Picture the terror she would have felt, knowing that any action she took could end in violence. If she chose to intervene or not, if she knew the men or not—in any scenario, she risks losing her hand, her pregnancy, or even her life. Even in the twenty-first century, we live in a society in which pregnant women find their choices restricted by the violence of the men around them. When we read these passages from Exodus and Deuteronomy in tandem, we see beyond the permission for reproductive choice to the structures in society that must be healed to make such choices real.

A second way to give the woman of *Mishpatim* greater voice and agency is to turn to midrash. No traditional midrash gives greater insight into this woman's story, so we are called to create our own. We might be aided in this endeavor by a final technique for bringing fuller justice to this narrative: we cannot ask this woman of the Torah for the truth of her experience, but we can come to a better understanding of it by asking those in the present day whose own stories could help uncover that which is hidden in this text.

Every family has stories of reproductive choices. Some are shared between mothers and daughters, between parents and children. Others are kept secret or lost. Our work of justice is rooted in the telling of these stories. For every woman caught in a fight between two men, there was one miscarrying at home and one in a strange land, one in a happy marriage and one whose relationship was violent, one alone and one surrounded by her family, one desperately wanting to save the fetus and one desperately wanting it gone. Every pregnancy has its own story with its own ending. Each time we listen with compassion and curiosity to a new narrative, we strengthen our ability to discuss pregnancy and its termination without judgment, guided by the voices of those who have actually experienced it. Sharing these stories has the power to lift up marginalized voices and create public empathy and awareness.

For us as activists and advocates, these stories we read alongside our ancient texts—and which we view as equally sacred—inspire our passion for justice. For Josh, the act of telling his grandmother's story compels him to work toward a world in which abortion might be legal, accessible, and destigmatized. For Emily, the stories of her ancestors and friends drive her to affirm abortion as a morally acceptable choice. Justice for all those who carry such stories, whether spoken or unspoken, must be reflected in our laws and in our culture. This text in *Parashat Mishpatim* gives us a blueprint for those laws. The personal narrative it omits calls us toward creating a more just culture, one in which we see the humanity of all those who choose to end a pregnancy.

Notes

1. Pew Research Center, "Views about Abortion among Jews," Religious Landscape Study, 2014, https://www.pewforum.org/religious-landscape-study/religious-tradition/jewish/views-about-abortion/.
2. *Mishnah Ohalot* 7:6.
3. We recognize the complexity of this term and acknowledge that it is not only women who experience pregnancy and abortion and also that not all women can experience pregnancy. We offer this word for simplicity but intend it to include a broad range of experiences and identities.
4. Many trace the split between lenient and strict positions to Rashi and Maimonides, respectively. See Rashi's comment on Babylonian Talmud, *Sanhedrin* 72b; Maimonides, *Mishneh Torah, Hilchot Rotzei-ach Ushmirat Nefesh* 1:9. Rashi defines the fetus as non-*nefesh* (in keeping with our passage in Exodus), while Maimonides focuses his discussion on the fetus as a *rodeif* (meaning only if the fetus is actively pursuing the life of the mother should the pregnancy be terminated). For fuller discussion of the halachic texts that flow from each side, see Daniel Schiff, *Abortion in Judaism* (Cambridge: Cambridge University Press, 2002).
5. Babylonian Talmud, *Y'vamot* 69b.

T'RUMAH—EXODUS 25:1–27:19

The Heart-Incited Offering: Interdependence, Economic Redistribution, and Community Care

RABBI MACKENZIE ZEV REYNOLDS

JUST BEFORE *Parashat T'rumah* begins, Moses receives the Decalogue (Exodus 20:1–17) and the Covenant Code (Exodus 21:1–23:33). He reads the terms of the covenant to the people, and they respond emphatically: *Naaseh v'nishma* (נַעֲשֶׂה וְנִשְׁמָע), "We will do and we will obey" (Exodus 24:7). God then brings Moses further up the mountain so that *B'nei Yisrael*, the Children of Israel, could be given a blueprint for the *Mishkan*, the Tabernacle, a space for God to reach down into this world and where community could be sustained. "*We* will do and *we* will obey," the Israelites said. The work of cohering and caring for the community is work they must share.

Parashat T'rumah is named after the offerings *B'nei Yisrael* are to bring: *V'yikchu li t'rumah me-eit kol ish asher yid'venu libo tikchu et t'rumati* (וְיִקְחוּ־לִי תְּרוּמָה מֵאֵת כָּל־אִישׁ אֲשֶׁר יִדְּבֶנּוּ לִבּוֹ תִּקְחוּ אֶת־תְּרוּמָתִי), "You shall accept gifts for Me from every person whose heart is so moved" (Exodus 25:2). The phrase *yid'venu libo* can also be translated as "whose heart incites them"—a person compelled by the needs of the community and responds to those needs with generosity. *T'rumah* comes from the *shoresh* (root) *resh-vav-mem* (*r-v-m*, ר-ו-מ), meaning something "set apart, lifted up." The Israelites are instructed to bring offerings of materials—gold, silver, copper; blue, purple, and crimson threads; textiles, skins, wood, spices, and more (Exodus 25:3–7)—everything needed for the *avodah* (service) to take place in the *Mishkan*. There is a double implication: we set these materials apart so that we can lift them—and our whole community—up. From this concept of offering *yid'venu libo*—the heart-incited offering—we might derive a new framework for redistributing resources to poor and working-class people.

Elsewhere in Torah, the word *t'rumah* describes a set, obligatory offering, a fixed-rate tax of a half-shekel of silver (Exodus 30:12–15). In contrast, the heart-incited freewill *t'rumah* of our *parashah* has no set financial amount and is not a monetary offering. *B'nei Yisrael* receive a list of materials needed for the construction of the *Mishkan*, the place that will allow God to dwell among them (Exodus 25:8), even as they move through the wilderness, allowing everyone to bring whatever they can from the list of what is needed. No offering is too small or too large. Each item is needed equally, and each person is free to give according to their means, their resources, and their inclination. This freedom creates space so that there could be no resentment. No one is forced to give beyond their means or desire, to take things they do not want or need. No one individual could produce the *Mishkan* on their own, obliging the community to them. The community joins in creating a place of sanctuary where God could dwell among them and they could dwell together.

Rabbeinu Bachya ben Asher pushes us further, teaching that the *t'rumah* of our *parashah* is an example of the *middah* of *chochmah* (the soul-trait of wisdom), by which the world is elevated.[1] How does this *t'rumah* elevates us through the *middah* of wisdom?

In his commentary on Ramchal's *M'silat Yesharim*, Rabbi Ira Stone comments that "*yirat ha-Shem*, usually translated 'God-fearing,' is the working definition of wisdom." The complex theological concept of *yirat HaShem* is not fully captured by "fear" or "awe," the two standard English translations. Stone proposes that *yirat HaShem* conveys the feeling of "overwhelming weight we take on when we recognize the infinite nature of our responsibility for others" and that *ahavah* (love) is "the infinite potential for joy we experience by our choices to implement the *yetzer ha-tov*."[2] Wisdom, he proposes, is functioning in this world in relation to *yirat HaShem*—orienting us toward a responsibility for meeting the burdens and needs of others, balancing our own needs (the *yetzer hara*, "evil inclination") with the needs of the world (the *yetzer hatov*, "good inclination"). Mussar, the Jewish ethical practice that aims to balance the *yetzer hara* and the *yetzer hatov*, does so by directing us to discern the needs and burdens of the other. "The other" is an expansive category: our closest family and friends, strangers, communities, people we have oppressed, people who have oppressed us, those who have wronged us or whom we have wronged—all are examples of "the other" in Mussar.

Through the *t'rumah* of this *parashah*, the offering "from anyone whose heart inclines them to give," we might construct a new framework for giving and sharing the material resources required to build and sustain community. The heart-incited offerings we give freely enable our community to cohere and sustain itself. In our world, where we function separately from the specific requirements of the Temple system, we can be expansive in thinking about what our communities need to cohere and sustain themselves. The Temple itself is the central piece of infrastructure of *B'nei Yisrael*. Similarly, we need resources for infrastructure, for beautifying, and for ongoing material costs. Communities are sustained through the care, support, and resources of their members, and no one person's offerings are more important than another's. Further, we support our communities by supporting the individuals in them—by offering, freely and with the incitement of our hearts, whatever resources are required.

This model stands in contrast to Maimonides's eight levels of *tzedakah*,[3] which focus on giving charity to individuals. In Rambam's model, the highest level suggests that a person with resources enters into a business partnership with a poor person or gives them a loan (or a gift) so that the poor person can build toward economic independence. In the middle, a person gives anonymously. At the lowest level, a person gives unwillingly. Rambam is ultimately concerned about the poor person's dependency and the shame of poverty, assuming that avoiding shame and nurturing individual financial independence are paramount. Rambam's model is deeply resonant with the American cultural ideal of independence. But independence is a class-stratified concept. Middle-class and wealthy people have greater access to resources and power than do working-class and poor people, and so the ideal of independence plays out at the level of individual choice, action, influence, and control. Working-class and poor people, on the other hand, have chaotic and unpredictable resources, often replete with contingencies. As a result, working-class and poor people rely on each other for resources and support, producing not shame, but strength, care, and resilience.[4] Independence in working-class and poor communities is exercised toward the needs of the community. This is very much like the giving practice of the heart-incited offering of *Parashat T'rumah*. Members of the community give what is needed of what they have in response to the community's needs.

A Mussar reading of this *parashah* might provoke us to ask ourselves: What are my community's needs? How might we be able to meet those needs? What might I be able to give? In a Mussar context, we would not start with what an individual *wants* to give, but with what is needed, and move from there to strategize how to meet those needs, including strategizing how each individual might contribute to the needs of the community through their own resources. This stands in contrast to normative models of giving that center around philanthropy, charity, and *tzedakah*—models that assume that people with resources have more wisdom, insight, and knowledge about how to organize, use, and distribute those resources than do poor and working-class people.

POOR Magazine, a Bay Area grassroots, poor-people-led organization, responds to philanthropic models of giving by reminding us that "people who have struggled to survive, feed, and clothe multiple family members and themselves in fact hold deep scholarship about the use and distribution of resources."[5] When we assess the needs of our community, we need to focus first around the needs of our people. Then, from there, we are motivated to give freely and generously of what we have, incited by our own hearts to bring about change in this world. The *POOR Magazine* organizers continue, "We believe that giving and donating is not a privilege, an option, or a nice idea for the donor; rather, it is a duty of people with class and/or race privilege, to give their time, their surplus income, their equity, and/or their support toward change for people struggling with poverty in the U.S. and across the globe." Our hearts are incited not only out of need but out of a sense of communal obligation. A lack of resources should not indebt a person to any individual or community. Resources should never come with strings or obligations. Sharing resources eases some of the burdens that poor and working-class people carry, by constructing safety nets through community care, mutual aid, and building strong and connected relationships.

Such is the wisdom that *Parashat T'rumah* teaches: Resource redistribution is best attended to through a thoughtful and honest accounting of our communities' needs, our own resources, and what we can do communally and individually to share resources broadly. We thereby create and sustain sanctuary and holiness in this world. And, through the vision that this wisdom nurtures, our hearts become incited to build this world anew.

NOTES

1. Bachya ben Asher ibn Halawa, Torah commentary on *Shemot*, 25:2:6.
2. Moses Hayyim Luzzatto, *Mesillat Yesharim: The Path of the Upright*, trans. Mordecai Kaplan, commentary by Ira Stone (Philadelphia: Jewish Publication Society, 2010), 10.
3. Moses Maimonides, *Mishneh Torah*, Hilchot Mat'not Aniyim 10:7–14.
4. Nicole M. Stephens, Hazel Rose Markus, and L. Taylor Phillips, "Social Class Culture Cycles: How Three Gateway Contexts Shape Selves and Fuel Inequality," *Annual Review of Psychology* 65, no. 1 (January 3, 2014): 615.
5. Lisa "Tiny" Gray-Garcia, Dee Garcia, and Poor Magazine Family, *Poverty Scholarship: Poor People-Led Theory, Art, Words, and Tears Across Mama Earth* (Oakland: POOR Press, 2019), 344.

T'TZAVEH—Exodus 27:20–30:10

Ending Wrongful Convictions:
A Divine Imperative

Kristine Henriksen Garroway, PhD

IN *PARASHAT T'TZAVEH*, God commissions Aaron and his descendants to serve as priests on behalf of Israel. Their task—an awesome one, indeed—is to manage the sacred precinct in which the presence of God dwells on earth, first in the wandering Tabernacle and later in the Temples of Jerusalem. Maintaining an abode holy enough for God's presence is a task beset with difficulties, because so many worldly forces threaten to profane it. The terrifying realities of death, sickness, decay, and disorder led to an elaborate system of ritual impurity that aimed to keep away those who had encountered them. Even more menacing was the defiling power of sin, which had the capacity to sully the sanctuary and repulse God's presence. When an Israelite committed a sin, the transgression somehow stuck to the altar and risked driving away the Divine. Without the atoning sacrifices mediated by the priests, especially the foremost sacrifice on Yom Kippur, God would withdraw the Divine Presence from Israel's midst.

Among the Israelite transgressions for which the priests effected atonement, the Talmud lists some usual suspects—for example, murder, idolatry, sexual misconduct—and explains how each of the priestly vestments atoned for one sin in particular: the tunic for bloodshed, the pants for illicit sex, the miter for arrogance, the ephod for idolatry, and so on.[1] The High Priest's "breastpiece of judgment" (*choshen mishpat*, חֹשֶׁן מִשְׁפָּט), we learn, was so called because it atoned for judgments—or, as Rashi would put it more specifically, for incorrect judgments (*kilkul hadin*, קִלְקוּל הַדִּין).[2] In other words, the

Israelites realized that even the best systems of human justice err on occasion, and they feared that miscarriages of justice in Israel would repel a just God. No less than murder and idolatry, then, mistaken verdicts sullied the sanctuary and required atonement. The breast-piece of judgment did the trick.

The Rabbis had no such garment, however, and no sacrifices with which to atone for erroneous verdicts. They therefore created an elaborate and rigorous judicial system so that miscarriages of justice would be as rare as possible. Emulating the demanding standards of the Divine Judge, who, for example, warned the Sodomites many times before condemning them[3] and even sent Abraham to plead their cause,[4] the Rabbis strove to establish a judicial system in which the innocent would be vindicated and only those truly guilty would be convicted. Such caution led them, on occasion, to limit the scope of a biblical law significantly. Consider the *ben soreir umoreh*, the "wayward and defiant son," whom Deuteronomy 21:18–21 says is to be executed. The Rabbis, apparently uncomfortable with the possibility that a son who was not truly rebellious might be killed for acting out on a little teenage angst, added so many qualifications to the definition of a rebellious child that it became necessary to concede that no such child could ever exist.[5]

The Rabbis also set strict stipulations regarding who could qualify as a witness or a judge. A case requires at least two eyewitnesses (Numbers 35:30; Deuteronomy 17:6), and neither can be a wicked person, a robber, or a person formerly impeached or convicted of perjury.[6] Maimonides would expand the list to ten classes of individuals unfit to offer testimony.[7] Witnesses and judges alike must be of the highest moral character—no gamblers, pigeon racers, or people who loaned money at interest qualified.[8] The sages believed judges who rule justly to be partners with God in creation, for "by means of a true judgment they uphold the world."[9]

The legal system envisioned by the Rabbis to replace the *choshen mishpat* was designed with the intention of providing as fair a legal process as possible given the fallibility of human actors. In keeping with the biblical injunction *Tzedek, tzedek tirdof* (צֶדֶק צֶדֶק תִּרְדֹּף),

"Justice, justice shall you pursue" (Deuteronomy 16:20), and believing that unjust verdicts repel the presence of God from their midst, they refused to take a life, or even impose a fine or diminish another's status, without a procedure deemed entirely fair.

We Jews have been taught to expect integrity, rigor, and reliability in a system of justice, and we therefore demand that justice be pursued with no less diligence by governments in the lands in which we reside. Judge Learned Hand wrote in 1923, "Our [criminal] procedure has always been haunted by the ghost of the innocent man convicted."[10] In the American justice system today, innocent defendants are too often convicted. False convictions are the result of a broken system. Misidentification by eyewitnesses, false confessions, fraud or human error in forensic analysis, police misconduct, incompetent defense attorneys, or overly zealous prosecutors—either individually or combined—can lead to false accusations.[11] In the case of eyewitnesses, police can unwittingly create biased lineups wherein the eyewitness is guided to pick a certain person. Police interrogations that use less than savory tactics or in which the defendant is detained for many hours or harassed into a confession can lead to a confession given out of fear. A shortage of resources, money, and equipment plays a part in faulty forensic analysis, while a desire to put someone—anyone— away for a crime can trump a quest for truth on the part of police and prosecutors. That police departments are not immune to insider malfeasance is evidenced by three infamous scandals, two in Texas and one in Los Angeles wherein "police officers were caught systematically framing innocent defendants for possession of illegal drugs or weapons."[12] The system is stuck in a vicious circle wherein many are prosecuted, but justice does not always prevail.

Change needs to happen. In the American justice system today, innocent defendants are too often convicted. Most false convictions that have been overturned are in cases of rape and murder, the two crimes that are overwhelmingly committed by men.[13] DNA evidence can play a definitive role in overturning convictions for these crimes. Consider that, as of 2012, DNA evidence had helped overturn seventeen death-row murder cases, while between 1989 and 2003, 121 men accused of rape had been exonerated.[14] Women, on the other hand, are most often convicted of drug crimes or crimes that involve family members, such as shaken baby syndrome or sex abuse.[15] A study of 148 women who were exonerated found that 63 percent were convicted for crimes that never occurred—events that were later found to be accidents or suicides.[16] Many times a desire to convict someone led to convictions based on sexist stereotypes. For example, upon the death of a child, an ex-husband testified that the ex-wife had once talked about getting an abortion. This was used as proof that she did not love her child.[17]

The case of the Central Park Five is perhaps the most notorious modern example of wrongful conviction in a rape case.[18] Five young men were charged and convicted of a crime because they were persons of color and in the wrong place at the wrong time. In their case, only after a serial rapist confessed to the crime and his DNA was found on the scene were the five exonerated—after serving their full term of thirteen years in jail. Other wrongfully convicted persons turn to a growing number of organizations dedicated, like the Rabbis envisioned, to bringing about justice: the Innocence Project, founded at Yeshiva University's Cardozo School of Law; the Bluhm Legal Clinic Center for Wrongful Convictions, at Northwestern University; and the Equal Justice Initiative.

Chester Hollman is one person exonerated through the work of the Innocence Project and cocounsel Alan J. Tauber. In Hollman's case, multiple factors went wrong. In 1991, a man was robbed and murdered on a Philadelphia street. Blocks away, Hollman and Deirdre Jones were stopped by police because Hollman was wearing the same color hoodie as the person who committed the crime. They were charged based on the testimony of a drug addict with a history of mental illness. Seven other eyewitnesses did not identify him as the murderer. In a case of unethical interrogation tactics and a desire to convict someone of the crime, the police coerced a false confession from Jones, who testified that Hollman committed the crime while she waited in a getaway car. Both the eyewitness and Jones later recanted their statements—in 2001 and 2005, respectively. Not until

2013 did the work of the Innocence Project reveal that the police had at the time actually investigated the real murderer but dropped the case because they had already convicted someone. Hollman was finally released in 2018 and exonerated in 2019.[19]

Such erroneous verdicts sully our national character no less than ancient miscarriages of justice in Israel sullied the sanctuary. We must demand, with our voices and our votes, reforms to the judicial system that will ensure every defendant competent representation, a fair trial, and reasonable sentencing. So, too, we might choose to support organizations that advocate for people who have been wrongfully convicted. No system of justice can eradicate mistakes altogether, but God's revulsion at injustice calls upon us to demand a system in which mistakes are both rare and reversible.

After all, there is no *choshen mishpat* to bail us out.

NOTES

1. Babylonian Talmud, *Z'vachim* 88b.
2. Rashi on Exodus 28:15.
3. *B'reishit Rabbah* 49:6.
4. *Midrash Tanchuma Buber, Vayeira* 9; Genesis 18.
5. Babylonian Talmud, *Sanhedrin* 71a.
6. Babylonian Talmud, *Sanhedrin* 27a; *Shulchan Aruch, Choshen Mishpat* 34:1, 7, 8.
7. Maimonides, *Mishneh Torah, Hilchot Eidut* 9:1.
8. *Mishnah Sanhedrin* 3:3.
9. Babylonian Talmud, *Shabbat* 10a.
10. United States v. Garsson, 291 F. 646 (S.D.N.Y. 1923).
11. Phoebe C. Ellsworth and Samuel R. Gross, "False Convictions," *University of Michigan Law School Scholarship Repository*, 2012, https://repository.law. umich.edu/book_chapters/96. Other issues identified by Ellsworth and Gross include perjury by informants who testify for exchange of favors and police misconduct.
12. Ellsworth and Gross, "False Convictions," 164.
13. M. Ruesink and M. D. Free, "Wrongful Convictions among Women: An Exploration Study of a Neglected Topic," *Women and Criminal Justice* 16, no. 4 (2005): 1–23, https://www.law.northwestern.edu/legalclinic/ wrongfulconvictions/exonerations/.
14. Ellsworth and Gross, "False Convictions," 164.
15. Molly Redden, "Why Is It So Hard for Wrongfully Convicted Women to Get

Justice?," *Mother Jones*, July/August 2015, https://www.motherjones.com/politics/2015/08/wrongfully-convicted-women-exonerations-innocence-project/.

16. Redden, "Why Is It So Hard?"

17. Redden, "Why Is It So Hard?"

18. Aisha Harris, "The Central Park Five: 'We Were Just Baby Boys,'" *New York Times*, May 30, 2019, https://www.nytimes.com/2019/05/30/arts/television/when-they-see-us.html.

19. Innocence Staff, "Philadelphia Exoneree Chester Hollman Featured in Netflix Series 'The Innocence Files,'" Innocence Project, April 1, 2020, https://www.innocenceproject.org/chester-hollman-facing-life-in-prison-exonerated-of-murder-to-be-featured-in-the-innocence-files/.

Ki Tisa—Exodus 30:11–34:35

May My Mercy Overcome My Anger: Ending America's System of Mass Incarcertion

Rabbi Deana Sussman Berezin, MAJE

> I don't like words that hide the truth. I don't like words that con-
> ceal reality. I don't like euphemisms or euphemistic language.
> And American English is loaded with euphemisms, because
> Americans have a lot of trouble dealing with reality. Americans
> have trouble facing the truth, so they invent the kind of a soft
> language to protect themselves from it."
> —*George Carlin*, "Doin' It Again"

COMEDIAN GEORGE CARLIN coined the phrase "soft language" to illustrate how we often use words to sterilize emotion and conceal the truth. The audience roars with laughter at his lighter examples, like when he points out that toilet paper has mysteriously become bathroom tissue, but applauds with appreciative fervor when he reminds us that poor people used to live in the slums, but now the "economically disadvantaged occupy substandard housing in the inner cities."[1] Toilet paper's advancement into polite society may be easily excused, but the same cannot be said in other instances. Over time, we have created phrases that take the passion (and the truth) out of language so that we may use it with emotional impunity.

Consider the "War on Drugs." At first blush, there is nothing particularly untoward about this phrase. A war on illegal substances may seem logical and even reasonable. Except that a War on Drugs is still a war, and the language around war requires an enemy that can only be brought to its knees through violent combat. And the casualties of war are not illicit substances; they are people. The casualties of war are *always* people.

President Ronald Reagan declared the current War on Drugs in 1982, resulting in a shameful system of mass incarceration that imprisons hundreds of thousands of nonviolent drug offenders. According to Michelle Alexander, author of *The New Jim Crow*, "The impact of the drug war has been astounding. In less than thirty years, the U.S. penal population exploded from around 300,000 to more than 2 million, with drug convictions accounting for the majority of the increase. The United States now has the highest rate of incarceration in the world, dwarfing the rates of nearly every developed country, even surpassing those in highly repressive regimes like Russia, China, and Iran."[2]

Failure to highlight the racial dimension of the War on Drugs and mass incarceration would be a glaring omission. According to Alexander:

> No other country in the world imprisons so many of its racial or ethnic minorities. The United States imprisons a larger percentage of its black population than South Africa did at the height of apartheid. In Washington, D.C., our nation's capital, it is estimated that three out of four young black men (and nearly all those in the poorest neighborhoods) can expect to serve time in prison. Similar rates of incarceration can be found in black communities across America.[3]

The casualties of this war are staggering. Hundreds of thousands of people find themselves behind bars for nonviolent crimes, their lives put on hold, absent from the lives of their families as they sit, waiting to come home. Many are unable to make amends or meaningfully contribute to society due to mandatory minimums, "three strikes" laws, and restrictions on release. The "tough on crime" policies related to the War on Drugs that have been fueling this system of mass incarceration are fundamentally unjust: They don't weigh personal stories and circumstances alongside missteps and poor choices. They don't create space for restorative justice, which both holds people accountable while allowing for reconciliation, focusing on retributive justice instead. They don't allow our judges to exercise their best judgment in sentencing. And they certainly don't account for the possibility of *t'shuvah* (repentance) and making right the wrongs that have been done.

In *Parashat Ki Tisa*, the Israelites commit the sin of the Golden Calf. In Moses's absence, they demand that Aaron create a god for them to worship (Exodus 32:1). To say that God is angry would be an understatement: "I see that this is a stiff-necked people. Now, let Me be, that My anger may blaze forth against them and that I may destroy them, and make of you a great nation" (32:9–10). Israel's transgression is blatant: they have forgotten *Adonai* and turned back to idolatry. So acute is God's displeasure that God is prepared to destroy the Israelites. Thankfully, Moses intercedes: "Turn from Your blazing anger, and renounce the plan to punish Your people. . . . And the Eternal renounced the punishment planned for God's people" (32:12–14).

What can the story of the Golden Calf teach us about the inhumane system of mass incarceration? First and foremost, we are reminded that people make mistakes. Even armed with the best intentions, individuals make poor choices and sometimes find their lives utterly derailed. Certainly, the Israelites did not set out to sin against God— they became frightened and felt alone in the world, making poor choices out of circumstance. The same can be said for the multitudes of offenders imprisoned for decades for a single nonviolent crime.

Second, anger and the call for swift, harsh punishment is natural. God's immediate response to the Golden Calf is to obliterate the Israelites. If God becomes this angry, then we ought not be surprised that human beings often act similarly. Punitive acts that feed our anger may seem like reasonable responses. But unlike God, who forgives the Israelites for their transgressions, nonviolent offenders are granted no such clemency. T'ruah: The Rabbinic Call for Human Rights, notes that "in addition to mandatory minimum sentences, federal truth-in-sentencing laws require a convicted person to serve at least 85% of his or her sentence, leaving no room for time off for good behavior."[4]

Third, every transgressor deserves an advocate. Upon hearing the harsh decree, Moses intercedes on behalf of the Israelites. In fact, commentaries and midrashim alike posit that God *knows* that this form of retributive justice is wrong and signals to Moses that he *must* advocate for the Israelites:

> "Now leave me to make an end of them." Had Moses caught the Holy One, Blessed be God, in his grip that God had to say, "Leave Me be"? But to what may this be compared? To a king who became angry with his son and took him to an anteroom and set about to try and kill him. There he shouted from the room, "Leave me alone to kill him!" The boy's tutor, who was standing outside, reasoned thus: "Both the king and his son are closeted together inside. Why then does he shout, 'Leave me alone'? The reason must be that the king really wants me to go in and make peace between him and his son. That is why he cries out, 'Leave me alone!'" Similarly, the Holy One, Blessed be God, said to Moses, "Now leave Me alone." Said Moses, "The Holy One, Blessed be God, wants me to make peace between God and Israel. That is why God says, 'Now—leave me alone.'" So he promptly began to intercede on their behalf.[5]

In our system of justice, lawyers act as advocates for their clients. But the unforgiving laws of the War on Drugs stymie their efforts when judges are unable to exercise discretion in sentencing. Take US district judge Mark Bennett: "These mandatory minimums are so incredibly harsh, and they're triggered by such low levels of drugs that they snare these non-violent, low-level addicts who are involved in drug distribution mostly to obtain drugs to feed their habit. They have a medical problem. It's called addiction, and they're going to be faced with five and 10 and 20-year and sometimes life mandatory minimum sentences. I think that's a travesty."[6] It is no wonder that the casualties of war continue to accumulate.

Finally, we learn that compassion and *t'shuvah* have the power to make us whole again. Slowly, the relationship between God and the

Israelites is repaired and the covenant is restored—reconciliation is possible. When Moses sees God's presence pass before him, God proclaims "Adonai! Adonai! A God compassionate and gracious, slow to anger, abounding in kindness and faithfulness, extending kindness to the thousandth generation, forgiving iniquity, transgression, and sin" (Exodus 34:6–7), a formula that the Talmud instructs us to recite whenever we err and require God's forgiveness.[7]

Our current system of justice simply does not make room for mercy or *t'shuvah*. It doesn't encourage our government to become a partner in facilitating reconciliation, and it doesn't make space for healing. *T'shuvah* is a chance to make oneself whole again and return to the right path. How can we emulate God—being merciful and kind, forgiving iniquity—if we do not create pathways for restorative justice?

In case we are still unclear about what God desires most, the Talmud asks, "What does God pray for?" The answer, it turns out, is simple: "May it be My will that My mercy will overcome My anger, and may My mercy prevail over My other attributes, and may I conduct Myself toward My children with the attribute of mercy, and may I put them before the letter of the law."[8]

When faced with retribution or mercy, God always chooses mercy. How can we do any less? The two million people trapped in our system of mass incarceration are worthy of mercy. They deserve for their humanity to be weighed in equal measure to their actions. They deserve advocates who see them as people and not as casualties of war. And most importantly, they deserve the opportunity to make *t'shuvah*, to make themselves and their communities whole again.

NOTES
1. George Carlin, *Doin' It Again*, HBO, June 2, 1990.
2. Michelle Alexander, *The New Jim Crow: Mass Incarceration in the Age of Colorblindness* (New York: New Press, 2011), 6.
3. Alexander, *The New Jim Crow*, 6–7.
4. Lev Meirowitz Nelson, ed., *A Handbook for Jewish Communities Fighting Mass Incarceration* (New York: T'ruah: The Rabbinic Call for Human Rights, n.d.), accessed September 8, 2020, https://www.truah.org/wp-content/

uploads/2016/10/MI-Handbook-complete-web.pdf, 46.

5. *Sh'mot Rabbah* 42:10.
6. Rachel Martin, "A Federal Judge Says Mandatory Minimum Sentences Often Don't Fit the Crime," *Morning Edition*, NPR, June 1, 2017, https://www.npr.org/2017/06/01/531004316/a-federal-judge-says-mandatory-minimum-sentences-often-dont-fit-the-crime.
7. Babylonian Talmud, *Rosh HaShanah* 17b.
8. Babylonian Talmud, *B'rachot* 7a.

Tzedakah: Putting Your Money Where Your Values Are

Rabbi Marina Yergin

Take from among you gifts to the Eternal; everyone whose heart is so moved shall bring them—gifts for the Eternal: gold, silver, and copper. . . . And everyone who excelled in ability and everyone whose spirit was moved came, bringing to the Eternal an offering for the work of the Tent of Meeting and for all its service and for the sacral vestments.

—*Exodus 35:5, 35:21*

IN *PARASHAT VAYAK'HEIL*, the Israelites, as an entire community, are asked to give gifts from their hearts to contribute to building the Tent of Meeting. Interestingly, the Hebrew delineates two different groups of people: *kol n'div libo* (כֹּל נְדִיב לִבּוֹ), "everyone whose heart is so moved" (Exodus 35:5); and *kol ish asher n'sao libo* (כָּל־אִישׁ אֲשֶׁר־נְשָׂאוֹ לִבּוֹ), "everyone who excelled in ability" (35:21). Rabbi Chayim ben Moshe ibn Attar (1696–1743), a Moroccan kabbalist and Talmudist who wrote the commentary *Or HaChayim*,[1] discusses the differences between the two categories.

Starting with Exodus 35:5, *Or HaChayim* explains:

When the Torah writes *y'vi-eha* (יְבִיאֶהָ), "[the generously minded donor] is to bring it," this means that the donor is to elevate the gift to such a spiritual level that it may merge with the *t'rumat HaShem* (תְּרוּמַת הַשֵּׁם), "God's contribution." When the Torah speaks of the *kol n'div libo* (כֹּל נְדִיב לִבּוֹ), "those whose hearts are so moved," it defines the kind of person whose gift will be of the caliber that can merge with God's intangible gift. If the human donor does not possess the spirit the Torah describes as *n'div lev* (לֵב נָדִיב), "their heart being moved," then the gift of such a person has no chance of merging with the divine contribution described here as the invisible contribution *t'rumat HaShem* (תְּרוּמַת הַשֵּׁם), "God's contribution."[2]

As the Torah's lessons inform our giving today, *Or HaChayim* reminds us not merely to contribute but to focus the intention behind our *tzedakah*. Then, and only then, will our gift truly have meaning. In our own context, we may see people giving money to organizations because they feel pressured to do so. This is not how *Or HaChayim* urges us to think about *tzedakah*. Instead, we should be giving in a way that is personally meaningful and significant. "Significant" refers not necessarily to a substantial monetary amount, but to the intention. The gift should be for something that "moves our hearts," that we truly care about and want to see succeed and thrive.

Or HaChayim continues the commentary by explaining that each of the thirteen materials listed in Exodus 35:5–9 is of equal importance and is "equally indispensable."[3] The point is not the item given, but the intent behind it. As Ibn Attar wrote, "The evaluation is based on the principle . . . that the quantity of a contribution does not determine how God evaluates it, but the intent does. As long as the intent is to please Heaven, that is all that matters."[4] Are we thinking about how our *tzedakah* pleases God—"Heaven," in the sage's words? Should we put more emphasis on the intent of the contribution?

We are reminded by our sages to think not only about ourselves but about others when donating. In Deuteronomy 15:7–8, Moses reminds the Israelites that if there is someone in need around you, "do not . . . shut your hand against your needy kinsman. Rather, you must open your hand." *Or HaChayim* explains:

> Moses referred to something we read in Proverbs 11:24 that "one person gives generously and winds up with more"; being charitable does not diminish one's wealth but increases it. When the Israelite "opens their hand," God "opens the gates of heavenly

bounty for them." This is why Moses said "in order that God will open [God's] hidden treasures, etc." He continues with "you shall lend a person whatever they lack, etc." The Torah means that when you open your hand for the poor all you are doing is giving them a loan, seeing that God will repay you with interest. This is certainly sufficient reason for Moses telling you to open your hand again and again.[5]

Whether we believe that God will repay us with interest or not, the focus is truly on the other person and how we should help them. *Or HaChayim* makes it seem like we are only talking about convincing the Israelites to give to those in need, but other commentators believe that we should be thinking about others and their hardship, not how it will impact our own lives.

Sifrei D'varim, a midrashic commentary written in Babylon around 200 CE, is one of the commentaries that shares a different perspective and is quoted by many commentators. The text reminds us that we must keep on opening our hand for those in need, no matter how many times. The midrash continues by explaining that the text offers a suggestion of a loan, because a handout may diminish a recipient's sense of self-worth. A loan offers an opportunity for the needy person to receive the help they need without sacrificing their dignity and self-respect. *Sifrei D'varim* then says that we are not required to make the person rich, but give them what they need, even if it is not a monetary need.[6]

I choose to focus on *Sifrei D'varim*'s idea that our gift should be chosen based upon how it can help other people and impact their lives. When we pair that with our own values, we can determine which organizations and causes are important and worthy of our donation. Our *tzedakah* impacts others—the ones we are moved to help, support, or organize around—when we contribute to the organizations that affect those people or causes directly.

In the simplest terms, people refer to *tzedakah* as "charity." However, much more than "charity" is implied by that Hebrew word. It is not just about giving money. The root of the word is *tzedek*, "justice" or "righteousness," so *tzedakah* implies necessary action to bring justice to the world. Monetary gifts are important, and at the same time, we must take a further step and do the work of making our world a better place every day. A text from Talmud highlights the importance of *tzedakah*: "What is stronger than death? Acts of *tzedakah*, as it is written: '*Tzedakah* delivers from death' (Proverbs 10:2)."[7] Whom does *tzedakah* deliver from death—the giver or the recipient? The text does not tell us, but I would argue that it is about the recipient. If we donate money or stand up for someone else's rights, it does not necessarily impact our lives profoundly—the experience might, but the act itself may not. Conversely, the person who receives the donation or sees you standing by them is deeply affected. *Tzedakah* is how we connect to others. It is the act that makes us think about others first and connects us with them. And it is something that we need to remind ourselves to do continuously, not just occasionally, so that we can take ownership of our actions. We need to make *tzedakah* a habit, a practice, for all times, just as the *Sifrei D'varim* on Deuteronomy 15:7–8 reminds us.

Instead of focusing on the dollar amount, we should look inside ourselves and give *tzedakah* to those organizations and causes that inspire us to be *n'sao libo* (נְשָׂאוֹ לִבּוֹ), carried away by our heart. This means not giving only to the organizations that our friends support, but also to do the research on our own. Our findings can then propel us to move from *nadvah rucho* (נָדְבָה רוּחוֹ), our spirit moving us, to *n'sao libo* (נְשָׂאוֹ לִבּוֹ), being truly carried away by what is in our heart.

When making a decision, these questions may guide us as we identify the organizations and causes that merit our support:

1. What value do I hold most dear that I would like to support?
2. What organization's work inspires me?
3. How much of my donation goes to the causes about which I am passionate, and how much is absorbed by administrative costs?
4. How much can I feasibly contribute to make a difference for the organization that inspires me?
5. How can I support this organization beyond a financial contribution?

The last question is important to consider. None of the Israelites' contributions to the Tent of Meeting were monetary; they were in the form of materials and artistry. We tend to think of *tzedakah* only as money, but we can and should stretch our imagination to think about other ways to support causes that are important to us.

When we do focus on *tzedakah* as a monetary donation, as in our religious schools and *b'nei mitzvah* programs, we should also encourage our students to ask themselves the above questions. *Parashat Vayak'heil* gives us the space, encouragement, and textual basis that giving from your heart is what is most important—be the gift monetary, in-kind goods or services, or volunteer effort. This process can be meaningful for all ages. Let *Vayak'heil*, the entire Torah, and the wise words of our sages guide us.

NOTES

1. Chayim ben Moshe ibn Attar, *Or HaChayim: Commentary on the Torah*, trans. Eliyahu Munk (Jerusalem and New York: Lambda, 1999), referenced on Sefaria (sefaria.org).

2. Adapted from Ibn Attar, *Or HaChayim*, https://www.sefaria.org/Exodus.35.5?lang=bi&aliyot=0&p2=Or_HaChaim_on_Exodus.35.5.1&lang2=bi.

3. Ibn Attar, *Or HaChayim*, https://www.sefaria.org/Exodus.35.5?lang=bi&aliyot=0&p2=Or_HaChaim_on_Exodus.35.5.3&lang2=bi&w2=all&lang3=en.

4. Ibn Attar, *Or HaChayim*, https://www.sefaria.org/Exodus.35.5?lang=bi&aliyot=0&p2=Or_HaChaim_on_Exodus.35.5.3&lang2=bi&w2=all&lang3=en.

5. Ibn Attar, *Or HaChayim*, https://www.sefaria.org/Deuteronomy.15.8?lang=bi&aliyot=0&p2=Or_HaChaim_on_Deuteronomy.15.8.1&lang2=bi&w2=all&lang3=en.

6. *Sifrei D'varim* 116:13–17, https://www.sefaria.org/Sifrei_Devarim.116.13-17?lang=bi.

7. Babylonian Talmud, *Bava Batra* 10a.

P'KUDEI—EXODUS 38:21–40:38

Equity in Education:
Let Every Student Shine

RABBI CRAIG LEWIS

IN *PARASHAT P'KUDEI*, we learn about the breastplate worn by the High Priest:

> The breastpiece was made in the style of the ephod: of gold, blue, purple, and crimson yarns, and fine twisted linen. . . . They set in it four rows of stones. The first row was a row of carnelian, chrysolite, and emerald; the second row: a turquoise, a sapphire, and an amethyst; the third row: a jacinth, an agate, and a crystal; and the fourth row: a beryl, a lapis lazuli, and a jasper. (Exodus 39:8–13)

Twelve gemstones, nicely spaced into four rows, represent the twelve tribes. It seems an equitable representation for this priestly garment. Rabbi Levi Yitzchak of Berditchev, an eighteenth-century teacher of *chasidut*, describes the breastplate as a great equalizer.

> Aaron was chosen as priest from among the Children of Israel. We must assume . . . that he was especially beloved, and this implies normally that by comparison the community at large was relatively despised; in order to counter such an assumption, the Torah commanded that the names of all the tribes be inscribed on the breastplate to show clearly that God loved all of them.[1]

The evenness, the balance, and the inclusiveness of the gemstones, at first glance, make a statement: all are equal before God. However, the Torah does not always treat the Children of Israel or their tribal descendants as equals. Land is not apportioned in equal amounts, and favor is shown in the tribes' placement around the Tent of Meeting, as well as in their marching order through the wilderness. We further see inequality in the way tribal identities are attached to the various gemstones on the breastplate of the High Priest. However, upon further examination, we find in the gemstones a subtle yet persuasive argument for equity over simple equality. Before we address gemstones, let us first identify the cost of neglecting equity.

In his critique of the American education system, *Savage Inequalities*, Jonathan Kozol highlights the sharp contrast between poorly funded and wealthy public schools. It is surprising that, in many cases, two schools receive the same funding per student—creating the perception of equality—while the actual costs of providing education are substantially higher in poorer areas. In one South Bronx high school, trash bags have replaced ceiling tiles, wood panels have replaced broken windows, dead light bulbs go unreplaced, a barrel collects rainwater in the school counselor's office, and students remark about fungus growing in the corner. Alexander, a sixteen-year-old recent immigrant from Jamaica, observes that parents and students in wealthier schools become locked "into the idea of always having something more. After that, these [extra] things are seen like an inheritance. . . . They get used to what they have. They think it's theirs by rights because they had it from the start. So it leaves those children with a legacy of greed." Reflecting on the perceptivity of her students, a counselor offers this analysis: "It's quite remarkable how much these children see [despite evaluation of their academic performance]. There is a tremendous gulf between skills and capabilities. This gulf, this dissonance is frightening . . . it says so much about the *squandering of human worth*."[2]

These last four words should remain with us, haunt us, and compel us toward actions that would correct historical and systemic injustices in our education system. Whether or not we are directly involved in education, we can take responsibility. With so many children denied a quality education, we collectively participate in squandering human worth—a value prohibited by our tradition.

We find this lesson in the details of *Parashat P'kudei*, specifically in the tribal gemstones on the High Priest's breastplate. The stones are not equal in value. The amount of lapis lazuli needed to match the amount of emerald in value would destroy the balance. The stones would all be different sizes, rendering even rows impossible. Still, by virtue of being on a priestly adornment, each gem is considered beautiful, worthy to shine alongside the other gems. As sacred objects, they must be kept sparkling; neglecting any one of them would be an unpardonable sin. For proper presentation, each gem demands its own unique treatment before being displayed, and ongoing maintenance for each gem is likewise unique. Cleaning agents used to polish amethyst could cause turquoise to fade. Heat treatments used on rubies could prove harmful to porous gems like lapis lazuli. Brushes used to clean emeralds are not recommended for use on carnelian.[3] If all gems were handled uniformly, with the exact same resources in equal quantities, some would shine brightly while others would be dimmed into oblivion. The gems need to be treated with equity rather than equality.

The gap between poor and affluent schools[4] is like the relative vibrancy of the gemstones when one polishing method is too broadly applied. Gloria Ladson-Billings, a past president of the American Educational Research Association, calls the discrepancy an "education debt." It is "the damage done to particular communities by 'the historical, economic, sociopolitical, and moral decisions and policies that characterize our society.'"[5] Elimination of that debt would require a collective effort to rethink the way we fund education.

A midrash on the life of Joseph provides a clue about how to achieve this:

> [Fulfilling his duties managing Egypt's grain reserves during the drought,] Joseph had been equipped with a degree of prophecy so much so that he knew how much money every person still possessed. He used this knowledge to charge higher prices to the rich and lower prices to the poor, in order to preserve a certain degree of equality among the population when it came to obtaining the necessities of life.[6]

Our ancestor Joseph knew to provide the best for each person regardless of their means. Still, knowing their specific needs guided every decision. This same wisdom can be applied to our schools.

If students were treated as precious gemstones, according to their unique needs, they would have equity of opportunity. The more we squander human worth, the more we increase our educational debt, perpetuating cycles of poverty that education has the best chance of breaking.

Every student deserves to shine brightly. Rather than treating students as the same raw material, we can consider them holistically—their backgrounds, their parents' education levels, their financial realities, and the specific pressures they experience. Ensuring educational equity begins, as does our passage of Torah, by envisioning the end goal: a shining array of precious individuals, their needs provided for in a way that allows each to be brilliant.

Notes

1. *K'dushat Levi* on Exodus 28:29.
2. Jonathan Kozol, *Savage Inequalities* (New York: Crown, 1991), 104–5, (emphasis added).
3. While I am not a gemologist or even a frequent purchaser of fine gems, I verified my intuition that each gem needs different treatment. These websites offered guidance in making my case: Gerald Wykoff, "Gemstone Care Guide," International Gem Society, accessed January 1, 2021, https://www.gemsociety.org/article/care-maintenance-gemstones/; and Robert Weldon, "An Introduction to Gem Treatments," GIA, accessed January 1, 2021, https://www.gia.edu/gem-treatment.
4. My focus is exclusively on public schools. While private schools are a great option for some, they remain beyond the reach of most American families, even in a system that would provide vouchers. Public schools have the opportunity and obligation to reach the widest range of American children.
5. Valerie Strauss, "How Covid-19 Has Laid Bare the Vast Inequalities in U.S. Public Education," *Washington Post*, April 14, 2020, https://www.washingtonpost.com/education/2020/04/14/how-covid-19-has-laid-bare-vast-inequities-us-public-education/.
6. Jacob ben Asher, *Tur HaAroch* on Genesis 47:15.

LEVITICUS

Harassment-Free Jewish Spaces: Our Leaders Must Answer to a Higher Standard

Rabbi Mary L. Zamore

Yes, it is awful that he said those things. They are totally inappropriate, but he is a beloved member of our clergy team, a founder of our congregation. We must recognize that he only yells at our professional staff and lay leaders when he is stressed.

She just has trouble with boundaries, but she's harmless. If we hold her accountable, she may leave the temple, which would be devastating. After all, she donates hours and hours to our synagogue. She is irreplaceable. The staff just needs to avoid her. We will remind her not to go to the staff members' homes without permission.

We all know his behavior is not right, so we will make sure he does not meet with women alone. He's going to retire soon. There is no reason to ruin his otherwise stellar reputation. Retirement is just a few years away. Maybe we can encourage him to leave sooner.

He has suffered enough by his sexual harassment coming to light. However, his contributions to the Jewish community are far too numerous not to quote him. Whom else could we cite? And why mention this dark spot on an otherwise sterling career?

ABOVE IS A COMPILATION of remarks reflecting many real cases in the Jewish community, conflated here to illustrate a theme. The common thread is a lack of accountability for the productive perpetrator. This is the professional or lay leader in a congregation or institution who is successful in their work, yet has substantiated accusations of sexual assault, harassment, or abusive/bullying behavior against them. They are trusted and beloved, generous with their time and/ or money; they excel in their field. And because of their success, their community will never hold them accountable for their bad behavior—even though it endangers the community's atmosphere of safety and respect—leaving a wake of damage in their path. Often working to keep the behavior and its negative impact unknown to the wider world, community leaders act as if the bad behavior is an unavoidable tax for the benefits the community reaps from the productive perpetrator's presence and work. However, *Parashat Vayikra* teaches us the exact opposite, commanding us to hold our leaders accountable to a higher standard.

Vayikra outlines the rituals for different types of sacrifices: *olah* (עוֹלָה), burnt offerings; *minchah* (מִנְחָה), meal offerings; *sh'lamin* (שְׁלָמִים), well-being offerings; *chatat* (חַטָּאת), purgation offerings; and *asham* (אָשָׁם), reparation offerings. While on the surface this portion reads like a simple instruction book for the sacrifices, it is infused with foundational values. Holding our leaders accountable for their actions is intrinsic to the biblical design of the ancient sacrificial cult and the accompanying priesthood, as we can observe in the *parashah*'s commandments.

The Israelite sacrificial cult is designed to function in an atmosphere of radical transparency. After the engaging narratives of Genesis and Exodus, it is easy to overlook the revolutionary nature of Leviticus. The laws regulating the sacrifices were given to the entire people of Israel, not just to the elite class of priests. There were no esoteric, secret rituals known only to the *kohanim*, the priestly class. Furthermore, sacrifices were performed publicly. As *The Torah: A Women's Torah Commentary* explains, "Although Leviticus preserves the priests' privileged monopoly regarding the service at the altar and its sacrifices, these instructions demystify the priests' role by making knowledge about their activities known to every Israelite."[1] Coupled with the prohibition against land ownership by priests (Numbers 18:20), universal access to the law equalized power in the Israelite community. *Kohanim* were supposed to facilitate the community's efforts to draw near to God rather than amass power for themselves. The public viewing of offerings also created accountability. The Hebrew term *eidah*, "community," is related to *eid*, "witness."[2] If a priest inadvertently made a mistake or knowingly deviated from the prescribed rites, the Israelites would know because they could witness the offerings in real time. The elevated status of the *kohanim* in the community required that they be held to a high standard. *Parashat Vayikra* demands a rigorous method of atonement for the priests' misdeeds, whether they were known to the public (Leviticus 4:3) or not (Leviticus 4:13). It should be noted that the Torah also holds chieftains to a standard higher than that of ordinary Israelites (Leviticus 4:22), but not as high as the priests. This portion clearly teaches that the greater one's status is in the community, the more accountable one must be for one's actions.

Laws concerning the *chatat*, purgation offering, exemplify the exacting standard required of the priests: "If it is the anointed priest who has incurred guilt, so that blame falls upon the people, he shall offer for the sin of which he is guilty a bull of the herd without blemish as a purgation offering to the Eternal" (Leviticus 4:3). Addressing no less than Aaron and his successors, this text continues with the intricate details required to perform this sacrifice.[3] In fact, the priest must offer an unblemished bull, the most expensive offering; his sacrifice is costlier than that of a regular Israelite. This recognizes that the priest's actions had an impact far beyond his own reputation; his guilt became his community's guilt.

Reflecting on this passage, Rabbi Shai Held points to the importance of leaders recognizing their failings:

> Like it or not, we learn from our leaders—so do our children. A generation whose leaders are incapable of apologizing is a generation devoid of a potentially powerful model; a generation whose leaders respond to charges of misconduct by denying, obfuscating, or shifting incessantly to the passive voice ("mistakes were made") is a generation whose children learn to offer an honest, straightforward apology for bad behavior only when their backs are against the wall—only, that is, when all other

(self-exonerating) tactics have failed. But a generation whose
leaders step forward and say, "Yes, I really blew it, and I'm sorry"
just might learn the importance of integrity and accountability.[4]

Rabbi Held is correct. When our leaders are willing to face their
wrongs and publicly admit the negative impact of their behavior, they
set an invaluable example for community members of all ages. However, when the leaders themselves are not forthcoming, the community must serve as a vocal *eid* (witness) and hold them accountable,
even when the leader has contributed much to the community's success. This is the most important model for the members of the Jewish
community, young and old. We are commanded, "You shall be holy,
for I, the Eternal your God, am holy" (Leviticus 19:2). Striving to be
holy requires the integrity to hold every member of the community
responsible for their actions.

Despite the checks and balances built into the priesthood by Torah
law, power differentials enabled the priests to amass great influence,
sometimes leading to corruption. The prophet Ezekiel exhorted on
behalf of God, "Her priests have violated My law and have profaned
what is sacred to Me; they have made no distinction between the holy
and the profane, and they have not taught the difference between the
unclean and the clean; and they hide their eyes from My sabbaths,
and I am profaned in their midst" (Ezekiel 22:26). This indictment
should serve as a warning to the modern Jewish community. Our
professional and lay leaders must never be considered above the law,
Jewish or secular. It is not enough for our congregations and institutions to have policies, standards, and procedures to guard against
harassing, abusive, and disrespectful behaviors. The community
must be willing to uphold these institutional policies and standards,
as well as to report wrongdoing to Jewish professional organizations,
which often have ethical oversight—and, when appropriate, to law
enforcement or other appropriate local, state, or federal agencies.
Unchecked misdeeds undermine the entire Jewish community,
destroying our ability to strive to be a holy people. The productive
perpetrator is perceived as too valuable, too irreplaceable to be held

accountable. However, it is the pain of their victims, the impact on bystanders, and the integrity of the Jewish community that are too valuable to be compromised. *Parashat Vayikra* demands that we hold our leaders to a higher standard, knowing that their actions affect us all.

NOTES

1. Tamara Cohn Eskenazi, *The Torah: A Women's Commentary*, ed. Tamara Cohn Eskenazi and Andrea Weiss (New York: Reform Judaism Publishing, an imprint of CCAR Press, and Women of Reform Judaism, 2007), 571.
2. Eskenazi, *The Torah: A Women's Commentary*, 580.
3. W. Gunther Plaut, ed., *The Torah: A Modern Commentary*, rev. ed. (New York: CCAR Press, 2005), 666.
4. Shai Held, *The Heart of Torah: Essays on the Weekly Torah Portion* (Philadelphia: Jewish Publication Society, 2017), vol. 2, p. 11.

Sacred Work Requires Sacred Infrastructures: Including People with Disabilities

Rabbi Ruti Regan

THE TORAH TEACHES US that we are all created in God's image—and yet, our communities do not always treat everyone equally. All too often, Jews with disabilities are excluded from both Jewish and secular spaces or treated unequally within them. Rabbi Hillel taught us, "That which is hateful to you, do not do to others. That is the whole Torah. Now go and learn it."[1] In other words, doing right by others is easier said than done. If we approach all Torah as an opportunity to go and learn how to do the right thing, we can better live up to our values. This is as true of the descriptions of the ancient sanctuary as it is of the more popular stories in the Torah.

Alongside the description of Moses consecrating the first priests, *Parashat Tzav* describes procedures for bringing personal offerings to the sanctuary. Those with a reason to bring an offering to the sanctuary acted on their own initiative, but they also relied on the sanctuary infrastructure and the ongoing work of the priests to make their offerings possible. Individuals, professionals, and communal institutions all played a critical role. So, too, the sacred practice of building disability equality into our communities depends on individual initiative, communal infrastructure, and ongoing work. The sanctuary does not maintain itself. Whatever our role in our communities, we all have a role to play in making them equitable.

"A handful of the choice flour and oil of the meal offering shall be taken from it, with all the frankincense that is on the meal offering, and this token portion shall be turned into smoke on the altar as a pleasing odor to the Eternal" (Leviticus 6:8). Doing the right and necessary thing can be expensive. Those who brought grain offerings were required to use the highest quality flour, investing a valuable resource into sustaining the sanctuary. In the words of Ibn Ezra, "It is not fitting to offer a meal offering to the Most High that is not of the highest quality."[2] Similarly, failing to "bring our best" to ensure equal access is an affront to the One we seek to serve. In the times of the ancient sacrifices and today, desire to proclaim our values is not enough. We have to put our money where our mouth is. On both an individual and communal level, budgetary priorities embody our values. Equality is only possible when communities are willing to devote resources to accessibility. In order to build equality into our most sacred spaces, we have to be willing to pay for it.

In addition to money, there is a spiritual price we need to pay as we strive toward equality. If disability equality is a mitzvah, then treating people with disabilities unequally within our communities is a sin for which we must do t'shuvah (repentance). We need to be prepared to face the fact that our communities have long made choices that have hurt Jewish people with disabilities very badly. When we exclude people, we don't have to see the consequences. When access to Jewish spaces is so rare that people feel the need to smile and express gratitude for anything at all, we can tell ourselves that they are always happy. When people with disabilities are so marginalized within our communities that they are afraid to speak up, we can ignore their pain. As we move toward greater equality, we are going to have to feel the weight of this pain and trauma. We have to accept the vulnerability that comes along with t'shuvah. We have done wrong, and we need to do better.

Grappling with sin and guilt has always been part of the sacred work that sustains our communities. In the ancient world, this sometimes involved bringing sin offerings to the sanctuary. In Parashat Tzav, the sanctity of sin and guilt offerings is taken for granted and used to illustrate the holiness of the grain offering: "It [the meal

offering] shall not be baked with leaven; I have given it as their portion from My offerings by fire; it is most holy, like the sin offering and
the guilt offering" (Leviticus 6:10). Even though the sins themselves
were shameful, the sin offerings were both as sacred and as routine as
other types of offerings. The priests offered them on a regular basis
and even ate of them. Not only is the work of *t'shuvah* possible; it sustains us.

Sin is shameful. *T'shuvah* is sacred. When we take that to heart, the
emotional price of *t'shuvah* becomes more bearable. Everyone makes
mistakes, and facing up to them is better than letting them stand.
T'shuvah requires that we bear certain kinds of pain, but it also gives
us the means to relieve it. As with any other type of *t'shuvah*, the first
step is facing reality as honestly as possible and then figuring out what
we need to do to fix the harm that we have done. We also need to keep
in mind that seemingly small details can make the difference between
a sacred offering and an offensive offering: "If any of the flesh of the
sacrifice of well-being is eaten on the third day, it shall not be acceptable; it shall not count for one who offered it. It is an offensive thing,
and the person who eats of it shall bear the guilt" (Leviticus 7:18). In
the times of sacrificial worship, those with something to celebrate
could bring a well-being offering of meat, somewhat akin to a sacred
barbecue party. Within the time limit, eating the food was accepted
as a sacred practice; eating the food after the time had elapsed was
offensive. Even if the food was still perfectly edible, and even if those
eating it still had the same intentions, continuing to eat made them
guilty of a serious sin.

In modern times, it may not be entirely clear why this particular
detail mattered, but we know that the failure to follow sanctuary rules
to the letter could result in severe consequences. When Nadab and
Abihu offer strange fire instead of the commanded incense, they pay
for that mistake with their lives (Leviticus 10:1–2). The dedication of
the sanctuary should have been a time of communal celebration, but
instead the community is forced to bear the trauma of the very public
deaths of two sacred leaders. When we are in a position of power, we
must attend to the consequential details, even when they seem small.

When we have the power to provide or deny access, it is of the utmost importance that we listen to people with disabilities about the details that matter to them. Proper attention to detail can be a matter of life and death. To give a direct example, the difference between a ramp that is compliant with the Americans with Disabilities Act and a somewhat steeper ramp might not be obvious to a walking person who designs a building. For a wheelchair user, it could mean the difference between having safe access to a building and risking serious injury every time they enter.

Beyond this direct kind of danger, it is very difficult to survive isolation from community. Just as LGBTQ-affirming community saves lives, so too does disability-affirming community save lives. In addition to his golden rule, Hillel also taught, "Do not separate yourself from the community."[3] The same is true in reverse: we need to build communities that people are not separated from.

Inclusive education is a critical part of keeping people connected to community, and this is another place where the details can make the difference between a sacred offering and an offensive offering. For example, if someone who needs an electronic format is repeatedly offered large print instead, they may be completely unable to read class materials. Similarly, videos automatically captioned with voice recognition software are not accessible to people who rely on captions. It is necessary to correct the captions and make sure that every word is accurate so that people can understand it. Even with the best of intentions, offerings that fail to facilitate access to education are offensive, and we are responsible for the consequences. People who are repeatedly excluded from Jewish educational settings and told to find "somewhere more equipped to meet their needs" rarely find that place. If we want it to exist, we need to create it, everywhere.

Details can also make the difference between a mutually respectful community and a humiliating community. For instance, using the r-word to refer to people with intellectual disabilities will lead a lot of people to the conclusion that they can't trust their communities to see them as fully human. Once that trust is broken, it is very hard to regain.

More subtly, the way that identity is or is not respected sends a message about how people are or are not valued. For instance, disability professionals and disability communities often use different language. Just as it is humiliating to women when men are treated as the gatekeepers of language, so too it is humiliating when non-disabled disability professionals are treated as the gatekeepers of language. When someone identifies as "disabled," a "person with a disability," "autistic," "d/Deaf," or any other language, they are describing themselves in relation to communities they are part of. Respecting these identities is a core part of building equality into our communities.

The details matter—including the nuances of how we seek out information. For instance, even with the intent to use the information to facilitate accessibility, asking a series of invasive personal questions sends the message that the right to be part of the community is contingent on giving up privacy. We should instead ask about access more directly, seek out expertise without making people come to us first, and, in all cases, listen.

Even when the difference a detail makes is no more obvious from the perspective of a decision-maker than the difference between eating an offering on the second day or the third, getting the detail wrong can make a well-intentioned offering offensive. Even when we have every intention to create equal access, sometimes we fail, and we bear responsibility for our failures.

When disabled people talk about details that seriously affect our lives, it is important to acknowledge that we know what we're talking about. When others do things on our behalf that are unhelpful or even harmful, it's important not to expect us to treat these offensive offerings as though they constituted equal access. In our efforts to build disability equality into our communities, we must make a priority of actually succeeding, not merely displaying good intentions. When we inadvertently offer offensive offerings, it's important to recognize them as offensive and do *t'shuvah*. Ongoing work, including ongoing *t'shuvah*, makes it possible for us to embody our most sacred values.

Notes

1. Babylonian Talmud, *Shabbat* 31a.
2. Ibn Ezra on Leviticus 2:1.
3. *Pirkei Avot* 2:4.

SH'MINI—LEVITICUS 9:1–11:47

Kashrut and Food Justice

RABBI DR. SHMULY YANKLOWITZ

THE LAWS OF KASHRUT, found in *Parashat Sh'mini*, are, for some, the most spiritually powerful among everyday Jewish rituals. For others, the system seems archaic and out of touch with their food choices. How might our Torah teachings on kashrut inspire a moral and spiritual revolution, both for those committed to traditional dietary laws and those who are not?

Parashat Sh'mini lays out famous rules such as requiring that a kosher animal have split hooves and chew its cud (Leviticus 11:3) and that fish have fins and scales (Leviticus 11:9), forbidding birds (Leviticus 11:13–19) and forbidding insects (Leviticus 11:20–23). For vegans, like myself, it is all intellectual and not practical. For other traditional Jews, of course, these explicit rules determine which animals they will eat and which they will not.

In the depths of Jewish tradition, one refrain echoes through each and every story, each and every law: to do what is *yashar v'tov*, what is "right and good." For millennia, the purpose of living a Jewish life has been to uplift the soul to perform its heavenly duties here on earth and bring about positive change to a world occupied with conflict.

Yet the contemporary reality of kashrut poses a pronounced difficulty for the Jewish people.

A commitment to the timeless ritual of kashrut is a powerful vehicle for Jewish survival and continuity. However, the fact that food is kosher does not always mean that eating it is ethical, per se. For many, kashrut involves a commitment to a Torah tradition without any deeper moral relevance. The spiritual enterprise of kashrut can be reframed to meet humanity's ethical obligation to tend to the earth and the heavens, including tending to workers' dignity and animal welfare.

At heart, kashrut is about dignity. An anecdote about a rabbinic ethicist helps us understand this concept. Rabbi Yisrael Salanter was the founder of Judaism's modern character development movement, Mussar. The story goes that one spring, before Passover, he was called to certify the kosher status of a matzah factory. As he inspected the factory, he observed the conditions thoroughly. He saw that the matzah, the unleavened bread, was made according to the letter of halachah (Jewish law). Yet, after inspecting every aspect of the factory, Rabbi Salanter refused certification. Why?

Rabbi Salanter explained that he refused to certify the factory's products because of the poor treatment of its workers. The women were overworked, their pay was insufficient, and their needs were ignored. Because his moral compass would not allow the consumption of products prepared unethically, Rabbi Salanter refused to certify the factory's matzah as fit for use on the holiday when Jews tell the story of their ancestors' release from enslavement.[1]

When we see immigrant workers in restaurants, or even when we don't see these invisible people, do we understand how easily they may be exploited for their work because they do not enjoy the rights and protections that citizens have?

In all we do, dignity must be at the forefront of our minds. Human dignity was a central issue in the philosophical thought of Rabbi Joseph B. Soloveitchik (known popularly as "the Rav") and was a dominant theme in his extensive writings. Indeed, he writes:

> There are . . . two moralities: a morality of majesty and a moral-
> ity of humility. The moral gesture of cosmic man aims at majesty
> or kingship. The highest moral achievement for cosmic man is
> sovereignty; man wants to be king. God is king of the world;
> man, imitating God, quests for kingship, not only over a limited
> domain, but over the far and distant regions of the cosmos. . . .
> Man is summoned by God to be the ruler, to be king, to be vic-
> torious. Victory, as the most important aspect of kingship, is an

ethical goal and the human effort to achieve victory is a moral one, provided the means man employs are of a moral nature.[2]

Contrary to the seemingly contradictory nature of those two positions, the morality of majesty and that of humility, the Rav argues that these worldviews are not, in fact, in competition. Rather, from his vantage point, the differences between God and humanity are complementary forces that people are supposed to harness, preserve, and keep in balance. Soloveitchik writes:

> Nature surrenders voluntarily to man's control and rule; she entrusts man with her most guarded secrets. It is more cooperation than dominion, more partnership than subordination... Let us watch out for moments of tension and conflict, when nature begins to hate man and to resent his presence. . . . If nature refuses to be dominated, man is left helpless and weak. . . . This is man's freedom: either to live at peace with nature and thus give expression to a natural existence in the noblest of terms, or to surpass his archaic bounds and corrupt himself and nature.[3]

For the Rav, the need to work and the action of working are deemed not only moral but a key part of Jewish practice. In respecting work, we respect the worker. Rather than being confined to the private sphere and study hall, the Rav argues that halachah "penetrates into every nook and cranny of life. The marketplace, the street, the factory, the house, the meeting place, the banquet hall, all constitute the backdrop for the religious life."[4]

Some of the Rav's most devoted students took this message of ethical kashrut to another level. Consider, for example, a 2008 interview with Rabbi Haskel Lookstein and Rabbi Dr. Yitz Greenberg in the *Jerusalem Post*. When asked why they called for a boycott of lettuce and grapes from nonunion farms, they responded:

> From him [Rabbi Soloveitchik] we learned the idea that Halacha is not just a list of ritual dos and don'ts, but a comprehensive worldview that applies to everything that happens around us. The Torah prohibits the exploitation of workers—so why shouldn't that apply to migrant farm workers picking lettuce or

grapes? They were being mistreated, so it was natural for us to apply the principle of non-exploitation to their situation, too. It seemed obvious.[5]

Not long ago, there was an assumption that kosher laws were not "a higher standard" but morally problematic. Indeed, in the late 1950s, there were many attempts at the state and federal levels to ban kosher slaughter. The Rav was appointed by the Synagogue Council of America to be the spokesperson for the American Jewish community. While the Rav, of course, defended the right to maintain Jewish ritual, he also challenged the Jewish community to establish more humane methods for animal treatment, opposed shackle and hoist (hanging an animal upside down, increasing the pain and trauma), and worked in partnership with the ASPCA to develop a more humane animal pen.[6]

Further, the Rav believed vegetarianism to be a Torah ideal. One commentator writes in Yeshiva University's *Kol Hamevaser*, "Unlike Rabbis Kook and Albo, R. Soloveitchik has no reservations concerning vegetarianism, and affirms it both as an ideal and a practice. He believes that all life, even animal life, is sanctified. . . . Hence, according to R. Soloveitchik, vegetarianism should be practiced, yet man, too desirous for meat, refuses to stop eating animal flesh."[7]

Such a commitment to ethical concerns, while technically separate from the kosher laws themselves, shows that supplemental but vital moral mandates should always be interwoven with ritual laws. Indeed, when we don't remember that we are here to respect and cherish the works of the Divine, we concede our moral primacy as human beings. With an ethical commitment, kosher consumers must move toward greater concern for animal welfare, which will impact all corners of the meat industry.

The ever-growing number of kosher consumers who wish to make the industry more accountable should be agitating for change. The American kosher industry will continue to import meat from Uruguay, Argentina, and other major exporting countries—where cruel methods of slaughter will continue unabated—if kosher consumers keep purchasing it. The elevation of the bottom line over godly respect for animals should bring about greater communal introspection about our sacred duty as stewards of the earth.

Nachmanides (also known as the Ramban) wrote that a person can be *naval birshut haTorah*, a repulsive person with the permission of the Torah. It is not enough, he argued, to follow the letter of the law. If we wish to be moral and holy, we must go further. His specific example, in fact, is one who keeps kosher but is morally oblivious and gluttonous with kosher meat.[8] Kashrut is indeed about far more than some technical ritual preparation. Rabbi Soloveitchik has been credited with expounding on the thought that halachah is a "floor, not a ceiling."[9] Fulfilling basic ritual requirements is merely the beginning. We only truly serve God when we consider the moral and spiritual dimensions involved with each religious act.

When we read *Parashat Sh'mini*, let us be inspired by the timeless traditions to keep the Jewish people nourished. At the same time, let us reflect on the ethical dimensions of food consumption that help enable us to thrive morally.

NOTES

1. The historicity of this story is disputed. For another version, see Rabbi Bonnie Margulis, "Worker Justice and Ethical Kashrut," Worker Justice Wisconsin, April 7, 2014, https://workerjustice.org/2014/passover-reflection-2014/.
2. Joseph B. Soloveitchik, "Majesty and Humility," *Tradition: A Journal of Orthodox Jewish Thought* 17, no. 2 (1978): 33–34
3. Joseph B. Soloveitchik, *The Emergence of Ethical Man* (New York: KTAV Publishing House, 2005), 60.
4. Joseph B. Soloveitchik, *Halakhic Man* (New York: Jewish Publication Society, 1983), 94.
5. Dr. Rafael Medoff, "'These Olympics Are Not Kosher" *Jerusalem Post*, May 1, 2008, https://www.jpost.com/Magazine/Features/These-Olympics-are-not-kosher.
6. See Joseph B. Soloveitchik, *Community, Covenant and Commitment: Selected Letters and Communications*, ed. Nathaniel Helfgot (Jerusalem: KTAV, 2005), 61–71.
7. David Errico-Nagar, "Vegetarianism and Judaism: The Rav's Radical View," *Kol Hamevaser* 5, no. 3 (February 2014).

8. Ramban on Leviticus 19:2.
9. Countless students of Rabbi Soloveitchik quote him as saying this famous line.

TAZRIA—LEVITICUS 12:1–13:59

Facing Mortality in Childbirth

MAHARAT RORI PICKER NEISS

IT IS STRIKING to find that in a Jewish tradition that seems so focused on reproduction, birth is something treated with repulsion rather than reverence.

In the Torah, procreation is simultaneously an obligation, a blessing, and a deep desire. God commands not once but twice that the people be fruitful and multiply (Genesis 1:28, 9:7), Abraham is promised that his descendants would be as numerous as the stars in the sky and the sand on the earth (Genesis 22:17), and we experience time and again the suffering of a mother unable to conceive in the stories of Sarah, Rebekah, Rachel, and Hannah. Yet, as this Torah portion opens with the laws pertaining to one who has given birth, the reader is left feeling neither joyful, hopeful, nor even content. The verses read:

> The Eternal One spoke to Moses, saying: Speak to the Israelite people thus: When a woman at childbirth bears a male, she shall be impure seven days; she shall be impure as at the time of her condition of menstrual separation.—On the eighth day the flesh of his foreskin shall be circumcised.—She shall remain in a state of blood purification for thirty-three days: she shall not touch any consecrated thing, nor enter the sanctuary until her period of purification is completed. If she bears a female, she shall be impure two weeks as during her menstruation, and she shall remain in a state of blood purification for sixty-six days.
>
> On the completion of her period of purification, for either son or daughter, she shall bring to the priest, at the entrance of the Tent of Meeting, a lamb in its first year for a burnt offering,

and a pigeon or a turtledove for a purgation offering. He shall
offer it before the Eternal One and make expiation on her behalf; she shall then be clean from her flow of blood. Such are the
rituals concerning her who bears a child, male or female. (Leviticus 12:1–7)

These verses are deeply unsettling, raising significant questions.
Why should this performance of a commandment, this gift of life,
render a person "impure," *tamei* (טָמֵא)? Even more outrageously, why
would a person be required to bring a sin offering to make expiation?
What is inherent in the act of conceiving and bearing a child that
could possibly necessitate atonement?

These questions have disturbed the rabbis for centuries. In particular, the latter question has sparked the rabbinic imagination to
envisage that in a state of intense anguish during the pains of labor,
one might have expressed evil thoughts that they later regretted[1] or
even made an oath to never again engage in sexual intercourse in
order to avoid bearing future children.[2] These inappropriate statements and improper oaths would, in the mind of the Sages, justify the
need for the sin offering.

Yet this answer is deeply unsatisfactory. Earlier in Leviticus, the
Torah already outlines the processes for bringing a sin offering,
with great detail regarding the status of the person who incurred the
guilt—whether a priest, a chieftain, and so forth—and whether it was
a singular or communal transgression. It seems impossible that the
Torah can here make a blanket statement about the myriad of people
who would give birth to a child. Moreover, can the Torah truly assume
that everyone who goes through labor should be presumed to have
made an inappropriate oath or voiced improper thoughts?

Rabbi Moses ben Nachman, commonly known as Nachmanides
or Ramban, who lived in thirteenth-century Catalonia, offers a very
different reading. Rather than understand the root of the Hebrew
word *v'chiper* (וְכִפֶּר), *kaf-pei-resh* (כ-פ-ר), as "expiation" as translated
in Leviticus 12:7 above, he understands the root to mean "ransom,"
as in Exodus 30:12, "When you take a census of the Israelite men
according to their army enrollment, each shall pay the Eternal a

ransom [*kofer*, כֹּפֶר] for himself on being enrolled, that no plague may come upon them through their being enrolled." Nachmanides does not understand the child-bearer as one in need of atonement, but instead restoration. In essence, Nachmanides, a physician as well as a philosopher and biblical scholar, recognizes that pregnancy, labor, and birth are each life-threatening. The one carrying the fetus and delivering the newborn has, in a sense, relinquished some control over their own life, giving up of their own body, physical functions, and consumed nutrients to grow and develop the future child. As the Talmud teaches, the fetus is considered "as its [parent's] thigh," meaning a part of the body of the one carrying it.[3] And so, according to Nachmanides, the sacrifice is a ransom paid for returning the child-bearer's body to its original owner.

It is significant to note that this ransom exchange can only take place after both the birth and the "period of purification" (*y'mei tohorah*, יְמֵי טָהֳרָה) (Leviticus 12:6), and not before. One might think that a ransom should be paid in advance, that the sacrifice would be offered during the pregnancy as a request or even a demand for a healthy and safe pregnancy, labor, and delivery. This delay highlights that the safety of the individual can never be guaranteed, that the body is not always returned. Indeed, far too many die in the course of childbirth. The sacrifice is a reminder that in the course of bringing life, death is far too often the result.

The Torah commands this offering for all those who give birth, with no distinction for the status, the wealth, the age, or any other defining feature of the individual. In this way, the Torah imagines a reality in which the risk facing each person who bears a child is the same risk, and thus the ransom paid must be the same ransom.

Yet, in our world today, the risk is not the same for all people. According to the United States Centers for Disease Control and Prevention, considerable racial and ethnic disparities in pregnancy-related mortality exist. From the years 2011 to 2016, the pregnancy-related mortality rates showed staggering variance: the CDC recorded 42.4 deaths per 100,000 live births for Black non-Hispanic individuals, whereas white non-Hispanic individuals had less than one-third of that number, at 13.0 deaths per 100,000 live births.[4]

These figures are sobering in their barbarity. The pregnancy-related mortality rate for a Black non-Hispanic individual is more than that of Asian/Pacific Islander non-Hispanic individuals, white non-Hispanic individuals, and Hispanic individuals *combined*. This disparity currently represents the largest disparity among all the conventional population perinatal health measures. Non-Hispanic Black individuals have had the fastest rate of increase in maternal deaths between 2007 and 2014 and have maternal death rates up to twelve times higher in some cities than non-Hispanic white individuals. Pregnancy-related mortality is also elevated among Native Americans/Native Alaskans, Asians/Pacific Islanders, and for certain subgroups of Hispanic individuals including Puerto Ricans in specific regions of the United States. Moreover, for every pregnancy-related death, one hundred individuals suffer a severe obstetric morbidity, have a life-threatening diagnosis, or undergo a lifesaving procedure during their delivery hospitalization. Non-Hispanic Black individuals have the highest rates for twenty-two of twenty-five severe morbidity indicators used by the CDC to monitor population estimates for severe maternal morbidity.[5]

These discrepancies do not result from natural differences between child-bearers of different ethnicities, but are byproducts of structural racism and the disparities that exist within our community and differential access to all the resources of society. Research shows that Black individuals are more likely to have pregestational diabetes and chronic diabetes, which sets them and their children up for complications and poor health outcomes. These conditions are often attributed to poor behaviors and personal health management, when they would be better blamed on environments that lack healthy foods, open spaces for safe recreation, quality and affordable health insurance to access care before and during pregnancy, education and job opportunities that permit time for leisure, and other factors intensified by structural racism.[6] Solving this crisis requires a holistic approach that includes combating implicit bias, institutional racism, lack of tracking or awareness of disparities, lack of cultural and linguistically appropriate care, and fragmentation of care.[7] In addition, our community must also address social determinants of health such as housing, environmental justice, safety and freedom from violence, transportation equity, and clean water, among others.[8]

The sacrifice brought in Leviticus 12 is a recognition of all that might have been sacrificed, that could have been lost, in the course of bringing a new life into the world. This ritual marks a moment of transitioning, leaving behind danger and fear to move forward with this new life. It is not coincidental, then, that this ritual also marks the moment of transition in which the individual exits their prior status as one who was in a state of *tum'ah* (טֻמְאָה), impurity, and enters the status of one who is in a state of *taharah* (טָהֳרָה), purity.

Rabbi Jonathan Sacks, z"l, the former chief rabbi of Britain, taught that a state of *k'dushah* (holiness) is a point in time or space in which we stand in the unmediated presence of the Divine. To do that, one needs a supreme consciousness of life. A person is rendered *tamei*—often translated as "impure" but legally referring to a status in which one cannot enter spaces of *k'dushah*—by that which reminds them of their own mortality, such as a dead body or a bodily emission. The one who gives birth has faced their own mortality, whether because to see the start of life is to recognize that there is an end or because the start of one life is itself too often another's end. It is the one who is *tahor*, who is called "pure," who has the capacity to enter into the holiest of spaces.

We cannot enter the immortal realm of the infinite when our mind is constrained by our own limitations, thoughts of our own mortality. That fact is not a flaw in our physical design but a feature. As humans, we cannot exist in the transcendent world. Though we might be able to attain glimpses of the incomprehensible, ultimately we always return to our corporeal space.

Bringing the sacrifice after childbirth is simultaneously standing with one foot in two spaces: looking back at all that could have gone wrong and the two lives that might not have been, and looking forward to reach toward the holy, aspiring to transcendence. A birth parent is uniquely qualified to bridge these two worlds, working to bring the image of the infinite into our finite space. It is only when we recognize the potential of the infinite that we can refuse to accept the finite world as it is, instead working to remake the world into what it can be, for all people.

NOTES

1. Ibn Ezra on Leviticus 12:6.
2. Babylonian Talmud, *Nidah* 31b.
3. Babylonian Talmud, *Gittin* 23b.
4. "Pregnancy Mortality Surveillance System," Centers for Disease Control and Prevention, accessed September 14, 2020, https://www.cdc.gov/reproductivehealth/maternal-mortality/pregnancy-mortality-surveillance-system.htm.
5. E. A. Howell, "Reducing Disparities in Severe Maternal Morbidity and Mortality," *Clinical Obstetrics and Gynecology* 61, no. 2 (2018): 387–99, https://doi.org/10.1097/GRF.0000000000000349.
6. K. A. Scott, L. Britton, and M. R. McLemore, "The Ethics of Perinatal Care for Black Women: Dismantling the Structural Racism in 'Mother Blame' Narratives," *Journal of Perinatal Neonatal Nursing* 33, no. 2 (April–June 2019): 108–15, doi: 10.1097/JPN.0000000000000394, PMID: 31021935.
7. Scott, Britton, and McLemore, "The Ethics of Perinatal Care for Black Women."
8. *Black Mamas Matter: Advancing the Human Right to Safe and Respectful Maternal Health Care* (New York: Center for Reproductive Rights, 2018), 53–56.

M'TZORA—LEVITICUS 14:1–15:33

The Inequities Revealed by Plagues and Pandemics: Confront the Problems, Don't Blame the Victims

RABBI ASHER GOTTESFELD KNIGHT

IN THE MID-NINETEENTH CENTURY, Italians discovered that the ankles of Michelangelo's famous statue, David, were slowly cracking. Hairline fissures extend up the statue's legs. Scientists have demonstrated that the cracks are so precarious that if the statue is tilted slightly, six tons of marble will bear down, breaking the ankles and causing the statue to crumble.[1] Italian authorities responsible for the statue's upkeep are monitoring the cracks and undertaking efforts to keep the statue upright and protected from earthquakes. There is little margin for error. The slightest tilt in one direction may destroy the Renaissance masterpiece.[2]

The world in which we live, like Michelangelo's statute, is profoundly beautiful. But our society is also precariously balanced upon significant cracks. When trauma happens—from a natural disaster to a tragic example of systemic racism to a global pandemic—those cracks become larger and more visible. COVID-19, for example, has revealed many of our society's inequities. The lack of paid sick leave for thirty million Americans has increased infection rates.[3] Food and housing insecurity has skyrocketed. One in seven households with children, including disproportionate numbers of Blacks and Latinos, lack sufficient food. One in six renters cannot not pay their rent, with Black, Asian, and Latino families facing the greatest hardships and eviction crises. Low-wage industries have seen the worst rise in unemployment, exacerbating a range of societal ills—mental illness, substance abuse, educational disparities, and homelessness.[4] Many people of color have reported increased racial animosity and discrimination.[5] Without access to affordable child care, those who have work are in crisis.[6]

Much like COVID, pandemics throughout history, from the Black Death to the 1918 influenza outbreak to HIV/AIDS, have also exposed deep fissures within society. Plagues magnify issues of economic disparity, access to quality health care, and food and housing insecurity.[7] Fears caused by pandemics have often been used by those who would assign blame and further the harm of their homophobia, xenophobia, racism, and antisemitism.[8]

Parashat M'tzora provides an important model for discussing how we confront inequalities in society when tackling infectious disease. Our *parashah* lists various laws dealing with *tzaraat* (צָרַעַת), often mistranslated as "leprosy." *Tzaraat* is a scaly infection that, according to the Torah, affects the human body, clothing, and the walls of houses in the Land of Israel.

Much of Jewish traditional commentary focuses on the cause of *tzaraat*. The idea was straightforward: if we know the cause, we can avoid the plague. The Talmud explains that *tzaraat* afflicts people "for malicious speech, for bloodshed, for an oath taken in vain, forbidden sexual relations, arrogance, theft, and stinginess."[9] In Numbers 12, Moses's sister Miriam is afflicted with the scaly infection after she and Aaron speak poorly of Moses. Jewish sages interpreted *m'tzora* as *motzi shem ra*—one whose speech is intended either to be evil or to take advantage of others.[10] *Vayikra Rabbah* explains that the scaly infection is a punishment for sin,[11] which may explain why our *parashah* includes the *asham* (אָשָׁם), the guilt offering, among the remedies for *tzaraat* (Leviticus 14:12).

This "blame-the-victim" analysis is troubling. When coupled with the idea that both Leviticus 13:46 and Numbers 5:2 require isolation and quarantine upon the detection of infection, the victim is not only culpable for the illness but also a clear and present danger to the health and well-being of the society. Further, if infection with the scaly disease is a result of divine retribution for infected persons' bad deeds, then they are culpable and responsible for everything that happens and the pain they bring to themselves and others. Still, the Torah offers the possibility of redemption: if they make restitution through the priests, then they may be healed.

As COVID-19 disproportionately kills members of racial and ethnic minority groups, too many in our society blame the victims, pointing to preexisting conditions or questioning what people were doing to contract the disease. Yet larger structural issues are at play. Many people of color suffer from systemic poverty and lack of access to health care and proper nutrition. People of color disproportionately hold lower-paying frontline positions within the service sector and health-care system, making them more vulnerable to exposure. Some suffer from chronic toxic stress due to racism, housing insecurity, insufficient income, and lack of access to education.[12] Preexisting conditions such as cardiovascular disease, diabetes, obesity, and chronic lung disease make COVID considerably more fatal, and members of minority groups face these health challenges at a higher rate than the general population.[13] Higher-density regions and the crowded conditions in which many of its citizens can afford to live were initially blamed for the spread of COVID-19. Many of the early victims of the virus were already victims of our society's failures.

Our modern-day medical treatments are vastly improved from biblical times. Still, we can learn from how the community approached *tzaraat*. First, we are all responsible. Our *parashah* says that the afflicted have a personal responsibility to warn others by saying, *K'nega nirah li babayit* (כְּנֶגַע נִרְאָה לִי בַּבָּיִת), "Something like a plague has appeared upon my house" (Leviticus 14:35). Second, there is a communal responsibility as well. The Talmud explains that the reason *tzaraat* appears in the Torah is to help us learn about the serious societal failings that could produce such a plague and what is required to remedy the situation.[14] The *Zohar* points out that the punishment of *tzaraat* can come about because of our failure to speak out against the ills of society: "Just as a person is punished for an evil word, so too is one punished for a good word which they could have spoken but did not speak. . . . All the more so when people follow crooked ways, and one could have said something to them and removed them, and instead one held their peace and did not speak."[15]

We are culpable for choosing to remain silent, avoiding taking action to right the wrongs afflicting our society. In contrast to the misguided blame-the-individual philosophy, recognizing a society's moral failings can be the first step to sparking large-scale change. Perhaps we should be asking why our health-care system does not care for all people, especially when the Torah is clear that access to remedies must be available to all, regardless of financial status.[16] Why did so many of COVID's victims have comorbidities and preexisting conditions correlated with income? Why is there so much disinformation, encouraging people to take unnecessary risks? While some perceive COVID-19 as the issue, the virus may be a symptom of much larger problems facing humanity.

Ignoring the failing systems and injustices that have added immeasurably to the misery and pain of the pandemic will likely lead to even greater calamity. Unfortunately, with the long-term effects of climate change looming, scientists predict that we will face more pandemics and natural disasters in the coming years.[17] If the present presages the future, the cracks upon which our society is insecurely balanced will be widened by destruction of the environment, warming temperatures, losses in biodiversity, and unknown microbes released in the fast-melting permafrost of the polar regions. The balance of human society is in danger.[18]

The COVID-19 pandemic has reminded us how interconnected we really are. We share this earth with everyone on it. A sickness that begins on one side of the globe can affect us all, and one country's carbon emissions can have worldwide consequences. The cracks are real, and the process to protect and repair our world will be long and complex. Our Torah portion insists that the responsibility falls upon each of us. What happens in our own home can affect others. What happens to our neighbors matters to each of us. We will be measured by how we confront the problems we face and care for everyone in our society.

NOTES

1. Giacomo Corti, et al., "Modelling the Failure Mechanisms of Michelangelo's David through Small-Scale Centrifuge Experiments," *Journal of Cultural Heritage* 16, no. 1 (2015): 26–31.

2. Sam Anderson, "David's Ankles: How Imperfections Could Bring Down the World's Most Perfect Statue," *New York Times* August 17, 2016, https://www.nytimes.com/2016/08/21/magazine/davids-ankles-how-imperfections-could-bring-down-the-worlds-most-perfect-statue.html.

3. Elise Gould, "How the Lack of Paid Sick Leave Will Make Coronavirus Worse," Economic Policy Institute, accessed October 13, 2020, https://www.epi.org/multimedia/coronavirus-paid-sick-leave-explainer/.

4. "Tracking the COVID-19 Recession's Effects on Food, Housing, and Employment Hardships," Center on Budget and Policy Priorities, updated December 18, 2020, https://www.cbpp.org/research/poverty-and-inequality/tracking-the-covid-19-recessions-effects-on-food-housing-and.

5. Neil G. Ruiz, Juliana Menasce Horowitz, and Christine Tamir, "Many Black, Asian Americans Say They Have Experienced Discrimination Amid Coronavirus," Pew Research Center's Social & Demographic Trends Project, July 1, 2020, https://www.pewsocialtrends.org/2020/07/01/many-black-and-asian-americans-say-they-have-experienced-discrimination-amid-the-covid-19-outbreak/.

6. Megan Leonhardt, "Affordable Child Care Is Increasingly Difficult to Find in the U.S.—Coronavirus Could Make It Harder," CNBC, May 15, 2020, https://www.cnbc.com/2020/05/15/affordable-child-care-is-tough-to-findcoronavirus-may-make-it-harder.html.

7. G. Alfani and T. Murphy, "Plague and Lethal Epidemics in the Pre-Industrial World," *Journal of Economic History* 77, no. 1 (2017): 314–43.

8. Aviya Kushner, "Pandemics Have Always Incited Anti-Semitism: Here's the History You Need to Know," *Forward*, May 4, 2020, https://forward.com/culture/445419/pandemic-anti-semitism-coronavirus-black-death-typhus-cholera-immigrants/. Also see Joseph Guzman, "New Report Says Coronavirus Pandemic Is Fueling Anti-Semitism," *The Hill*, April 20, 2020, https://thehill.com/changing-america/respect/equality/493671-the-coronavirus-crisis-is-fueling-anti-semitism-report-says.

9. Babylonian Talmud, *Arachin* 16a.

10. *Vayikra Rabbah* 16:2; see the end of the story of the man who peddles false cures as someone who is *motzi shem ra*.

11. *Vayikra Rabbah* 17.

12. "Health Equity Considerations and Racial and Ethnic Minority Groups," Centers for Disease Control and Prevention, updated July 24, 2020, https://www.cdc.gov/coronavirus/2019-ncov/community/health-equity/race-ethnicity.html#fn2.

13. "Coronavirus Disease 2019 Case Surveillance—United States, January 22–May 30, 2020," Centers for Disease Control and Prevention, June 18, 2020.

14. Babylonian Talmud, *Sanhedrin* 71a.

15. *Zohar* 46:2–47:1.

16. Leviticus 14:21–32, which repeats the sacrificial rites discussed in Leviticus 14:1–20, making substitutions for individuals who cannot afford to sacrifice more expensive animals. This follows the Levitical principle of Leviticus 27:8, "If one cannot afford the equivalent . . . the priest shall make the assessment according to what the vower can afford."

17. Abrahm Lustgarten, "How Climate Change Is Contributing to Skyrocketing Rates of Infectious Disease," *ProPublica*, May 7, 2020, https://www.propublica.org/article/climate-infectious-diseases.

18. Melody Schreiber, "The Next Pandemic Could Be Hiding in the Arctic Permafrost," *New Republic*, April 2, 2020, https://newrepublic.com/article/157129/next-pandemic-hiding-arctic-permafrost.

Mental Illness and Incarceration: Cutting People Off or Bringing Them Home?

RABBI JOEL MOSBACHER

PARASHAT ACHAREI MOT holds out the idea that we can be transformed, describing rituals and practices that make change possible. However, some of the key rituals of change in the *parashah*—the concepts of *kareit* (Leviticus 17:4), of being permanently cut off from one's people, and of the goat sent out to Azazel (Leviticus 16:20)— are so foreign to us as to seem irrelevant to our modern sensibilities. As Jews, we believe that repentance and return to wholeness are possible. Especially as Reform Jews, we don't cut people off from our community; instead, we seek to have a tent open on all sides.[1] And we certainly do not believe in the ancient idea that we can symbolically put our sins on the head of a goat and send it out to the wilderness. These punishments and rituals are anathema to us; they make us recoil when we read them.

But how foreign to our modern experience are they, in reality? How much differently did the ancients treat their fellow human beings than we do? When it comes to approaching citizens facing mental illness, we are still cutting people off from society. We are still putting the sins of society on God's creatures, still sending them, like the scapegoat in Leviticus, off into the wilderness, hoping they will not come back.

The Mishnah includes a list of actions that entail the punishment of cutting off a person from their kin:

[There are] thirty-six acts for which the Torah [prescribes] *kareit*:
. . . [including] one who blasphemes, or who worships idols, or
who sacrifices one's children to Molech; . . . one who violates
Shabbat, or an impure person who eats consecrated food; one
who enters the Temple when impure, or one who eats forbidden
fat, or who eats blood . . . or who eats leavened bread on Pesach, or who eats on Yom Kippur. . . . Positive commandments
[whose neglect warrants *kareit* are]: the Passover offering, and
circumcision.[2]

Yitzchak Abravanel, in his commentary on another text about *kareit*,
notes that "we see that there are various sins that invoke *kareit* that
are quite different in their severity, but the punishment is nevertheless the same, and this cannot be according to God's just and righteous ways."[3] Abravanel acknowledges, as might we, that there may
be people who commit acts that are so heinous, so violent, so unfor-
givable, that being cut off from the community feels like the only fitting punishment. But he also asserts, as we might similarly, that not
every crime listed in the Mishnah deserves the same level of severity
in punishment.

In our modern context, it is important to note that merely 4 percent of interpersonal violence in the United States stems from mental
illness.[4] And yet, nearly 40 percent of news stories on mental illness
link it with violent behavior. In reality, the US Department of Health
and Human Services reports that individuals with serious mental illnesses are over ten times likelier to be victims of violent crimes than
those in the general population.[5]

Instead of focusing on their vulnerability to others' criminal acts,
America has constructed a society in which individuals with severe
mental illness are overrepresented in the criminal justice system
when compared with the rest of the population. In the United States
each year, approximately one million detentions in county jails
involve persons with serious mental illnesses. These individuals are
imprisoned about ten times more frequently than they are admitted
to state mental hospitals[6] and are incarcerated for significantly longer periods than other inmates.[7]

In New York City, the proportion of inmates at municipal jails who are mentally ill has increased to nearly 40 percent in recent years, even as the overall number of people incarcerated has shrunk.[8] Many of these inmates are so-called frequent fliers, constantly cycling in and out of Rikers Island, the city's main jail complex. A task force commissioned by Mayor Bill de Blasio identified more than four hundred people who had been jailed at least eighteen times in the last five years, accounting for over ten thousand jail admissions during that period. It said that 67 percent of these inmates had "a mental health need"; 21 percent were severely mentally ill, meaning they had diseases like schizophrenia or bipolar disorder; and 99 percent had a substance abuse problem.[9]

When we treat people with serious mental illness as we are today, it is as if, in the words of Rashi, we are cutting their life and the life of their children short.[10] We are thus acting in place of God, and not in a good way; just as God "set[s] [God's] face against them,"[11] so do we. We are dealing with them as we might deal with someone who has committed an irredeemable crime and deserves life in prison.

The shame of this should weigh heavily on us, for the Torah imagines that people can be transformed. In today's United States, it is as if we have lost that imagination, giving up hope on people who need our help. We have relegated them to a life of endless incarceration without the support they need. And in sending them off to prison, we believe we are absolving ourselves of responsibility for them.

In the Torah, Azazel "is the name of the wilderness beyond the boundaries of settled life. . . . Azazel in this case is best imagined as the antithesis of the Tabernacle/sanctuary, a place of disorder."[12] When we send people living with mental illness to prison instead of treatment, it is as if we are banishing them to Azazel. Prisons are not designed for mental health care, yet we express shock and surprise when, unlike the goat in Leviticus, people with mental illness who are incarcerated return again and again.

Decades of local, state, and federal disinvestment in mental health care has turned police into ad hoc psychiatric caregivers of last resort. Between 2014 and 2018, New York City lost 10 percent of its psychiatric hospital beds, even as the city population increased. Too often, those with severe, treatment-resistant mental issues wind up in jails.[13]

Fortunately, models and practices exist to help break these cycles, get people the treatment they need, and massively reduce recidivism. Universal Crisis Intervention Team (CIT) training for law enforcement officers—usually the first responders when individuals suffering episodes caused by mental illness act in ways that could bring harm to their families, their neighbors, or themselves—is the first step. Police must be properly trained to identify and de-escalate encounters with people facing mental illness and/or addiction. Combining this training with the availability of crisis stabilization centers and mental health diversion centers—where police can quickly offer treatment, support services, and housing in place of expensive and ineffective incarceration—has proved effective in addressing the need for treatment while reducing recidivism and all of its ancillary costs.

Over the past two decades, nearly nine thousand people have been referred to a program, created by Judge Steven Leifman in Miami-Dade County, Florida, to divert individuals with serious mental illnesses away from the criminal justice system and into comprehensive community-based services. Annual recidivism rates among participants went from 75 percent to 20 percent. The jail population dropped by 45 percent, allowing the county to close one of its jails and save $12 million a year.[14]

There are a growing number of mental health courts and diversion centers in our country attempting to approach this issue from a different angle. No doubt, this kind of care requires thoughtful planning and major investment, but such efforts will yield returns much greater than our current lack of coordination and massive expenditure on a prison industrial complex that is simply not designed to provide people living with mental illness the help they need.

One potent verse in our *parashah* points to what should be our approach to Americans struggling with mental illness: "You shall keep My laws and My rules, by the pursuit of which human beings shall live: I am the Eternal" (Leviticus 18:5). Our Sages emphasize the phrase *vachai bahem* (וָחַי בָּהֶם), "by which human beings shall live," interpreting that the performance of mizvot should lead us to life, not death.[15] Maimonides further interprets: "We see that the laws of the Torah are not designed to bring hardships but compassion, loving-kindness, and peace into this world."[16]

As Maimonides suggests, we have a question to resolve as a society: Are our laws meant to help people with mental illness so they might live among their neighbors? If not, then the current system of incarceration is working exactly as designed. If so, however, we must work to unlock the system that incarcerates people on a mass and recurring scale, cutting them off from society and sending them into the wilderness. Instead of *kareit*, we must provide the compassionate treatment that they need.

Notes

1. Rabbi Rick Jacobs, "As Numerous as the Stars of Heaven," address to the URJ Biennial, December 12, 2019, https://urj.org/blog/2019/12/12/numerous-stars-heaven-0.
2. *Mishnah K'ritot* 1:1.
3. Abravanel on Numbers 15:22.
4. Alexandra Sifferlin, "Most Violent Crimes Are Wrongly Linked to Mental Illness," *Time*, June 6, 2016, https://time.com/4358295/violent-crimes-mental-illness/.
5. Sifferlin, "Most Violent Crimes Are Wrongly Linked."
6. "Facts," Greenburger Center for Social and Criminal Justice, Greenburgercenter.org/facts.
7. "Facts," Greenburger Center for Social and Criminal Justice.
8. Michael Winerip and Michael Schwirtz, "New York City Plans Focus on Mental Health in Justice System," *New York Times*, December 1, 2014, https://www.nytimes.com/2014/12/02/nyregion/new-york-city-to-expand-health-services-for-mentally-ill-inmates.html.
9. "Task Force Report on Mental Health in New York Justice System," *New York Times*, December 2, 2014, https://www.nytimes.com/interactive/2014/12/02/nyregion/mental-health-justice-report.html.
10. Rashi on Leviticus 17:9.
11. Leviticus 10.
12. Rachel Havrelock, in *The Torah: A Women's Commentary*, ed. Tamara Cohn Eskenazi and Andrea L. Weiss (New York: CCAR Press and Women of Reform Judaism, 2008), 682.

13. "Task Force Report," *New York Times*.

14. "Steve Leifman: A Judge on the Mental Health Frontlines in Miami," accessed January 3, 2021, The Stepping Up Initiative, https://stepuptogether.org/people/steve-leifman.

15. Babylonian Talmud, *Sotah* 85b.

16. Maimonides, *Mishneh Torah, Hilchot Shabbat* 2:1–3.

K'doshim—Leviticus 19:1–20:27

What We Leave for the Poor

Rabbi Barry H. Block

As part of the daily morning service, Reform Jews say these words:

> These are things that are limitless,
> of which a person enjoys the fruit of the world,
> while the principal remains in the world to come.
> They are: honoring one's father and mother,
> engaging in deeds of compassion,
> arriving early for study, morning and evening,
> dealing graciously with guests,
> visiting the sick,
> providing for the wedding couple,
> accompanying the dead for burial,
> being devoted in prayer,
> and making peace among people.
> But the study of Torah encompasses them all.[1]

A note at the bottom of the page in *Mishkan T'filah* indicates that this liturgy is based on *Pei-ah* 1:1, a reference to a tractate of the Mishnah, the code of Jewish law committed to writing around the year 200 CE. Specifically, *Pei-ah* refers to a law in the Torah's Holiness Code, found in *Parashat K'doshim*, requiring that Israelites leave the corners of their fields for the poor and the stranger (Leviticus 19:9–10).

Our prayer book does not include the corner of the field among the list of acts that are limitless. However, in *Mishnah Pei-ah*, that mitzvah is listed first. Specifically, though the Rabbis insist that the corner left for the poor must be no less than one-sixtieth of the field,[2] they pointedly do not set a maximum.

A thirteenth-century commentator, Rabbi Jacob ben Asher, notes that the commandment to leave the corner of the field is immediately followed in our Torah portion by the words *lo tignovu* (לֹא תִּגְנֹבוּ), "You shall not steal" (Leviticus 19:11), a quotation from the Ten Commandments. Rabbi Jacob suggests that the proximity of two seemingly unrelated passages is "to warn the owner not to steal from what belongs to the poor."[3] In other words, the corner of the field is already the property of the poor, not of the landowner. A sixteenth-century rabbi, Moses Alshich, goes even further: "You shouldn't think that you are giving to the poor person from your own property, or that I have despised [the poor] by not giving bread to [them] as I have given to you. For [the poor are] also my child[ren], just as you are, but [their] portion is in your produce."[4]

In ancient Israel, providing for the poor was not optional. In a society that measured wealth in agricultural produce, all property owners were required to leave a corner of their fields unharvested and to consider a portion of their crop as if it were not their own. Contemporary commentator Jeffrey Spitzer emphasizes that the farmer did not give anonymously: "While we tend to think of an ideal of anonymous giving, this [mitzvah] points out the importance of transparent, public giving. Knowing that other people are giving is crucial in order to maintain widespread support for any system of [*tzedakah*]."[5]

One additional aspect of the mitzvah merits our attention: "The owner of the field does not distribute the *peah*; rather, the poor come and take it for themselves."[6] The poor retain their dignity in the process, earning the produce by harvesting it.

Most contemporary Jews are not farmers. Technically, most commandments regarding the land in Israel are not in force today, and they will not be until the messianic era arrives. However, as Rebbetzin Chana Bracha Siegelbaum teaches, "The Rabbis ruled that we must keep these mitzvot today . . . to ingrain within the corners of our being the limitation of ownership . . . through the mitzvot of allowing the poor to take what is rightfully theirs."[7]

Paying taxes is one way we fulfill this commandment today. Just over a third of our American federal tax dollars are directed toward programs that benefit the poor and needy. About three-quarters of that is for health care, including Medicare for those age sixty-five and over, poor or not.[8] As in ancient Israel, part of Americans' income belongs to the poor as a matter of law.

Many Americans oppose the requirement to provide for the poor. Libertarian Bryan Caplan states the case:

> Consider the best-case-scenario for forced charity. Somebody is absolutely poor through no fault of [their] own. . . . Even here, the moral case for forced charity is much less plausible than it looks. Patriotic brainwashing notwithstanding, our "fellow citizens" are strangers—and the moral intuition that helping strangers is [beyond the call of duty] is hard to escape. And even if you think the opposite, can you honestly deny that it's debatable? If so, how can you in good conscience coerce dissenters?[9]

Judaism would answer: The obligation to care for the poor is not debatable. No less authority than God commands it. Moreover, Judaism agrees that those whom we help may include strangers. Caplan is correct: an obligation to assist strangers is not necessarily intuitive. That's precisely the reason the Torah requires it explicitly.

Judaism does not deny that providing for the poor may cost us. After all, the farmer would profit by harvesting the corners of the field and bringing all of the land's produce to market.

In fact, the mitzvah is not fulfilled when charity does not cost us anything. We all engage in that kind of giving, and there's nothing wrong with doing so. We bring carloads to Goodwill, giving away clothing and other items we can no longer use. When a food drive comes around, at least some of the canned goods we prune from our pantries may be items we would never consume. That kind of giving is a mitzvah, namely *bal tashchit*, the obligation not to waste. It also helps the poor. When we perform that good deed, though, we are not giving up a portion of what we have.

When we pay for public education, especially if we do not have children in public schools or are taxed an amount more than the state pays to educate our own offspring, we are giving the corner of our field to the poor and the stranger. When we pay for SNAP, the food stamp program that provides subsistence nutritional assistance, mostly for the working poor, we are leaving the corner of our field. When we provide health insurance for our fellow citizens who cannot afford basic medical care, we are leaving a corner of our field. And when we support college acceptance or hiring preferences for those who don't enjoy the benefits we and our children do, we are also leaving a corner of our field. It's a mitzvah, a religious obligation binding on every Jew.

The Poor People's Campaign, led by Rev. William Barber, calls itself "A National Call for Moral Revival . . . uniting . . . people across the country to challenge the evils of systemic racism, poverty, . . . ecological devastation, and the nation's distorted morality."[10] America's distorted morality includes the so-called prosperity gospel, teaching that "'health and wealth' are the automatic divine right of all Bible-believing Christians . . . since the Atonement of Christ includes not just the removal of sin, but also the removal of sickness and poverty."[11] Many Christians find this theology repulsive; Judaism utterly rejects it. Remember, Rabbi Moses Alshich taught that the mitzvah of *Pei-ah* reminds us that God has provided for the poor, quite the opposite of spurning them.

What should we leave for the poor? Like ancient Israelite farmers before us, we are enjoined to provide the needy a portion of what we hold most precious, reserving a meaningful percentage of what we have. It's already theirs, having been provided by God. Let its reward, like the mitzvah itself, be limitless.

Notes
1. *Mishkan T'filah*, ed. Elyse D. Frishman (New York: CCAR Press, 2007), 44.
2. *Mishnah Pei-ah* 1:2.
3. *Baal HaTurim*, quoted in Jeffrey Spitzer, "Pe'ah: The Corners of Our Fields," My Jewish Learning, accessed April 27, 2018, https://www.myjewishlearning.com/article/peah-the-corners-of-our-fields/.
4. *Torat Moshe*, quoted in Spitzer, "Pe'ah: The Corners of Our Fields."
5. Spitzer, "Pe'ah: The Corners of Our Fields."
6. Rabbi Jack Abramowitz, "216. Peah I: The Obligation to Leave a Corner of

the Field for the Needy," OU Torah, accessed April 27, 2018, https://www.ou.org/torah/mitzvot/taryag/mitzvah216/.

7. Rebbetzin Chana Bracha Siegelbaum, "Ingrained Giving," *Nature in the Parasha*, accessed April 27, 2018, www.berotbatayin.org/wp-content/uploads/2015/04/NatureAchareiKedoshimGiving.pdf.

8. "Policy Basics: Where Do Our Federal Tax Dollars Go?," Center on Budget and Policy Priorities, updated October 4, 2017, https://www.cbpp.org/research/federal-budget/policy-basics-where-do-our-federal-tax-dollars-go.

9. Bryan Caplan, "12 Reasons to Oppose the Welfare State," Foundation for Economic Education, March 7, 2016, https://fee.org/articles/12-reasons-to-oppose-the-welfare-state/.

10. Poor People's Campaign, https://www.poorpeoplescampaign.org.

11. Joe Carter, "What You Should Know About the Prosperity Gospel," The Gospel Coalition, May 3, 2017, https://www.thegospelcoalition.org/article/what-you-should-know-about-the-prosperity-gospel/.

EMOR—LEVITICUS 21:1–24:23

Does the Torah Require Vegetarianism?

RUHAMA WEISS, PhD

TWO ADJACENT LAWS in *Parashat Emor* deal with a unique aspect of kashrut. While most of the rules classify food as permitted for eating (all plant foods) and prohibited for eating (certain types of animals), these two laws enact special time limits for slaughtering sheep and cattle: "When an ox or a sheep or a goat is born, it shall stay seven days with its mother, and from the eighth day on it shall be acceptable as an offering by fire to the Eternal. However, no animal from the herd or from the flock shall be slaughtered on the same day with its young" (Leviticus 22:27–28).

The first law states that sheep or cattle aged less than eight days must not be sacrificed—in the first seven days of life, we must let these animals be with their mothers. During those seven days, slaughtering the mother is forbidden as well, since we must allow the mother-newborn unit to live together throughout the first week. The contemporary reader should note that Leviticus does not distinguish between slaughter for sacrifice and slaughter for eating—meat to be eaten was to be sacrificed first.

If we take this law one step further, we can deduce that the Torah also forbids the practice of keeping newborn animals away from the mothers in order to use mother's milk for human needs during the first week, since the mother and child must be together.

This law is mentioned, in similar words, once again in the Torah: "You shall give Me the first-born among your children. You shall do the same with your cattle and your flocks: seven days it shall remain with its mother, on the eighth day you shall give it to Me" (Exodus

22:28–29). This verse, which equates the firstborn of the Israelites with the firstborn of sheep and cattle, bolsters the sense that before God, one system includes all living beings: humans, cattle, and sheep.

The second law also deals with the timing, prohibiting the slaughter of an animal and its offspring on the same day. Neither law has an explanation in the Torah itself.

We may nevertheless glean a biblical reason for these two laws. A common denominator is the description of family relationships between animals in terms typically reserved for human relationships: mother, child, father. Furthermore, the observance of the law requires those who raise the animals to locate families in their herds, since identifying the parent of each sheep is not easy.

The first law concerning cattle requires maintaining family ties for at least seven days, in contrast to what we see on most farms today. Torah laws require us to treat edible animals as families, not merely pieces of property. The language of the rules and the content of the guidelines obligate us to address the emotional world of animals, to be aware of the parent-child relationship among livestock.

Two other biblical laws, also related to animals as food, take the same approach: "If, along the road, you chance upon a bird's nest, in any tree or on the ground, with fledglings or eggs and the mother sitting over the fledglings or on the eggs, do not take the mother together with her young. Let the mother go, and take only the young, in order that you may fare well and have a long life" (Deuteronomy 22:6–7); and "You shall not boil a kid in its mother's milk," appearing three times in the Torah (Exodus 23:19, 34:26; Deuteronomy 14:21).

In the verses dealing with the commandment to send the mother from the nest, the title *eim* (אֵם), "mother," is mentioned three times. The title *banim* (בָּנִים), "children," is mentioned twice, denoting the relationships familiar to us from human language: mother and children.

Much discussion has been devoted to the text in an attempt to explain the essence of the prohibition "You shall not boil a kid in its mother's milk." This law has become a cornerstone of kashrut, and its application in halachic culture has affected the structure of the

Jewish kitchen and the relationship between the Jewish community and non-Jews. It is hard to locate another example of five Hebrew words that are more consequential for Jewish culture.

Yehuda Amichai wrote a poem suggesting a problem with the implementation of this meaningful commandment:

> **Instead of a love poem**
> From "thou shalt not seethe a kid in its mother's milk,"
> They made the many laws of Kashrut,
> But the kid is forgotten and the milk is forgotten and
> the mother
> Is forgotten.
>
> In this way from "I love you"
> We made all our life together.
> But I've not forgotten you
> As you were then.[1]

Amichai demands that we return to the simple and primary intention of the short law, expressed in its concise language and yet absent from the way it has been traditionally implemented: There is a goat, the goat has a mother, and the mother has milk. The only moral way to arrange the goat-milk-mother triad is in a situation where the goat suckles milk from its mother's teats. This is nature, the way God created the world. In contrast, the image of the pot of milk in which a little goat's meat is cooked is distorted and cruel.

The biblical scholar Menachem Haran seeks to emphasize the humanitarian rationale of compassion underlying the four laws:

> The law of the Torah forbade only the cooking of the goat in its mother's milk, and for an obvious reason: because of the cruelty and the feeling of abomination in this combination. In this respect, this prohibition of the Torah is similar to the warning "until seven days after calving, an ox or a sheep or a goat must be with his mother, and only from the eighth day onwards is it permissible to bring it as a sacrifice" (Exodus 22:29; Leviticus 22:27). It is also similar to warnings not to slaughter an ox or a sheep or a goat and its child in one day (Leviticus 22:28) and to send away the bird when taking its chicks or eggs (Deuteronomy

22:7), and all these warnings are based on a humanitarian reason.[2]

Compassion for animals is also the focus of a Talmudic story about Rabbi Y'hudah HaNasi:

> The afflictions of Rabbi Y'hudah HaNasi came upon him due to an incident and left him due to another incident. What was that incident that led to his suffering? There was a certain calf that was being led to slaughter. The calf went and hung its head on the corner of Rabbi Y'hudah HaNasi's garment and was weeping. Rabbi Y'hudah HaNasi said to it: Go, as you were created for this purpose. It was said: Since he was not compassionate, let afflictions come upon him.
>
> And suffering left him due to another incident. One day, the maidservant of Rabbi Y'hudah HaNasi was sweeping the house. There were young weasels lying about, and she was sweeping them out. Rabbi Y'hudah HaNasi said to her: Let them be. It is written: "The Eternal is good to all; and God's mercies are over all God's works" (Psalm 145:9). They said: Since he was compassionate, we shall be compassionate toward him.[3]

The words of Rabbi Y'hudah HaNasi to the calf that came to ask for salvation sound particularly cruel. Is Rabbi Y'hudah God, who can rule on the destiny of every creature? Is it appropriate for a rich person like this sage, living a comfortable life, to see the suffering of an animal and condemn it on the grounds that there is order in the world and suffering is the fated lot of certain beings? Heaven thought otherwise and decided to cause Rabbi Y'hudah HaNasi suffering in order to teach him to have mercy on all creatures. Rabbi Y'hudah learned his lesson.

Can we say that these sources required their ancient readers to avoid eating animals? I must admit that I do not think so. The sources ask us to face ambivalence: they allowed us to eat animals but at the same time demanded that we remember that this act is morally distorted because we and the animals belong to the same family. We have all experienced a parent-child relationship, whether biological or otherwise. All children want protection from their parents, and all

parents are supposed to take care of their children. We all want to live and are afraid to die. No one wants to find themselves on a friend's dinner plate. No living entity is meant to be food. The idea that we humans, as those in power, are allowed to take newborn animals from their parents and eat them is chilling if we are willing to put it in the simple and true way the Torah formulates.

One can explain that the Torah permits eating animals because the quantity and variety of plant foods were limited in ancient times. By contrast, there is no escape from the determination that in our time, in places where plant foods are in great variety, we must be careful to avoid eating animals and thus walk in God's way, as "God's mercies are over all God's works" (Psalm 145:9).

NOTES
1. Yehuda Amichai, "Instead of a Love Poem," in *The Great Tranquility: Questions and Answers* (New York: Sheep Meadow Press, 1997), 48.
2. Menachem Haran, "A Kid in Its Mother's Milk," in *Eretz Yisrael Yad Tishlach* [Hebrew], 12–18 (my translation).
3. Babylonian Talmud, *Bava M'tzia* 85a.

B'HAR—LEVITICUS 25:1–26:2
"The Land Is Mine"

RABBI JILL JACOBS

IN SPRING 2001, I sat in a *beit midrash* (study hall) in southern Jerusalem, listening to a lecture on *Parashat B'har*. From outside, we could hear the exchange of fire between snipers in the Palestinian town of Beit Jala and the Israeli army responding with heavy artillery. "But the land must not be sold beyond reclaim." *Boom.* "*Ki li haaretz.* The land is Mine." *Boom, boom.* "You are but *gerim* [sojourners] resident with Me."[1] *Boom, boom, boom.*

Nobody in the room that day acknowledged aloud the discordance between the words of the text and the battle outside to lay permanent claim to the land on which we sat.

Throughout the Torah, God makes clear that permission to settle in the Land of Israel comes by divine grace alone and that failure to comply with the conditions of this gift will result in expulsion:

> Do not defile yourselves in any of those ways, for it is by such that the nations that I am casting out before you defiled themselves. Thus the land became defiled; and I called it to account for its iniquity, and the land spewed out its inhabitants. But you must keep My laws and My rules, and you must not do any of those abhorrent things, neither the citizen nor the stranger who resides among you; for all those abhorrent things were done by the people who were in the land before you, and the land became defiled. So let not the land spew you out for defiling it, as it spewed out the nation that came before you. (Leviticus 18:24–28)

The language used here, *vataki haaretz et yoshveha* (וַתָּקִא הָאָרֶץ אֶת־יֹשְׁבֶיהָ), "and the land spewed out its inhabitants" (Leviticus 18:25), literally conjures up an image of the land vomiting up its residents, like food gone rotten. The land, God reminds us, belongs only to God. Human beings may dwell there, but as *gerim*—sojourners with rights and responsibilities, but without a permanent claim.

We often translate *gerim* as "immigrants," "refugees," or "strangers." While each captures a facet of this word, none proves sufficient. In the Bible, *ger* connotes someone who came from one place and has settled—perhaps for a lifetime—in another.[2]

As such, the Torah describes the Israelites as having been *gerim* in Egypt—an initially tolerated minority who never became fully Egyptian, and thus ultimately fell victim to the politics of fear that insisted on enslaving the dreaded other. The status of the *ger* remains precarious, as shifting political winds can easily turn tolerance into enslavement. For this reason, the Torah teaches, the experience of being *gerim* must compel the Israelites to protect vulnerable *gerim* in their own land.

But the experience of being a *ger* is not limited to immigrants and refugees. Indeed, as Leviticus reminds us, the Israelites' very possession of the land of Israel rests on divine grace. God alone possesses the land, and God reserves the right to expel its residents. The Psalmist takes this sense of impermanence even further, declaring, "I am only *ger* in the land; do not hide Your commandments from me" (Psalm 119:19). Explaining this verse, the twelfth- to thirteenth-century commentator Radak (David Kimchi) comments, "A person in this world is like a *ger* who has no status in the place, for a person will travel from this world, having no standing or permanence there."[3]

Human beings, says Radak, must always act as *gerim*, aware of our perpetual impermanence. This sense of our own lack of ownership becomes more difficult—and more necessary—when we come into possession of our own land, as the Torah warns us:

> When you have eaten your fill, and have built fine houses to live in, and your herds and flocks have multiplied, and your silver and gold have increased, and everything you own has prospered, beware lest your heart grow haughty and you forget the Eternal your God . . . and you say to yourselves, "My own power and the

might of my own hand have won this wealth for me." (Deuteronomy 8:12–14, 17)

The Jewish people, God warns, should never take for granted the right to dwell in the land of Israel. *Ki li haaretz* (כִּי־לִי הָאָרֶץ), "for the land is Mine" (Leviticus 25:23), says God.

The foremost sin that can result in expulsion from the land is the crime of bloodshed: "You shall not pollute the land in which you live; for blood pollutes the land, and the land can have no expiation for blood that is shed on it, except by the blood of the one who shed it. You shall not defile the land in which you live, in which I Myself abide, for I the Eternal abide among the Israelite people" (Numbers 35:33–34).

The Talmud makes this warning even more dire: "For the sin of bloodshed, the Temple is destroyed, and the Divine Presence leaves Israel, as it says: 'You shall not pollute the land in which you live' and 'You shall not defile the land in which you live, in which I Myself abide.' If you defile the land, you will not inhabit it, and I will not dwell in it."[4] Murder, the Rabbis assert, not only results in the expulsion of the Jewish people from the Land of Israel and the destruction of the center of our religious life, but also in the departure of the Divine Presence from the land. Bloodshed so tarnishes the land that even God must flee, leaving the Land of Israel stripped of its status as the dwelling place of the Divine.

This idea returns in the response of Rabbi Moshe Avigdor Amiel (Lithuania/Israel, 1883–1946) to the policy of *havlagah*, "restraint," in the face of the Palestinian uprising against the British in the 1930s. David Ben-Gurion, later the first prime minister of Israel, argued that Jews should show restraint for practical reasons, to enamor themselves to the British and to secure international support for the Zionist cause. Amiel instead insisted on morality, not political pragmatism, as the driving force for restraint:

"Do not murder," without any conditions, and without any exceptions. "Do not murder" because "whoever sheds human blood, by the human hand shall that person's blood be shed; for in the image of God, God made humanity." Every single person is included in this, whoever they may be. . . . It is not appropriate for Israel to achieve its goal—the establishment of a national home in the Land of Israel—if the means of realizing this goal are invalid, for the final goal of Zionism is not only a majority of Jews in the Land of Israel, but rather the goal of "the end of days" for *tikkun olam b'malchut Shaddai* [the restoration of the world under divine sovereignty].[5]

Amiel's warning, that Zionism must not accept bloodshed or invalid means to achieve the dream of a national home in the Land of Israel, has gone unheeded as the State of Israel has prioritized land over human life in carrying out an occupation that has lasted more than half a century. Today some five million noncitizen Palestinians live under Israeli sovereignty[6] and under a jumble of legal statuses. Palestinians in the West Bank live under military law; the Israeli Defense Forces control the entire West Bank, though the Palestinian Authority (PA) maintains limited control in certain areas. At the same time, Israeli citizens living in West Bank settlements carry their citizenship with them and live under Israeli civilian authority, sometimes mere meters from Palestinian neighbors governed by an entirely different legal system. In Gaza, the Hamas government over-sees all aspects of daily life, though Israel controls Gaza's perimeter, its imports and exports, the population registry, and all movement of people in and out—including people and products headed to the West Bank or to other countries altogether. The Israeli army regu-larly operates both inside of Gaza and in West Bank cities officially under PA control. In East Jerusalem, annexed by Israel soon after its capture, Palestinian residents live in a sort of limbo. Most hold East Jerusalem residency cards but not citizenship. This status allows them to vote in municipal, but not national, elections and to travel between Israel proper and the West Bank. East Jerusalem residents regularly lose their residency status as a result of long absences from the city, and those who marry nonresidents must choose between moving to the West Bank or wherever their spouse resides, thereby forfeiting their residency status, or living alone in East Jerusalem.

In accordance with international law prohibiting annexation[7] and consistent and clear rejection of other annexations, the international community has never accepted the annexation of East Jerusalem,[8] though the Trump administration deviated from this international consensus in moving the US embassy to Jerusalem before a final status agreement on the city.

Occupation, in and of itself, is not illegal per international law, but it is meant to be temporary. Occupying powers must follow certain laws, including maintaining existing law, not moving civilians into the occupied territory, and refraining from collective punishment or the confiscation of property.[9] Israel has violated these conditions, including by promoting settlement through government subsidies and other assistance; declaring private Palestinian land "state land" or required for military use in order to seize such land, often then transferring it to settlements;[10] and employing collective punishment such as closures and the demolition of homes belonging to the families of Palestinians who carry out terror attacks.[11]

In prioritizing land over the lives of human beings, the State of Israel violates the biblical warning against defiling the land and the Talmudic threat that God will flee if there is bloodshed in the land.

Lest the reader of the biblical text—or the observer of the modern State of Israel—be disheartened by the command to maintain a sense of our own impermanence in the land, the midrash, commenting on *Parashat B'har*, offers some encouragement: "Do not take it badly that I forbid you to sell the land in perpetuity, for 'you are but strangers resident with Me' (Leviticus 15:24). Do not make yourself foremost [*ikar*]. . . . 'With Me.' 'When you are Mine, the land will be yours.'"[12] Prioritizing the land and holding onto a belief in one's own power, the midrash says, will only lead to dispossession. But putting God and the divine commandments—including those regarding how to live ethically in our land—first will ultimately grant us permanence there.

Notes

1. All quotations in this paragraph are from Leviticus 25:23.
2. Rashi to Exodus 22:20.
3. Kimchi, Commentary on Psalm 119:19.
4. Babylonian Talmud, *Shabbat* 33a.
5. Dror Greenblum, *From the Bravery of the Spirit to the Sanctification of Power* [in Hebrew] (Raananah: HaUniversitah HaPetuchah, 2016), 13–14 (translation mine).
6. "Palestinian Population 2020," World Population Review, accessed September 25, 2020, https://worldpopulationreview.com/countries/palestine-population.
7. United Nations Charter, Article 2:4, Fourth Geneva Convention Article 47 (Inviolability of rights), Security Council Resolution 242 (land for peace resolution), UN General Assembly Resolution 68/262 (on territorial integrity of Ukraine).
8. Security Council Resolution 478.
9. Fourth Geneva Convention, Section III (Articles 47–78).
10. Isabel Kershner, "In West Bank, 99.7% of Public Land Grants by Israel Go to Settlers," *New York Times*, July 17, 2018 , https://www.nytimes.com/2018/07/17/world/middleeast/west-bank-public-land-israel-palestinians.html; Adam Aloni, *Expel and Exploit: The Israeli Practice of Taking Over Rural Palestinian Land* (B'tselem, 2016), https://www.btselem.org/publications/summaries/201612_expel_and_exploit; Yehezkel Lein, *Land Grab: Israel's Settlement Policy in the West Bank* (B'tselem, 2002), https://www.btselem.org/publications/summaries/200205_land_grab.
11. "Home Demolition as Collective Punishment," B'tselem, November 11, 2017, https://www.btselem.org/punitive_demolitions; Efraim Benmelech, Claude Berrebi, and Esteban F. Klor, "Counter-Suicide-Terrorism: Evidence from Home Demolitions," April 2011, https://scholar.harvard.edu/files/benmelech/files/hd_april_9_2011.pdf.
12. *Sifra, Behar* 4:8.

B'CHUKOTAI—LEVITICUS 26:3–27:34

Fatness Is the Blessing, Not the Curse

RABBI RACHEL GRANT MEYER

THE OPTIONS BEFORE US at the beginning of *Parashat B'chukotai* appear dauntingly unambiguous. "If you follow My laws and faithfully observe My commandments" (Leviticus 26:3), the *parashah* begins, you will receive abundant blessing as outlined in the verses that follow. But, if not, less than a dozen verses later, we learn that horrific curses will befall us: consumption and fever, infertility, domination by our enemies, barren lands, wild beasts, insatiable hunger (Leviticus 26:16–26). These harsh realities raise many questions. Are these the only two outcomes? Does everything live at the pole of blessing or the pole of curse? Moreover, in a postbiblical era, who gets to declare what is deserving of blessing and what is deserving of curse? Can one person's blessing be another's curse and vice versa?

There is no shortage of things that society pathologizes that are not actually so cut and dried. Growing up as a fat child and then a fat young adult, I internalized the impossible-to-miss messages from every corner of my life: My body was a sight of curse rather than blessing. I learned quickly that my physical cursedness centered specifically on my fatness. When my positive attributes were named, they were named in juxtaposition to my fatness. "But you have such pretty eyes," I heard. "But you have such a good sense of humor." When the "but" was not explicitly articulated, it was implied. I grew to understand that my fatness was a curse—presumably caused by a lack of willpower or overindulgence. At best, my fatness could be neutralized by my other positive qualities. At worst, it meant that I was to be shunned, made invisible, and encouraged to change; others were to avoid succumbing to my fate at all costs. Somehow, though, even amid the clear message that my fat body was unacceptable, I continued to question whether there was actually anything wrong with me or whether the real problem lay in spewing hatred toward fat bodies—marginalized bodies—that, like thin bodies, are created in the divine image.

The biblical commentators seem to share my hesitancy to divide the world into a blessing-curse binary. Over time, the commentators shift the way they describe the section of negative consequences enumerated in Leviticus that will befall those who violate God's commandments. In the Mishnah, we learn about the customs for reading these sections of the Torah on public fast days, and the Mishnah uses the word *k'lalot* (curses) to refer to the negative consequences of violating God's commandments.[1] By the time the midrash on this section of Torah is written, the Rabbinic commentators complicate the Mishnah's understanding of these consequences as wholly negative. Unlike the straightforwardness of the Mishnah, the midrash gets into the emotional life of the text to help us understand how these consequences are experienced, which is not entirely bad. *Kohelet Rabbah* recounts the story of Rabbi Levi reciting these verses in front of Rabbi Huna: Rabbi Levi mutters his way through the verses, and Rabbi Huna responds by telling Rabbi Levi to raise his voice, because these verses "are not curses [*k'lalot*], but reproofs [*tocheichah*]."[2] Thus, the midrash is teaching us that while a *k'lalah* (curse) is understood as singularly awful, *tocheichah* (reproof), a corrective for bad behavior, can lead to personal growth—a positive outcome. Centuries later, for some Chasidic teachers, "the admonishments [*tocheichah*] were viewed as curses which embedded in them great blessings . . . [a] notion . . . apparently derived from the *Zohar*."[3] The *Zohar* recounts an exchange between Elijah and Rabbi Shimon in which Elijah offers the idea that even though God uttered curses, God's words were said lovingly. Therefore, though outwardly these words may appear to be curses, they are actually evidence of God's kindness and compassion.[4] Perhaps, given the way that the Rabbis' understanding of these negative consequences evolves over time from something categorically bad to something more complex, we might also understand the consequences of our actions as existing on a spectrum rather than at two opposite poles. Not everything is exclusively good or bad.

Moreover, even as the categories of blessing and curse are complex, determining which end of the spectrum something lies on may also depend on the eye of the beholder. That which originally seems to be a curse may, in fact, be shaded in blessing if we look at it from another perspective. Rabbi Jack Bieler refers to this as "a stark application of the biblical terminology" v'nahafoch hu, "and it was just the opposite," from the Book of Esther (9:1).⁵ One person's curse can, indeed, be another person's blessing; furthermore, blessing can even exist within what we are told is a curse. Not until my adulthood did I find fat activist communities that turned my idea of fatness as a curse on its head. The fat justice movement teaches that we have to be accepting of and loving toward all bodies—including fat bodies. The movement seeks to root out size discrimination in general and anti-fat bias in particular. Dismantling fatphobia means not just destigmatizing fatness but also depathologizing fatness as a physical and moral disease. This means seeing "fatness as a healthy form of bodily diversity," in the words of scholars Michael Orsini and Deborah McPhail.⁶ V'nahafoch hu—and it was just the opposite. The curse is not fatness; the curse is fatphobia.

Yet, as we learned from the ancient Rabbis, blessing and curse are not a binary. Even fatphobia has its blessings. As Rabbi Minna Bromberg, the author of the blog Fat Torah, teaches:

> What I find so deeply compelling about the work of Fat Torah is that the insidious pervasiveness of weight stigma—harming so many different people in so many different ways—also means that the healing and liberation can start from anywhere. Fatphobia is woven so thoroughly into so many corners (and wide open spaces and cul-de-sacs and schools and offices and homes and, yes, houses of worship) of our society that one can pull any single thread to start its unraveling.⁷

It follows from Rabbi Bromberg's words that our mission, then, is not only to defang the curse—where possible, we should actually turn the curse into blessing. In every negative word weaponized against our fat bodies, in every interaction with a medical professional who cannot get past the number on the scale as the cause of every malady, in every way that fatphobia roots itself in white supremacy to "both degrade Black women and discipline white women,"[8] in every space not designed to comfortably accommodate all types of bodies, we can encounter the blessing of speaking out and ridding the world of the limitations placed on those living in fat bodies and the harm caused by our marginalization.

The adverse effects—the curse—of fatphobia, though, cannot be overstated, as fatphobia pervades every corner of the world we live in. According to journalist Michael Hobbes, "[Fat-shaming] is visible and invisible, public and private, hidden and everywhere at the same time." A 2017 survey reported that 89 percent of fat adults experienced bullying from their romantic partners connected to their weight.[9] Research consistently "finds that larger Americans (especially larger women) earn lower salaries and are less likely to be hired and promoted."[10] Fat patients also receive inadequate medical care, as doctors have shorter appointments and show less emotional rapport in the limited time they do spend with fat patients, if they are willing to see them at all. Regardless of what seems to be ailing them, doctors persistently tell fat patients that they need to lose weight to feel better, often before an examination even takes place. Fourteen percent of OB-GYNs polled by the *Sun-Sentinel* in South Florida had barred all new patients weighing over two hundred pounds.[11] The damage these experiences cause is multilayered, holding fat people back from living their fullest lives. One woman interviewed about the impact of her weight on her self-esteem shared that she waited until she was thirty-eight to get a master's degree and fifty-five to get a PhD because she thought "fat people couldn't do [those things]."[12] It took me more than thirty years to feel comfortable wearing a two-piece bathing suit or a pair of shorts, because I internalized the message that those articles of clothing were not meant for fat bodies. The curse of fatphobia ranges from limiting and hurtful to lethal.

The blessing and the curse live in the very word "fat," which I have used throughout this essay but heretofore left unaddressed in and of itself. For so many, "fat" carries an implied negative value judgment. What if, instead, we understood the word to be a celebration of the ingenuity and boundless inventiveness of God's creationary talents? Rather than smiting fat bodies as a cursed mistake to be erased from the earth, may we come to see them as the purposeful creation of a God who loves us in the fullness of who we are, not in spite of it.

NOTES

1. *Mishnah M'gillah* 3:6.
2. *Kohelet Rabbah* 8:3.
3. Haim Talbi, "Turning Curses into Blessings," Bar Ilan University's Parshat Hashavua Study Center, accessed September 4, 2020, https://www.biu.ac.il/JH/Parasha/eng/bechuko/alb.html. The trajectory of this argument—the evolution from understanding the verses from Leviticus 26 as *k'lalot* to understanding them as *tocheichah*—is taken from this essay.
4. *Zohar Chadash, Parashat Ki Tavo*, 3: 9–10.
5. Jack Bieler, "Curses as Blessings," *Contemporary Explorations of Jewish Texts and Thinkers*, May 19, 2017, https://yaakovbieler.wordpress.com/2017/05/19/curses-as-blessings/.
6. Michael Orsini and Deborah McPhail, "Ending Fatphobia Isn't Enough—We Need to Stop Pathologizing Obesity," *Globe and Mail*, August 20, 2020, https://www.theglobeandmail.com/opinion/article-ending-fatphobia-isnt-enough-we-need-to-stop-pathologizing-obesity/.
7. Minna Bromberg, "A Torah That Is Fat," *Fat Torah: Your Path from Narrowness to Freedom*, August 7, 2020, https://www.fattorah.com/post/a-torah-that-is-fat.
8. Sabrina Strings, *Fearing the Black Body: The Racial Origins of Fat Phobia* (New York: New York University Press, 2019), 28, Kindle. This is an excellent resource for learning more about the racialization of the female body, fear of fat Black women, and the racist nature of the contemporary ideal of slenderness.
9. Michael Hobbes, "Everything You Know about Obesity Is Wrong," *Huffington Post*, September 19, 2018, https://highline.huffingtonpost.com/articles/en/everything-you-know-about-obesity-is-wrong/.
10. Hobbes, "Everything You Know about Obesity Is Wrong."
11. Hobbes, "Everything You Know about Obesity Is Wrong."
12. Hobbes, "Everything You Know about Obesity Is Wrong."

NUMBERS

B'MIDBAR—NUMBERS 1:1–4:20

Counting Justly:
Lifting Up Every Head

ILANA KAUFMAN

FROM GRADE FOUR through my senior year in high school, I was required to declare my enrollment status, personal, academic, and life interests, gender, and race to the San Francisco Unified School District. The forms asked me, among other questions, to rank the types of professional roles most appealing to me and whether my race was white, Black, Asian, Latino/Hispanic, or Native American. This exercise allowed for me to be counted and sorted by grade level, hobbies and pursuits, and identity characteristics. Counting and sorting students allowed SFUSD and the school to know how many students were in my class, and it enabled the alignment of interests with academic and intelligence tests scores to help school counselors assign me to the correct programs.

Counting, sorting, weighing, measuring—all can serve important purposes. Seeing an individual, providing them with a sense of purpose, location, and context, has the potential to be a life-affirming experience. Because this is important, holy work, those counting bear serious responsibilities—not only to count, weigh, and measure, but also to understand the limitations of their imagination, their capacity to count, and to make meaning of numbers beyond what the numbers themselves, at first blush, reveal. When counting is done with humility and intentionality, those counted can feel seen, known, and valued; those counting can be left with a sense of awe and wonder about not only what has been counted and sorted but also what can't be seen or known—what is hidden among and beyond what is counted.

Parashat B'midbar begins with God in conversation with Moses in the Tent of Meeting. God tells Moses to take a count, a census, of the Israelites. Count them by name. Count the men, twenty years and older (Numbers 1:2–3). Instruct them as to where to plant their flags, pitch their tents, what role they will have among the Israelite tribes. Through the process of being counted, these men knew their role, that they were part of a family and tribe, of an army, of a people. The opening verse notes that the people are *b'midbar* (בְּמִדְבַּר), "in the wilderness" (Numbers 1:1). By counting and sorting, Moses offers an important experience of identity establishment and personal validation during a time of literal and metaphoric uncertainty.

Each year at SFUSD, as my #2 Ticonderoga pencil made its way down the long, narrow Scantron, I'd proudly declare my graduation year, select three clubs in which to participate, and then happily navigate my way to the section where I'd proclaim my interest in being a lawyer, librarian, carpenter, or priest (the closest multiple-choice option to rabbi at the time). I was excited to be part of my class, to be assigned to a school professional who would value me, and to be part of formal groups with friends and peers. For me, among giant classes and on enormous campuses, San Francisco public schools were not a *midbar*, a wilderness. And the opportunity to be enrolled, enlisted, included gave me a powerful sense of personal value and identity.

Counting in a way that gives and affirms identity, that invites one into a sense of value and purpose, is deep and important work. Unlike my public school experience, which was more focused on crowd control than identity affirmation, in *Parashat B'midbar* God gives Moses careful instructions about how to approach the census: *S'u et rosh kol adat B'nei Yisrael* (שְׂאוּ אֶת־רֹאשׁ כָּל־עֲדַת בְּנֵי־יִשְׂרָאֵל), "Take a census [literally, 'Lift up the heads'] of the whole Israelite company" (Numbers 1:2). Do not begin your count with an estimate. As the counter, do not start your effort with a mindset about your own needs and objectives. Rather, begin your counting by letting each child of Israel know they are individually seen, acknowledged, and that they matter. Each individual is unique; the instruction to "lift the heads of all" is an invitation to know each name, each family, each Israelite. Therein,

God gives the counters the essential tool to ensure each person who is counted knows they matter and to whom they matter. By providing role and context as well as identity, validation, and affirmation, counting is a holy practice that infuses in others a sense of deep value.

This task of counting must be held with care and caution. People are vulnerable, and how we hold our identities is deeply personal.

The scratch of my pencil and the pace of my Scantron bubble-filling would always slow as I made it to the race questions. White, Black, Asian, Latino/Hispanic, or Native American? I would shift my weight in my seat as I evaluated the options. Understanding the question as literal rather than political, an awareness that would come to me at a later age, I was annually presented with racial categories never reflective of the complexity of my reality. Those five categories tried to force me into the narrowness of the mind of the counters. The counters should have made space for the treasures they, their minds, their questions could neither reveal nor see. But at this they failed.

This human flaw—our lack of ability to see, and sometimes to even be curious about, that which is beyond our self—makes real the danger of counting, which by extension imparts value on another. As if doling out value is not precarious enough, counting becomes riskier when intersected with the reality that we are vulnerable as humans; identity is very personal. But this is also what makes counting holy.

To help us understand the depth of responsibilities and opportunities found in the act of counting, the Rabbis provide tools—tools that help reveal blessings that until the moment of counting are unseen and unknown. Through prayer, the Rabbis enable counters to transcend the narrowness of their minds and limited imaginations. Rabbi Yitzchak said, "A blessing is found only in an object that is hidden [samui] from the eye." Similarly, Rabbi Yishmael taught, "A blessing is found only in an object that is not exposed to the eye," and he goes further to remind us that God ensures that we have the capacity for prayer before counting, stating, "The Eternal will command blessing upon you [while measuring new grain] in your barns."[1]

The Rabbis know that counting is careful, important, and sometimes mysterious work. When entering a workspace—be it a barn to measure new grain or, in our days, a Jewish Federation to count a community's population—one should ask God to bless the work of the hands and mind. Once the measuring begins, we pray for blessings to come to the heap of grain or the Jews being counted. The counter's prayer is in vain, however, when the counting comes before the prayer. Doing so encumbers the counted with a narrow identity, an assigned, imposed role before an opportunity for the counted's natural, inherent blessings, treasures, or true self can emerge. Frontloading the blessing demonstrates to God, to the grain, and to the one who is counted that counters know their mind is narrow, their imagination limited. The act of counting, absent the opportunity for hidden blessings to emerge, is in fact a prevention of the blessing itself.

Jews have been counting Jews since Exodus 30:11–12. Hundreds of modern studies in the United States, commissioned by reputable Jewish institutions, claim to count Jews. To understand the number of Jews of Color in the United States, and expecting those studies to reflect the diversity of US Jews, the Jews of Color Initiative commissioned Stanford University to undertake a study in 2018. *Counting Inconsistencies* sought to analyze and draw conclusions from the data found in the twenty-five best-quality Jewish community demographic studies. *Counting Inconsistencies* revealed that an estimated 12 to 15 percent of US Jews are people of color—one million out of the total Jewish population of 7.2 million.[2] The number was reaffirmed by Atlantic 57's report *Unlocking the Future of Jewish Engagement.*[3] What was perhaps even more significant was the finding that the previous studies themselves were deeply flawed. Designed by and for a "mainstream" Jewish community and developed based on their own experiences, views, and perspectives of Jews, the previous research had neglected to imagine a racially diverse Jewish people. As a result, it failed to ask reliable questions about race and ethnicity. We were left with inconsistent data on the racial or ethnic identities of American Jews and systematic undercounting of Jews of Color.

While the results of *Counting Inconsistencies* have validated the existence of one million members of our Jewish community, thereby "lifting up each head" of Jews of Color, the revelation that sizable population was omitted suggests the counters failed to meet their obligation of pre-counting prayers and blessings, squandering the opportunity to "find blessing in that which is hidden from the eye."[4] First they counted, weighed, and measured, forgetting their roles and responsibilities—the full scope and gravity of their work. People are fallible, and prayer alone is insufficient as an antidote to our failings as humans. To make space for the hidden blessings, those who count must be equipped beyond good intentions with not only the tools for counting and the possibilities revealed through prayer, but also research, humility, and the capacity see beyond the self.

They asked: White, Black, Asian, Latino/Hispanic or Native American? But what about the nine million Americans who identify as multiracial? They asked: Ashkenazi, Sephardic? But what about our Mizrachi, Bene Israel, Beta Israel, and Bukharan family? They inquired about being Yiddish or Russian-speaking, never wondering about our speakers of Ladino, Spanish, Mandarin, Quechua, and Diné Bizaad. They asked us to check boxes clarifying our denomination, level of engagement, perspectives on Zionism, and rate of Jewish communal giving, but where does one check the box claiming identity as a *kohenet*, a Hebrew priestess? Not until Jews of Color asked, an act of lifting up our own heads, did any leader assigned the role of counter thoroughly consider our existence.

We hope, we plan, we pray that the counting of the future will hold space for all, with the highest levels of skill, the greatest capacities, and the best intentions. Aware of our own narrow minds and limited imaginations, with the profound understanding of counting as holy work, we pray for God to bless the efforts of our minds and hands, our demographic surveys, our #2 pencils, our Scantron sheets, knowing, appreciating, deeply understanding that "blessing is not found in anything weighed, measured or counted, but only in that which is hidden from the eye."[5]

NOTES

1. Babylonian Talmud, *Taanit* 8b.
2. Ari Y Kelman, Aaron Hahn Tapper, Izabel Fonseca, and Aliya Saperstein, *Counting Inconsistencies: An Analysis of American Jewish Population Studies, with a Focus on Jews of Color* (Stanford, CA: Stanford University, 2019), https://jewsofcolorfieldbuilding.org/wp-content/uploads/2019/05/Counting-Inconsistencies-052119.pdf.
3. Atlantic 57, *Unlocking the Future of Jewish Engagement* (March 2020).
4. Babylonian Talmud, *Bava M'tzia* 42a.
5. Babylonian Talmud, *Taanit* 8b.

The Death Penalty: From Jealous Rage to Dubious Deterrence

Rabbi Ronald Stern

At the center of *Parashat Naso* is the rather bizarre—and, to modern eyes, offensive—ritual of the *sotah*: the woman accused by her husband of adultery. Overcome by a fit of jealousy, the husband turns to the priest and God for truth and justice. The priest follows a prescribed ritual that will discern the woman's guilt or innocence. After the priest utters a strange magical incantation, the woman drinks a vile elixir composed of dirt from the sanctuary floor combined with the ink from a parchment upon which a priest has written the words of his imprecation. If she is guilty, her belly distends and her thighs sag; if innocent, we imagine she will gag a bit and move on (Numbers 5:11–31). This cannot be our Torah! That's not what our people practice or believe! After all, this same Torah teaches: "Let no one be found among you who consigns a son or daughter to the fire, or who is an augur, a soothsayer, a diviner, a sorcerer, one who casts spells, or one who consults ghosts or familiar spirits, or one who inquires of the dead. For anyone who does such things is abhorrent to the Eternal" (Deuteronomy 18:10–12). Is this strange *sotah* ritual not a spell of some kind? Is the priest not attempting to divine the truth from the woman through the ritual? And yet, this particular rite and its apparent magic are not only permitted but prescribed.

Viewed through our contemporary lens, without the larger context of the Torah's historical origins and complex documentary sourcing, it is possible to classify the *sotah* ritual as an archaic, albeit obscure, example of the objectification of women—a ritual that, yet again, forces a woman to submit to humiliation not imposed on men. Even an exploration of the possible rationale behind such an abhorrent practice in no way seeks to affirm it by explaining it away through context. Having said that, the *sotah* ritual could quite possibly be an ancient attempt to limit the extrajudicial femicide arbitrarily practiced in the ancient Near East, a practice that tragically still lingers in the region.[1] Though prohibited by most religions, the indiscriminate killings of women at the hands of overzealous fathers, husbands, and brothers is a result of the marital culture in which women are property of the men in their household. That magic is prescribed despite the unequivocal prohibition of Deuteronomy might point even more directly to the text's attempt to eliminate this violent practice by bringing it under the Temple's management.

At the same time, legally prescribed killing is the Torah's way of ensuring adherence to many precepts a modern reader would hardly feel any inclination to observe, even as others are universally abhorred. Unsurprisingly, one who kills another (man) is put to death. Note that the Torah specifically—and disturbingly—says "man" and *not* "man or woman."[2] Death is prescribed for kidnapping (again, a man), insulting one's parents, bestiality, and—most often— violating the Sabbath.[3] And those examples are taken only from the Book of Exodus!

No ambiguity about gender or consequence occurs when adultery is the crime. The punishment is death for both the wife and her partner. This legislation is found in Leviticus 20:10 and Deuteronomy 22:22. Both offenders are put to death because they have violated the husband's proprietorship over the wife. An illustrative scenario occurs in the story of Pinchas (Numbers 25:1–13). Pinchas follows an Israelite and Midianite into a tent as a plague is raging in the Israelite camp. Using a single thrust of his spear, he pierces both through the belly, indicating that they are *in flagrante delicto*. While it is not at all clear that the offense is an adulterous liaison, it is certainly a prohibited union. Administering capital punishment extrajudicially, Pinchas is commended for faithfulness to God and the law; he is given a pact of eternal peace for his action.

Taking another look at the *sotah* ritual, we may consider the possibility that it is actually a form of ancient satire to critique a common practice.[4] Perhaps the late author, acutely aware of the Deuteronomic prohibition against the use of magic, knows that the ritual is specious at best.[5] By prescribing an ineffective and elsewhere prohibited ritual—which would, on some level, restore the relationship—the source writer is suggesting that retributive femicide arising from spousal jealousy is ridiculous and contrary to God's will. Surely the outcome of drinking the solution in the bowl would be a minor stomachache at worst and easily foreseeable. Thus, the account in Numbers serves a dual purpose: on one hand acknowledging an ancient ritual that ultimately sought to preserve a marriage and a life, while on the other pointing out that such magical rituals, when examined carefully, are contrary to the more contemporary Deuteronomic theology that prohibits magic. Interestingly, the Talmud parses and expands on the administration of the ritual in a way that seeks to reflect the Creator's perfect administration of justice. The effect is to essentially obviate the ritual by establishing such a high bar of prerequisites for witness testimony that the wife's guilt is nearly impossible to affirm.[6] Ultimately, the Talmud's requirement for due process had the effect of making honor killings unfathomable in a Jewish context.

The Talmud's resolution of the *sotah* ritual reveals the Sages' much-discussed propensity to eschew death as tool for the human administration of justice. This mirrors the Torah's own recognition of the potential for overreaching in the oft-cited passage "A person shall be put to death only on the testimony of two or more witnesses" (Deuteronomy 17:6). Our Rabbis sought to mitigate the Torah's relatively wide range of capital violations, famously declaring, "All violators of capital offenses can only be convicted based on witnesses who warned them before the act and told him that it was a death penalty offense."[7] The Talmud continues by delineating the many ways that one might not hear the warning and thus be exempt from prosecution. Notably, the Jerusalem Talmud declares that were Sages present when Pinchas perpetrated his wanton act of homicide, he would have been excommunicated had not God intervened.[8]

Jewish tradition's ambivalence is reflected in the United States as well. Our country's on-again, off-again, on-again relationship with the death penalty displays a core discomfort. The truth is that in its application in the United States, there are many reasons why the death penalty is both ineffective and counterproductive. Over the forty-four years since the death penalty has been reinstated in the United States, 1,516 people have been put to death by state governments.[9] This number pales in comparison to the number of homicides in that period, with 16,214 reported in 2018 alone.[10] Arguments that it serves as a deterrent are undermined by the evidence that states with the death penalty have a consistently higher murder rate than do states without it.[11]

Does it serve justice? To the contrary, the data suggests that Blacks are far more likely to be charged with capital murder in all circumstances—and, should the victim be white, the likelihood of a capital charge increases significantly.[12] That significant numbers of death row inmates have been exonerated upon review of their cases through the efforts of justice-seeking experts indicates that the state may execute the innocent.[13] Could we stomach an expanded use of the death penalty, bringing with it the likelihood of many more innocent being put to death as a result of the proven failure of our justice system to protect the falsely accused?

Though the Torah prescribes stoning or impaling on a stake as a means of execution, we moderns would judge those methods to be inhumane. We live under the illusion that we have achieved progress, yet current mechanisms are equally vile. Death by lethal injection is "preferred" because it is less gruesome for the witnesses than other methods. Ideally, the victim just appears to "go to sleep." However, lethal injections rarely go smoothly, as medical personnel are seldom the ones to administer the dose—doing so would clearly violate their principles and is discouraged by the American Board of Anesthesiologists.[14] Reports of victims writhing in pain or requiring secondary applications of the toxic chemicals reveal the dubiousness of claims of its humanity.[15] Death by the electric chair is equally heinous and is certainly visually jarring, possibly causing initial suffering and often causes severe burns to the victim.[16]

Tragically, it is difficult to trace a trajectory of human progress from the days of death by stoning to methods used today. Nor can we maintain that we have achieved more perfect justice, given the failures of our justice system referenced above. So, left with centuries of failure, we have reached a time for a reckoning with this most imperfect application of human justice. Now, we must bring humanitarian considerations to bear on the ambiguous yet troubling legacy we have inherited. Capital punishment in the United States today is administered no more justly than the *sotah* ritual. Much as women were singled out for punishment for adultery, people of color and the poor face discrimination in the application of the death penalty. If the trajectory of resistance to the indiscriminate use of this vile practice reflected in Rabbinic writings is our inheritance, the flaws of our current society are our possession. We must endeavor to fashion a world in which one human being's death at the hands of another is not only a rare crime, but also abhorred by individuals and the state in the pursuit of justice.

NOTES

1. For example, consider Laws #129–133 of the Code of Hammurabi here: https://en.wikisource.org/wiki/The_Code_of_Hammurabi_(Harper_translation). For honor killings today, see, for example, Bijan Pirnia, Fariborz Pirnia, and Kambiz Pirnia, "Honour Killings and Violence against Women in Iran during the COVID-19 Pandemic," *Lancet Psychiatry* 7, no. 10 (2020): e60, https://www.ncbi.nlm.nih.gov/pmc/articles/PMC7494269/.
2. To those who say that the term "man" implies a man or a woman, the text itself rejects that assumption. When the Torah means woman, it explicitly says so. When it refers to both genders, it says "man or woman."
3. Exodus 21:14–17, 18; 31:14–15; 35:2.
4. Satire is not unknown in the Torah. The account of Balaam in Numbers 22 is the most familiar. Esther is also a form of farcical satire.
5. "Late" in this context indicates the chronology of when the text was incorporated into the final version of the Torah—so in this case, among the last to be redacted. For a brief exploration of the assumptions used for dating the writing of books of the Torah, see Jeffrey Tigay, "Preserving Multiple

Opinions," TheTorah.com, 2014, https://thetorah.com/article/preserving-multiple-opinions.

6. Jacob Neusner, "Introduction to Tractate Sotah," in *The Babylonian Talmud: A Translation and Commentary* (Peabody, MA: Hendrickson, 2011).

7. *Tosefta Sanhedrin* 11:1–2; translation and insight from David Bernat, "Pinchas' Extrajudicial Execution of Zimri and Cozbi," TheTorah.com, 2018, https://thetorah.com/article/pinchas-extrajudicial-execution-of-zimri-and-cozbi.

8. Jerusalem Talmud, *Sanhedrin* 9:7.

9. CNN Editorial Research, "Death Penalty Fast Facts," CNN, August 4, 2020, www.cnn.com/2013/07/19/us/death-penalty-fast-facts/index.html.

10. "Total Number of Homicides in the United States in 2019 by State" and "Murders in the U.S. by State 2019," Statista, accessed November 18, 2020, https://www.statista.com/statistics/195331/number-of-murders-in-the-us-by-state/.

11. "The Death Penalty and Deterrence," Amnesty International, May 18, 2017, https://www.amnestyusa.org/issues/death-penalty/death-penalty-facts/the-death-penalty-and-deterrence/.

12. "Race and the Death Penalty by the Numbers," Death Penalty Information Center, accessed November 18, 2020, https://deathpenaltyinfo.org/policy-issues/race/race-and-the-death-penalty-by-the-numbers.

13. "About the Innocence Project," Innocence Project, August 20, 2020, https://innocenceproject.org/about/.

14. Rob Stein, "Group to Censure Physicians Who Play Role in Lethal Injections," *Washington Post*, May 2, 2010, https://www.washingtonpost.com/wp-dyn/content/article/2010/05/01/AR2010050103190.html; Noah Caldwell, Ailsa Chang, and Jolie Myers, "Gasping for Air: Autopsies Reveal Troubling Effects of Lethal Injection," NPR, September 21, 2020, https://www.npr.org/2020/09/21/793177589/gasping-for-air-autopsies-reveal-troubling-effects-of-lethal-injection.

15. Rick Rojas, "Why This Inmate Chose the Electric Chair Over Lethal Injection," *New York Times*, February 19, 2020, https://www.nytimes.com/2020/02/19/us/electric-chair-tennessee.html.

16. Michael A. Owens, "Robert Gleason Got Death the Way He Wanted It," *Bristol Herald Courier*, September 19, 2019, https://heraldcourier.com/news/robert-gleason-got-death-the-way-he-wanted-it/article_539a0bea-602d-11e2-9e30-001a4bcf6878.html.

B'HAALOT'CHA—NUMBERS 8:1–12:16

Shedding Light on Solidarity: A Candle Loses Nothing by Lighting Another Candle

Imani Romney-Rosa Chapman
and Rabbi Ellen Lippmann

HOW DO WE SHED LIGHT on an old system so we can see anew the devastation it caused? How do we raise that light high enough to allow a wide view, the "aha" moment that can lead to change? *B'haalot'cha.* Raising up the lamps. Our *parashah* shows us a way to shine a light on the challenges and opportunities of being in community and cocreating a new way of life.

We write in the fall of 2020/5781, as our society is increasingly fractured. The COVID-19 pandemic continues, neighbors turn against neighbors, communities are at odds with one another, and the lethal combination of white nationalism and militarized police poses a continuing danger to Black people across the country; meanwhile, confused white Americans, including white Jews, wonder how to move beyond fear and empathy to stand in solidarity. Writing and learning about solidarity in this time seems necessary. We recognize that readers of this commentary will have different reasons for learning about solidarity, be they straight folk who need to learn how to stand in solidarity with queer folk, white Jews who need to learn how to stand in solidarity with Jews of Color, or white Americans who need to learn how to stand in solidarity with Black and Brown Americans. We write about solidarity from the perspective of a white Jew and an Afrolatina Jew confronting the current horrors of

American racism. We are grateful to have the guidance of *B'haalot'cha*.

B'haalot'cha begins after the *Mishkan* (Tabernacle), the central gathering place for the people, the locus of divine connection, is physically complete. Yet it is not truly complete until the lights are turned on. In the previous *parashah*, we read, "On the day that Moses finished setting up the Tabernacle, he anointed and consecrated it and all its furnishings, as well as the altar and its utensils" (Numbers 7:1). It seemed the *Mishkan* was finished. But as we read at the beginning of our *parashah*, "The Eternal One spoke to Moses, saying: Speak to Aaron and say to him, 'When you mount the lamps, let the seven lamps give light at the front of the lampstand.' Aaron did so; he mounted the lamps at the front of the lampstand, as the Eternal had commanded Moses" (Numbers 8:1–3).

We so often think a matter is settled, yet when we shine a light on it again, we see that much remains to be done. The *Mishkan* is finished and consecrated, and tribal offerings have been made. However, God realizes that more light is needed—more awareness must be aroused to enable the people to gather with their leaders and the Divine. New light brings change right away. In our *parashah*, a new situation arises, requiring God to make a new ruling, creating a new reality. Pesach Sheini, a second Passover, the possibility of celebrating Pesach a month after its set date, is established to account for limited circumstances that may prevent one from observing at the usual time. God grants us not only the specific opportunity of Pesach Sheini, but also the broader possibility of second chances.

When we meet and work with people who experience the world in a radically different way than we do, or when we read or learn about them from afar, we will likely misunderstand, hurt, or harm one another. A second chance is a generous blessing. Yet many commentators note that the second chance comes with strict guidelines and boundaries.[1] Torah allows for Pesach Sheini but not *sh'lishi or r'vi-i*—a third or fourth Pesach. The limited allowance for Pesach Sheini teaches that not all failures deserve a second chance. You can't just blow off Pesach in Nisan and then celebrate it a month later. For us, too, there are no third, fourth, or fifth chances if we do not learn the lesson a second time. We have to put in the work and be more disciplined as we collectively seek greater equity and access for all.

To do that, we must stand in solidarity with each other, providing for everyone's unmet needs. God is our teacher. Several commentators, noting that the command to lift the lights comes immediately after an extensive passage about the consecration of the *Mishkan*, say that Aaron has been in despair at seeing his tribe of Levi not included in those rituals. God then prepares an additional ritual, lifting the lights, as if a kind of reparation to repair that omission.[2] It is a daily gift; fifteenth-century Moroccan commentator Or HaChayim says, "God wanted Aaron to know that the task of taking the candlestick apart daily . . . and then reassembling [it] constituted a daily inaugural."[3]

Before being given this gift, how must Aaron have felt to be unseen, overlooked, even marginalized, as the community created and carried out ritual together? What if the Levites had never been invited to bring their full gifts and hearts to the collective? In order to repair the hurt, God had to see Aaron's pain and recognize it. That re-cognition—"the mental action or process of" once again "acquiring knowledge and understanding through thought, experience, and the senses"[4]—is the beginning of moving into solidarity. In other words, lift the lights, see more clearly.

What else is required to be in solidarity with others? How does solidarity begin?

Awareness

We need to arrive at what the Rambam (Moses Maimonides) calls *hit'or'rut*, "awakening"—or, as many have said in recent years, "wokeness." The Rambam seems to have meant something like what we call discernment, the process of arriving at a best self, a clear moment of divine connection, an expanded awareness. The path toward that awakening is not easy, then or now. At every step, we must remember that our actions have consequences. Often, we need help. Rashi suggests that the lifting of the lights in our portion is actually the lifting of the priest doing the lighting and that the priest stood on some kind of stool or small ladder to lift the lights to their proper place.[5] Solidarity might mean something as seemingly minor as bringing the ladder. But it can take years for a person unaccustomed to noticing to realize that a ladder is needed and that she is the person who could find and bring it. We can't just wait to be asked or ask generally, "How can I help?" Look around, see when a small ladder, an outstretched hand, could make a difference, and bring that to where it is needed.

Listening

After we become aware, we do not broadcast how aware we now are. Instead, we need to get quiet and begin to listen and read to understand, releasing our sense of knowing, our skills for debating, and our intellectualizing. We need to attend to the aperture of the heart and practice cultural humility[6]—a commitment to self-critique, redress of power imbalances, and mutual care.

Recognition

We must recognize that the humanity of us all is diminished by injustice. In the words of Aboriginal leader Lila Watson, "If you have come here to help me you are wasting your time, but if you have come because your liberation is bound up with mine, then let us work together."[7]

Letting Go of Shame

We need to let go of shame—the shame that we didn't know sooner, that we are complicit, that we don't know how to take the next step forward. We also need to let go of shaming that stems from what social-change facilitator Gibrán Rivera calls "woke fundamentalism."[8] As scholar Brene Brown said, "Shame is not an effective social justice tool. Shame is a tool of oppression."[9] We have all made missteps and deserve to be called into the collective consciousness. Let us not be paralyzed by our shame. Learn from mistakes and keep going.

Feeling

While we need to move forward, we also should not simply rush to "do." We do more harm when our rush to fix means we avoid feeling the pain, grief, and anger of injustice and our role in it. We need to *feel* so that we can create a thoughtful approach to shifting power. We must look to community leaders to see what is needed and which of our own skills and resources could be useful. We must learn to take leadership from those whose lives are most immediately impacted by the injustice. This can be a challenge, since many of us have been socialized to "act for and not with" populations that have been sub-jugated. There is a difference between "social action" and "social justice."

Learning

While we can never be fully competent in the culture of another, especially keeping in mind that cultures shift, we can continue to learn and be curious, recognizing that directly affected people are the experts. Our job is to become knowledgeable but not expert in their experience, to become more cognizant of contributing factors from *our* cultural heritage, and to lend labor and power to the endeavor.

Persisting

We needn't be awestruck by the missteps we will inevitably make once we commit to action. Our goal is to avoid repeating them or enabling others to repeat them. We are reminded that *cheit*, which is often translated as "sin," is a term borrowed from archery, meaning, "to miss the mark." We do not give up when we miss the mark. Rather, we try again. Perfectionism, like shame, will keep us immobilized if we let it. By doing with our hands by way of our hearts as well as our minds, we begin to undo what has been done to all of us. We learn to ask for, and not demand, a second chance. When our knowledge, skill set, analysis, or awareness keeps us from showing up in community the way we both want and need to, we learn from this *parashah* that second chances are possible. That *is* a gift, but not one we can abuse. We must learn from our mistakes.

Finding Common Interest

Solidarity extends beyond simple empathy, which means "feeling with." Solidarity emerges from common interest. In the fight for justice, this interest can be grounded in *sh-l-m* (ם-ל-שׁ), the *shoresh*

(Hebrew root) that brings us to both *shalom* (שָׁלוֹם), "peace," and *shaleim* (שָׁלֵם), "wholeness," which come through the restoration of human dignity for us all. Many of us become overwhelmed by the learning process of simply recognizing injustice and are fatigued before approaching the stage of undoing injustice. We need the staying power—garnered from relationships, rest, and ritual—that keeps us from turning on one another and keeps us moving together.

Amplification
Ella Baker, the "brilliant, Black hero of the civil rights movement, was known for inspiring and guiding emerging leaders."[10] One aspect of solidarity is to amplify the work, the writing, the teaching of leaders from the community with which we stand. We can do this by sharing their voices on our online platforms, inviting someone with a(nother) minoritized identity to be an additional speaker when we are invited, footnoting another's work, connecting someone to a publisher, a school, a conference. Express pride in them. Then move back.

Like the ancient Rabbis, we end with a *nechemta*, a word of comfort or hope. We are taught in *B'haalot'cha*: God says to Moses, "Have two silver trumpets made; make them of hammered work. They shall serve you to summon the community and to set the divisions in motion" (Numbers 10:2). We yearn for a community united enough to gather and move forward together. The sixteenth-century Italian commentator Sforno tells us that the people were to be called by the trumpets to assemble before the Sovereign, that is, God.[11] We pray now to stand with one another in a way that moves us to God, or however we name our highest aspirations, and enables us to arrive at a place of true equity and justice.

Notes

1. For example, Chizkuni, Rabbi Hezekiah ben Manoah, the thirteenth-century French commentator, notes, "The person the Torah has in mind here is the one who reasons that they can always make up for their failure to observe the Passover in Nisan, by observing it in Iyar."

2. For example, Rashi, Rav Shlomo Yitzchak, the eleventh-century French commentator, explains, "Because when Aaron saw the dedication offerings of the princes, he felt distressed because neither he nor his tribe was with them in the dedication, whereupon the Holy One, blessed be God, said to him, 'By your life! Your part is of greater importance than theirs, for you will kindle and set in order the lamps.'"

3. Chayim ibn Attar or Chayim ben Moshe ibn Attar, also known as the Or HaChayim, quotes *Midrash Tanchuma* saying that "God told him that he, Aaron, would light the candlestick in the sanctuary on a daily basis and would prepare the oil and wicks both mornings and evenings." After a lengthy exploration of the construction of the lamp, Or HaChayim concludes that "God wanted Aaron to know that the task of taking the candlestick apart daily when he would clean the lamps and then reassemble them constituted a daily inaugural. In effect, Aaron put the candlestick together every single day. Every time he would light the candlestick would be like inaugurating the candlestick anew."

4. "What Is Cognition?," Cambridge Cognition, August 19, 2015, https://www.cambridgecognition.com/blog/entry/what-is-cognition#:~:text=The%20Basics,%2C%20experience%2C%20and%20the%20senses.&text=It%20is%20in%20essence%2C%20the,decisions%20and%20produce%2-0appropriate%20responses.

5. Rashi offers two thoughts on the "lifting" of the lights, both of interest; the second involves the step or small ladder: "*B'haalot'cha*, lit., WHEN YOU MAKE [THE LIGHTS] RISE — Because the flame rises upward (*olah*), an expression (*b'haalot'cha*) denoting 'ascending' is used of kindling them (the lights), implying that one must kindle them until the light ascends on its own (Babylonian Talmud, *Shabbat* 21a). — Furthermore, our Rabbis derived from here (from the expression *b'haalot'cha*) that there was a step in front of the candelabrum upon which the priest stood while preparing the lights (*Sifrei Bamidbar* 59). Other commentators suggest there was a stone with a step in it, or even more than one step. So is it the light that rises or the lighter of the lights?

6. M. Tervalon and J. Murray-Garcia, "Cultural Humility vs. Cultural Competence: A Critical Distinction in Defining Physician Training Outcomes in Multicultural Education," *Journal of Healthcare for the Poor and Underserved* 9, no. 2 (May 1998): 117–25, https://pubmed.ncbi.nlm.nih.gov/10073197/.

7. "Lilla Watson Quotes," Goodreads, 2020, https://www.goodreads.com/author/quotes/7166413.Lilla_Watson.

8. Terry Patten, "White Supremacy, Woke Fundamentalism, and Evolutionary, Accountability: A Conversation with Gilbran Rivera," *A New Republic of the Heart*, July 17, 2020, https://newrepublicoftheheart.org/podcast/038-gibrn-rivera-white-supremacy-woke-fundamentalism-and-evolutionary-allyship/.

9. Brené Brown, "Brené on Shame and Accountability," *Unlocking Us*, July 1, 2020, https://brenebrown.com/podcast/brene-on-shame-and-accountability/.

10. "About Us," Ella Baker Center for Human Rights, accessed January 7, 2021, https://ellabakercenter.org/about/about-us.

11. Obadiah ben Jacob Sforno comments on the uses of the trumpets to gather the people: *"V'hayu l'cha l'mikra ha-eidah* (וְהָיוּ לְךָ לְמִקְרָא הָעֵדָה), to assemble the people or their leaders in front of the Tabernacle. God wanted that the trumpets be used to render honor to the king."

B'HAALOT'CHA—NUMBERS 8:1–12:16

Scarcity, Abundance, and the Imagined Past

Rabbi Rachel Kahn-Troster

STORYTELLING IS ESSENTIAL to the fight for justice. A good narrative creates a sense of community, enabling us to build a shared platform of values and demands. But almost as essential as the "we" is the "what," the shared vision of what is possible. We tell a story that enables as many of us as possible to be sustained, even those called to sacrifice in order to achieve a greater good. But our narratives of inclusion must compete with counter-narratives of exclusion, scarcity, and fear. How do we respond? *Parashat B'haalot'cha* contains both warnings and options for living in a contested space where images of a rosier past threaten to undo the work of the present.

Being in the desert for years on end cannot have been easy, and as time wore on, the miseries of life in Egypt receded in favor of fiction. Toward the end of *Parashat B'haalot'cha*, we read one of many episodes when the Israelites rebel against God during their desert wanderings. Their frustration is understandable, born of the endless sand, heat, and exhaustion. God, who never has much patience for their complaining, hits the Israelites with a plague, which only ends because Moses intercedes on their behalf. In response to this punishment, the Israelites once again lose their patience and demand a return to Egypt. Canaan might be the promised land of the future, but the Israelites demand a return to a promised land of the past, a vision of Egypt that is focused on imagined luxury: "The riffraff in their midst felt a gluttonous craving; and then the Israelites wept and said, 'If only we had meat to eat! We remember the fish that we used to eat free in Egypt, the cucumbers, melons, the leeks, the onions, and the garlic. Now our gullets are shriveled. There is nothing at all! Nothing but this manna to look to!'" (Numbers 11:4–6).

Two elements of this complaint immediately stand out. The first is the potential undercurrent of xenophobia. This initial rejection is blamed in the Torah on "riffraff"—generally understood to be non-Israelites who followed the Israelites in their journey to freedom.[1] The riffraff's cravings cause an emotional dam to break for the Israelites, who pour out their resentments and concerns. The second element is the rejection of manna as a sustaining force. While life in the desert was difficult, so was life in Egypt; slaves would not necessarily have had easy access to the rich foods they are now yearning for. In the desert, God has provided them with a miracle food, in seemingly endless supply: "Now the manna was like coriander seed, and in color it was like bdellium. The people would go about and gather it, grind it between millstones or pound it in a mortar, boil it in a pot, and make it into cakes. It tasted like rich cream. When the dew fell on the camp at night, the manna would fall upon it" (Numbers 11:7–9).

When I was younger, I remember my teachers explaining that manna would taste like whatever food you wanted. Even if that is a midrash,[2] it seems clear that manna is not merely basic desert sustenance but a food of freedom. The Israelite rejection of this miracle is therefore a rejection of God and an insistence that following God toward redemption has made their lives ultimately poorer. Because of their despair, they cannot see reality for what it is.

Mobilizing around scarcity is a powerful force in American politics—for example, in the enunciation of the slogan "Make America Great Again" by white people of means who were actually fundamentally better off than they had been years before. They had prospered in the years after the Great Recession. What they were afraid of, a fear ultimately based in racism, was that those who were different from them would share in that prosperity. Americans' rejection of social welfare programs is often linked to concern that people whom they deem undeserving—usually immigrants, people of a different racial background, or those of a lower socioeconomic class—will benefit.

This scarcity narrative can also be seen when we claim that we have no money as a nation for spending on health care or education, but spend so much on the military. Pointing out that abundance exists yet is obscured by the way it's allocated is particularly difficult when people's perception of safety is invoked: trading a bigger military for better health care makes no sense in a world where we insist that aggression and might are primary values. A rejection of this mentality can be seen both in the platform of the Poor People's Campaign, which asks us to divest from the military and invest at home,[3] and in the movement to defund the police in favor of increased funding for social services and community development. It's easier to see curses than blessings, to wallow in nostalgia for a real or imagined past rather than try to reckon with the reality of the present, because that reckoning requires reprioritizing, making choices, and changing the narrative about what is possible.

At this juncture, the *parashah* explores the repercussions both of widening the "we" and of embracing a politics of fear. The tensions around the impact of this kind of choice resonate with me when I think about our contemporary political situation, which feels like a struggle between hope in the potential for change and the anxiety that change will create chaos or make what is already difficult worse. The first path in the *parashah* is obviously more positive. What does Moses do when faced with a nation that can only wallow in the past rather than build a shared sense of what is possible in the present? Understandably, he tries to opt out, reminding God that he never volunteered for the mission and is overwhelmed by the demands of the job (Numbers 11:10–15). God's response is to build Moses a better command structure, bringing the seventy tribal elders into more direct communication with God. God's stated reasoning is to ensure that Moses will no longer be isolated, bearing the burden of leadership alone (Numbers 11:16–17). By increasing entry points for the people's access to Moses, God is also rebuilding a shared sense of "we" in the relationship between the Israelites and the Divine. God is reinvesting them in the relationship so that they will be reinvested in the journey. The Promised Land cannot be reached if it can be seen and understood only by Moses, by a solitary charismatic figure. Moses immediately realizes the importance of this widening of leadership when two additional Israelites who are not among the chosen seventy also begin to speak the words of God in ecstasy (Numbers 11:26–28). He wonders, "Would that all the Eternal's people were prophets, that the Eternal put [the divine] spirit upon them!" (Numbers 11:29). If all of the people were invested in God's word, then harmony would be so much more possible.

But the second path, happening simultaneously, is darker. Even as God widens the circle of those sharing the direct line to divine wisdom, God ominously tells Moses to prepare the people for more meat than they can imagine, for days on end, until their imagined state of luxury becomes a curse: "You shall eat not one day, not two, not even five days or ten or twenty, but a whole month, until it comes out of your nostrils and becomes loathsome to you. For you have rejected the Eternal who is among you, by whining before [God] and saying, 'Oh, why did we ever leave Egypt!'" (Numbers 11:19–20). Moses meekly asks whether God's threat is even possible given the sheer number of Israelites involved, and God responds in words that boil down to "Is there anything I can't do?" (Numbers 11:21–23). This is more than just a statement of divine ego or power. By disparaging the blessing of manna as impoverishment—crying about alleged scarcity in an environment where literally anything was possible thanks to God—the Israelites have turned the present into a nightmare they claim to be living. And the empty blessing truly becomes a curse: not only do they eat until they are sick, but they are then struck by plague again (Numbers 11:32–33).

Willfully confusing abundance with scarcity has dire and deadly consequences, and when we are only out for ourselves—when we narrow, who should benefit or our sense of shared responsibility—these consequences only magnify. Justice activists must open our eyes to how narratives of scarcity inhibit the creation of both a bigger tent—a new community where the contributions of all are valued—and a realistic picture of the world as it is so all can benefit. This revisioning of reality has to be the antidote to a political rhetoric of scarcity and fear, a rhetoric that will persist no matter who is in government. *B'haalot'cha* warns us of the consequences of nostalgia for a nonexistent past, of literally hungering for illusions rather than seeing God's blessings in the world we inhabit. Those blessings may diverge from our dreams or they may be all that we have hoped; either way, by seeing them for what they are rather than wishing to replace them with the imagined blessings of the past, we can grapple with the challenges we face, journeying together toward a shared understanding of a collective promised land.

Notes

1. Rashi to Numbers 11:4.
2. See, for example, *Midrash Tanchuma Buber, B'shalach* 22:1.
3. "About the Poor People's Campaign: A National Call for Moral Revival," Poor People's Campaign, accessed January 7, 2021, https://www. poorpeoplescampaign.org/about/.

SH'LACH L'CHA—NUMBERS 13:1–15:41

The Rights and Duties of Citizenship

RABBI SETH M. LIMMER

There shall be one law for you and for the resident stranger; it shall be a law for all time throughout the ages. You and the stranger shall be alike before the Eternal; the same ritual [*torah*, תּוֹרָה] and the same rule shall apply to you and to the stranger who resides among you.
—*Numbers 15:15–16*

For the citizen among the Israelites and for the stranger who resides among them—you shall have one ritual [*torah*, תּוֹרָה].
—*Numbers 15:29*

ONE FUNDAMENTAL TRUTH of *Parashat Sh'lach L'cha* is that the stranger and the citizen should be bound by the same law. From a social perspective, we learn that polities have long been composed of citizens and strangers, of "insiders" and "outsiders." From a social justice perspective, we learn that Judaism demands equity before the law *even*, or perhaps *especially*, for those members of any nation who are not official citizens. In order for us to understand the implications of this principle for immigrants and resident aliens, we must first understand the related rights and duties of the citizen.

Numbers 15 intertwines the fates of citizens and strangers. The Hebrew here translated as "stranger," *ger* (גֵּר), literally means "sojourner," one not at home among a land's citizens and thus not necessarily protected by its practices. As Jacob Milgrom explains, the Hebrew *ger* specifies "a man [*sic*] of another tribe or district who, coming to sojourn in a place where he was not strengthened by the presence of his own kin, put himself under the protection of a clan or of a powerful chief."[1] A stranger is thus reliant upon citizens for certain safeguards. By contrast, an *ezrach* (אֶזְרָח), or "citizen," is a native member of a society, born into its protections and prohibitions.[2] Those are the protections Numbers 15 commands the citizen to extend to the stranger. But before we can see what this means for the stranger, we need to examine what it means to be a citizen.

The Israelites initially become a people, a political entity, in the Book of Exodus. That drama of redemption teaches us a great deal about citizenship from a biblical perspective. On the one hand, the sweeping narrative of the Exodus is the liberation from Egyptian oppression; on the other hand, the great epic teaches how the Jewish people go from being slaves (*avadim*) to Pharaoh and instead became servants (*avadim*, the same word!) of the Eternal. To be redeemed is to be restored to one's proper place: Jews are not freed from Egypt to live a libertine life doing whatever they see fit; Jews are redeemed from Egypt and brought to Mount Sinai so that they might freely bind themselves to Torah. Exodus explains that being a part of the Jewish body politic combines two kind of freedoms: "freedom from" the oppression and suffering of Egypt, and "freedom to" follow the laws of Torah as full participants in the covenant of the Jewish people. The meaning of the redemption from Egypt is that the Jewish people are now freed *from* outside interference so that they might freely choose *to* follow Torah.

In modern times, citizenship has also been understood as a contrasting set of "freedoms from" and "freedoms to." President Franklin D. Roosevelt, in his 1941 State of the Union Address, famously spoke of the "four freedoms" essential in human life: freedom *to* express ourselves; freedom *to* worship in our preferred manner; freedom *from* want; and freedom *from* fear.[3] For FDR, "freedom to" is about individual liberty, while "freedom from" is about societal responsibility. The president argues there are arenas in which individual choices should be the sole determinant in guiding personal practices: speech and worship. Of equal importance, there are areas where larger society has a role to play: protecting and nurturing the larger whole. Paradoxically, in order to ensure these important "freedoms from," FDR understood that there would need to be limits placed on individual freedom: he explicitly called for economic and military restraints to bring about an end to want and fear, respectively. Roosevelt illustrates the paradox that the best way to protect freedom is sometimes to curtail freedom.

Judaism has long understood that to be a member of our community is first to be free and then to be as entitled to rights as one is enjoined by responsibilities. This is clear from the sequence in Leviticus, where our liberation from Egypt is the premise enabling us to follow Torah's laws: "I the Eternal am your God who freed you from the land of Egypt. You shall faithfully observe all My laws and all My rules" (Leviticus 19:36–37). The Talmud expands upon this principle in teaching that only the free are able to observe the commandments, since a person cannot serve more than one master.[4] Furthermore, Jewish law is structured in such a fashion that, in dedicating one's life *freely* to divine service, a Jew assumes both opportunities and restrictions. The Rabbis categorized the 613 mitzvot as "positive" commandments as to what we *should* do and "negative" commandments that delimit our behaviors.[5] The Sages of the Talmud understood that to be truly free is to be limited: there are 365 negative commandments proscribing personal behavior, in contrast to only 248 that provide possibilities for exercising our freedom. Jewish law knows that human behavior needs at times to be limited—we cannot murder, steal, and much more—in order to protect the possessions and lives of others.

To be a citizen is to balance one's freedoms in counterweight to society's needs. In Judaism, the needs of the whole take precedence over the rights of the individual. In today's United States, this very question is up for debate. On the one side are those of libertarian bent, who advocate for the doctrine of personal responsibility. They contend the purpose of America is to guarantee its citizens every "freedom to" without encumbering their behaviors with limiting laws. Along these lines, Dennis Prager explains that America was founded on the ideal "You rise or fall on your achievement or your failure."[6]

Against this opinion are those who argue for social responsibility, the idea that the nation was established not just to be rid of English tyranny, but also to ensure the "life, liberty and pursuit of happiness" of every citizen. In this camp, Ibram X. Kendi teaches that society should be structured to preference communal needs—Rooseveltian freedoms from want—over personal liberty: "The individual should be restricted from harming the community. The individual should be free to aid the community."[7] Jewish tradition, which contains far more positive than negative commandments, is clearly on this latter side, demanding social responsibility. Judaism eschews the extreme doctrine of "personal responsibility" or any assertion that individual liberty is the highest value in our world. The heritage that teaches "All Israel is intertwined, each with the other" was committed to social responsibility for millennia before that phrase even existed.[8]

To be a citizen in Jewish law is to be a member of society, bound by laws that serve the purpose of both personal growth and societal success. To be a citizen is to be committed to the existence and evolution of the entire populace, even at the expense of self-restraint. The rights of citizenship are to live freely in a society that allows every member to fulfill their divine potential; the responsibilities of citizenship are to make the necessary personal sacrifices that grant to every other member of society that same right of fulfilling the most sacred that lies within every human being. Our biblical obligations are easily translatable into modern terms: our borders should receive refugees and those seeking asylum; immigrants should not only contribute to our economic system but also benefit from our social safety net; immigrants, even before they become (or if they never become!) naturalized citizens, should feel secure in their status and not fear deportation; our national discourse should, like our Bible, speak of the vital role the stranger plays in strengthening our communities.

Instead, the first two decades of the twenty-first century have demonstrated that the United States has failed to uphold our Jewish ideal of seeing to the needs of the stranger. We have made it nearly impossible for those fleeing tyranny and terror to take asylum in America.[9] We have reduced, and in some cases eliminated, regulations allowing refugees to build new lives on our shores.[10] We tax the temporary noncitizen workforce—deemed "essential" to our economy during the COVID-19 pandemic—but do not provide legal measures for their health care or social security.[11] We encouraged young people who only know America as their home, our "Dreamers," to come out of the shadows and participate fully in our society, only to pull the rug out from under them and work exhaustively toward their deportation.[12] Like the ugliest chauvinists throughout history, too many American leaders demonize the immigrant: they blame the stranger for society's failures in place of extending to them all of our nation's protections.[13] The US immigration policy of late has been one of gross social injustice.

The Book of Numbers and parallel passages throughout the Torah compel us to treat every human being in the same fashion, here expressed through the language of "the stranger the same as the citizen."[14] In our American context—as well as that of our Israeli family—this means those of us who are citizens need to extend to immigrants, foreign nationals, and all other noncitizens the same system of rights and responsibilities we enjoy. Since there is to be one Torah for citizen and stranger, we uphold a Jewish obligation to extend to noncitizens freedom from want and harm, the privileges citizens enjoy. The heritage that taught the world that every human being is created in the divine image likewise advocates that every human being—regardless of place of origin or current circumstances of living—deserves equal protection under the law.

NOTES

1. Jacob Milgrom, *JPS Torah Commentary: Numbers* (Philadelphia: Jewish Publication Society, 1996), ad loc. It should be pointed out that, by the Rabbinic period, the term *ger* had taken on a new dimension. Extending the notion of one not born to a place (or tribe) yet taking up status within that society, *ger* came to mean "convert." The preponderance of Rabbinic midrash and medieval commentary reads the Numbers passages as speaking of the later "converts" and not the original "strangers." Thus, for the purposes of this essay, many of these traditional passages—focused on religious boundaries—fail to address our question of political citizenship.

2. The etymology of *ezrach* is from the verb *zarach*, "to rise." Hence it is originally

understood as "one arising from the soil," which in ancient Israel likely meant "free tribesman" (*Brown-Driver-Briggs*).

3. In FDR's own words:

    In the future days, which we seek to make secure, we look forward to a world founded upon four essential human freedoms.

    The first is freedom of speech and expression—everywhere in the world.

    The second is freedom of every person to worship God in his own way—everywhere in the world.

    The third is freedom from want—which, translated into world terms, means economic understandings which will secure to every nation a healthy peacetime life for its inhabitants—everywhere in the world.

4. Babylonian Talmud, *Hagigah* 41a.

5. Babylonian Talmud, *Makot* 23b. The difference between these two types of commandments can be seen in a quick glance at the Ten Commandments at Exodus 20. Positive commandments point the direction toward proper behavior: "keep the Sabbath"; "honor your parents." Negative commandments restrict behavior: "thou shall not kill"; "thou shall not steal."

6. Dennis Prager, "The American Tradition of Personal Responsibility," Heritage Foundation, September 20, 1994, https://www.heritage.org/political-process/report/the-american-tradition-personal-responsibility.

7. He contrasts this with those who only seek "freedom to" and want to live in a society that frees them, as individuals, by subjugating the community. Aptly, and brilliantly, Kendi calls this the "psyche of the slaveholder." Ibram X Kendi, "We're Still Living and Dying in the Slaveholders' Republic," *The Atlantic*, May 4, 2020, https://www.theatlantic.com/ideas/archive/2020/05/what-freedom-means-trump/611083/.

8. Babylonian Talmud, *Sh'vuot* 39a.

9. "Asylum Seekers and Refugees," National Immigrant Justice Center, November 2020, https://immigrantjustice.org/issues/asylum-seekers-refugees.

10. Priscilla Alvarez and Geeva Sands, "Trump Administration Proposes Sweeping Changes to Asylum System in New Rule," CNN, June 10, 2020, https://www.cnn.com/2020/06/10/politics/us-asylum-draft-rule/index.html.

11. Miriam Jordan, "Farmworkers, Mostly Undocumented, Become 'Essential' Workers," *New York Times*, April 2, 2020, https://www.nytimes.com/2020/04/02/us/coronavirus-undocumented-immigrant-farmworkers-agriculture.html; Julie M. Weise, "Trump's Latest Immigration Restriction Exposes Key Contradiction in Policy," *Washington Post*, June 23, 2020, https://www.washingtonpost.com/outlook/2020/06/23/trumps-latest-immigration-restriction-exposes-key-contradiction-policy/.

12. Michael D. Shear and Emily Cochrane, "Trump Says Administration Will Try Again to End 'Dreamers' Program," *New York Times*, June 19, 2020, https://www.nytimes.com/2020/06/19/us/politics/trump-daca.html.
13. "Mainstreaming Hate: The Anti-Immigrant Movement in the United States," ADL, 2018, https://www.adl.org/the-anti-immigrant-movement-in-the-us.
14. The Bible commands a general sensitivity to the stranger thirty-six times. Four times, the Torah specifically states that strangers and citizens should be treated alike. Two instances occur in this chapter of Numbers, and the other two passages can be found at Exodus 12:49 and Numbers 9:14.

KORACH—NUMBERS 16:1–18:32

Dissent for the Sake of Heaven: American Jews and Israel

RABBI ETHAN BAIR

THE FAMOUS REBELLION of Korach begins when the descendant of the House of Levi complains to Moses and Aaron, "You have gone too far! For all the community are holy, all of them, and the Eternal is in their midst. Why then do you raise yourselves above the Eternal's congregation?" (Numbers 16:3). Reflecting on the first three verses of *Parashat Korach*, Nechama Leibowitz points to the difference between "All the congregation *is* holy"—in the singular, which we might expect—and the language the Torah employs: "All the congregation *are* holy," in the plural, meaning each member of the congregation taken individually. She writes, "Personal ambition outweighs [Korach's and his congregation's] feeling as a 'kingdom of priests and a holy nation.' They interpreted the mission of holiness, the role of 'chosen people' with which they had been charged by God, in the sense of conferring on them superiority and privilege, rather than as constituting a call to shoulder extra duties and responsibilities."[1] Korach and his congregation interpret God's command, "You shall be holy" (Leviticus 19:2), as a privilege rather than a call to action. They do not see that leadership comes with the responsibility to serve. Korach fixates on the status that comes with it, and he uses the language of equality to bolster his own jealous claim.

According to the Rabbis, the story of Korach demonstrates political ambition and a quest for raw power, both of which stem from feelings of profound entitlement. Korach protests that because he is the son of a firstborn Levite, he has a higher claim to leadership than his first cousins Moses and Aaron. Korach bands together with Dathan and Abiram—descendants of Reuben, the eldest son of Israel—who believe that *they* are destined to the highest spiritual and political offices. Little unifies Korach, Dathan, and Abiram other than their complaints against Moses and their disparate claims to power. This makes for the ugliest kind of family feud. Their attempted coup is not rooted in values but in the quest for personal gain, and their punishment is unsparing: God swallows them up into the earth.

The lesson from Korach is not to stifle values-based dissent, but rather to be wary of leadership pursued for the wrong reasons. Dissent based in values *is* encouraged and celebrated in Jewish tradition. The Mishnah teaches that minority opinions are not necessarily wrong even though they may not be accepted, and that is why the Talmud preserves them: "And why do they record the opinion of a single person among the many, when the halachah must be according to the opinion of the many? So that if a court prefers the opinion of the single person it may depend on it."[2] But Korach's rebellion is the prototype of dissent unworthy of preservation. *Pirkei Avot* teaches why that is: "Every controversy that is pursued in a heavenly cause [*l'shem shamayim*, לְשֵׁם שָׁמַיִם], is destined to be perpetuated; and that which is not pursued in a heavenly cause is not destined to be perpetuated. Which can be considered a controversy pursued in a heavenly cause? This is the controversy of Hillel and Shammai. And that not pursued in a heavenly cause? This is the controversy of Korach and his congregation."[3]

But who gets to decide when dissent is or is not *l'shem shamayim*, "for the sake of heaven"? Given that the Torah includes so many dissenting opinions, what is jarring about Korach is that his voice is shut down so unequivocally. I have not found a single commentator who takes Korach's side, adds any positive nuance regarding his character, or even gives him the benefit of the doubt. Yet how many times in Oral Torah do we see the Rabbis extrapolating from a single word, imagining psychological motives and nuances absent from the text, and filling in the gaps of the narrative to bring out an overlooked aspect of it? Aaron witnesses as his people worship the Golden Calf, and the Rabbis go to great pains to show that he was not the leader of this idol worship. They say that he sought to stop the people but feared for his own life.[4] Indeed, the Rabbis lift up Aaron as the model of the *rodeif shalom*, "pursuer of peace." Many other rabble-rousers and dissenters in the Torah—the seer Balaam (Numbers 24), the daughters of Zelophehad (Numbers 27:11), even Abraham (Genesis 18), who advocates for the innocent of Sodom and Gomorrah—are praised by the Rabbis for their courage. Biblical heroes, including all the Hebrew prophets, are those who challenge the status quo in order to advance moral change. Yet there are no extant examples of Rabbinic accolades directed at Korach. His fate is similar to that of Aaron's sons, Nadab and Abihu—who, according to the Talmud, plot to replace Moses and Aaron in the future.[5] The Rabbis see only treachery, a dearth of values undergirding Korach's rebellion. Is this a case of the winner writing history? Were there once-valid voices defending Korach that the Torah stifled? Or was Korach's rebellion as the simple meaning of the *Pirkei Avot* text asserts—an egotistical controversy lacking any higher purpose?

In contemporary Jewish life, there is hardly a topic as charged and polarizing as Israel's ongoing Occupation of the West Bank. There are those who are comfortable with the status quo or at least resigned to it, because they see no partner for peace in Palestinians. There are those who are committed to Israel as both a democratic state and homeland for the Jewish people and who would like to see a two-state solution, but worry whether Israel's withdrawal from the West Bank and the establishment of a Palestinian state would in fact bring peace. On both sides, there are maximalists who are against any compromises. And there are those who, frustrated by the lack of progress toward peace, support the Boycott, Divestment and Sanctions (BDS) movement to end the Occupation at all costs. For many in the Jewish community, BDS is an untouchable topic—the Korach of today. Some have decided that Israel is beyond certain limits of reproach, and that position animates not only their defense of their own positions, but leads them to silence or ignore fellow Jews with a different point of view. The same is true for the other side. And too often, the reason for that silencing is because the future of the Jewish people is at stake. It is an argument *lo l'shem shamayim*, they say. To which we can ask once more, who gets to decide when dissent is or is not for the sake of heaven?

The solution is not to decide which side you are on. The troubling story of Korach and its interpretation in the Torah is a warning that we should not stifle voices, no matter how radical they seem at first. Instead, we have to ask how we build coalitions that may be imperfect but that effectively lead to a common goal. How do we speak across chasms and create empathy for other people's perspectives without completely villainizing dissenting voices, even when we disagree? How can we appreciate the values that animate many of the people on both sides of the BDS debate, while reinforcing the more broadly shared goal of two states for two peoples? Listening to people's motivating values rather than jumping to villainize the dissenter is also a lesson of this *parashah*.

Just as Korach claimed that all the community "are" holy but did not pursue a holy end, we must be wary of a chauvinism that says Israel's government is beyond reproof. We would never seek to shield the American government against criticism. Critique and dissent bolster democracy, just as they have bolstered Jewish life and the halachic process for two thousand years. Whatever our view of Israel and BDS, our holiness as a people depends on constantly pursuing righteousness, justice, and improving our society rather than convincing ourselves that an unsustainable status quo can persist. Seeing the Jewish people and the State of Israel as intrinsically holy rather than holy as a result of the values—and actions—that God commands us to pursue would amount to the ultimate Korach-esque approach to God and Torah.

NOTES

1. Nechama Leibowitz, *Studies in Bamidbar* (Jerusalem: World Zionist Organization Department for Torah Education, 1980), 183.
2. *Mishnah Eduyot* 1:5.
3. *Pirkei Avot* 5:17.
4. Babylonian Talmud, *Sanhedrin* 7a.
5. "And it had already happened that Moses and Aaron were walking on their

way, and Nadab and Abihu were walking behind them, and the entire Jewish people were walking behind them. Nadab said to Abihu: When will it happen that these two old men will die and you and I will lead the generation, as we are their heirs? The Holy One, Blessed be God, said to them: We shall see who buries whom" (Babylonian Talmud, *Sanhedrin* 52a).

CHUKAT—NUMBERS 19:1–22:1

A Lesson in Trauma-Informed Care

RABBI SHOSHANAH CONOVER

HAVE YOU EVER NOTICED how one story of trauma begets another? You can be sitting with a group of friends and when one person shares a story about a car accident or devastating illness, suddenly everyone begins to share their own stories of trauma. I experienced this phenomenon a few years ago when co-facilitating a Peace Circle at the Juvenile Temporary Detention Center in Cook County, Illinois. I sat in this particular circle with eight youths just weeks after my parents died—one of them unexpectedly. They asked why I had been away for so long, and I told them about my parents' deaths. Their deaths were not tragic; they lived good, fairly long lives. Still, their loss left me bereft. After I shared about my loss, the boys began to talk about theirs. They had experienced deaths of parents, siblings, and good friends, all taken from them too soon by illness or violence. We cried together and supported one another. By the end of the circle, we noticed not only each other's pain points, but our courage, goodness, and motivation to live in such a way that would bring honor to the memories of those loved ones.

This kind of sharing of trauma is familiar to Jews. We take the multiplicity of traumas that have befallen our people throughout the span of time, bewailing them all on one day each year. Tishah B'Av, the ninth day of the Hebrew month of Av, commemorates tragedies that happened on or near that date, including the destruction of the First and Second Temples in Jerusalem, the biblical incident of the spies, the failure of the Bar Kochba revolt, the Crusades, the expulsion of Jews from Spain, the deportation of Jews from the Warsaw Ghetto to Treblinka,[1] and the bombing of the Jewish Community Center in

Buenos Aires, Argentina.[2] Each Tishah B'Av is a haunting echo of the Tishah B'Av of yesteryears. As Walter Benjamin once wrote, "A remembered event is infinite because it is only a key to everything that happened before it and after it."[3]

And this is the lesson of trauma: one moment of pain evokes another. As Bessel A. van der Kolk wrote in *The Body Keeps the Score*, "The past is alive in the form of gnawing interior discomfort."[4] Or, as James Baldwin chronicled poetically, "My memory stammers, but my soul is a witness."[5] In too many systems of our society—educational, health care, and criminal justice, to name a few—we ignore trauma's profound impact. We set levels of learning, norms of health, standards for behavior. Then, when certain individuals don't meet these standards, we ask, "What is wrong with you?" By contrast, a trauma-informed approach teaches us to ask instead, "What happened to you?" Through unpacking moments of trauma, real healing can begin to occur.

We encounter a stark moment of trauma and its aftermath in *Parashat Chukat*, with the incident of Moses striking the rock at Kadesh in the wilderness of Zin. Just after the death of Miriam, the community complains about the lack of water. Exasperated, Moses and Aaron seek out God. God instructs them to talk to a rock to yield its water. Instead, Moses yells at the people and strikes the rock—twice (Numbers 20:1–11).

Many of our classic commentators look at the actions of Moses and Aaron and ask, "What's wrong with you?" Chayim ben Moshe ibn Attar (ca. 1696–1743) detailed criticism by the sages. From Rashi's condemnation of the first strike to Ibn Ezra's condemnation of the second, and from Maimonides's critique of Moses and Aaron's misleading the Israelites to think that God was angry with them to Nachmanides's criticism that Moses and Aaron took credit for the miracle, no less than ten separate responses explain what was wrong with Moses and Aaron.[6]

Yet the question "What's wrong with you?" rarely yields instructive answers. Even the question itself enforces a type of blame that rarely leads to healing. What might we learn if we instead pose a trauma-informed question: "What happened to you?" The resulting response allows our text to speak to us in surprising ways. It opens our eyes to the multiple moments of trauma—and transformation—in Moses's childhood and adolescence.

Born into a society that sought his death from his first breath, Moses grows up in a palace as an outsider on the inside—raised by his mother yet given to Pharaoh's daughter to claim as her son (Exodus 2:7–10). Reared in isolation in a society that depended on the oppression of an entire people—his people, the Hebrews—Moses emerges as a young adult who lashes out. We read in Exodus, "He saw an Egyptian beating a Hebrew, one of his kinsmen. He turned this way and that and, seeing no one about, he struck down the Egyptian and hid him in the sand" (Exodus 2:11–12). Aviva Gottlieb Zornberg poignantly explains, "His circumspect glance takes in the systemic persecution that lies behind this moment."[7] Moses flees in mortal fear.

Time and again, often with Aaron (e.g., Exodus 7:10–13), Moses uses an unassuming shepherd's staff as a paradoxical instrument of both violence and redemption. First as a magic wand, transforming it into a snake; then as baton of death, turning the Nile to blood; then as a tool of our redemption, parting the sea; and twice more dealing death to our foes, drowning the Egyptians and defeating the Amalekites; and ultimately as an instrument used to nourish the Israelites in a waterless region—this humble staff carries the courage and strength as well as the trauma of our people.

Just before our incident in *Parashat Chukat*, we hear about this staff once more.[8] After Korach's rebellion and the plague that ensues, God commands a leader of each of the twelve tribes to bring forward a staff with their name inscribed upon it (Numbers 17:17–24). The staff of Levi with which we have become so familiar is inscribed with the name of Aaron. God charges Moses with depositing all the staffs inside the Tent of Meeting in front of the Pact of the Covenant. The next day, a miracle occurs: Aaron's staff sprouts almond blossoms. There, in the Holy of Holies, the staff becomes an instrument of healing and growth. Its intended purpose has finally sprouted. In this sacred space, it remains for decades.

However, thirty-eight years later,[9] when the Israelites arrive at Kadesh, Moses and Aaron's beloved sister, Miriam, dies. The text almost glosses over this tragedy. The thirst of the Israelites subsumes their grief. Without time to mourn, Moses and Aaron are thrown into the familiar traumatic territory of the Israelites' anger. The "remembered event is infinite," as Walter Benjamin would say. Time collapses, and Moses and Aaron act as before in Rephidim (Exodus 17:1–6): they strike the rock. Some ask, "What is wrong with them?" We should instead ask, "What happened to them?"

What happened to them? When we ask this question about Moses and Aaron, we see their lives and actions more fully and empathetically. The moments we are living through today call on us to transform our health system to provide trauma-informed care, defined as "a strengths based framework that is grounded in an understanding of and responsiveness to the impact of trauma, that emphasizes physical, psychological, and emotional safety for both providers and survivors, and that creates opportunities for survivors to rebuild a sense of control and empowerment."[10] The approach of trauma-informed health care enables this system to become one in which healing, resilience, self-confidence, and joy can grow among people of all economic backgrounds, ethnicities, and race. This approach has major implications in the realm of justice. Scholars point out, "What we see repeatedly across national crises and disasters is that the most disenfranchised among the U.S. population are disproportionately harmed physically, emotionally, economically, and educationally. These are the same communities already experiencing the toxic stress of poverty, crime, unemployment, racism, and discrimination . . . who then additionally bear the burdens and traumatic stress brought on by a crisis."[11] Racial and ethnic minorities have less access to mental health services than do whites, are less likely to receive needed care, and are more likely to receive poor-quality care when treated.[12] Too many people from communities of color continue to experience re-traumatization when seeking medical care.

In her book *The Deepest Well: Healing the Long-Term Effects of Childhood Adversity*,[13] California surgeon general Nadine Burke Harris delves into the adverse childhood experiences of her former patients to bring a more holistic and trauma-informed approach to health. In an interview, she cites an example of how this approach could produce better outcomes in maternal mortality. After explaining how the cumulative effects of childhood adversity dramatically increase the risk of chronic conditions such as diabetes and heart diseases, she asks, "What would it be like if every OB-GYN in the country were able to do some type of assessment of cumulative adversity of the patients they were caring for, assessing their risk and being able to proactively do interventions to support and protect the health of their patients?" We see again the lifesaving effects of asking someone, "What happened to you?" instead of "What's wrong with you?"[14]

Ultimately, trauma-informed health care requires a collaborative approach across all systems. Trauma-informed care calls on educators, medical professionals, police, lawyers, judges, parents, students, and friends to recognize that a person is so much more than who they appear to be in a single moment. A trauma-informed approach helps our youth—and the adults they become—to examine the sacred ark of the self. With holistic support, the soul—like the staff of Moses and Aaron—that has borne witness to violence and courage, terror and kindness, agony and hope, will sprout new life and blossom in healing.

NOTES

1. Sara Levine, "11 Tisha B'Av Calamities," Jew in the City, August 14, 2016, https://jewinthecity.com/2016/08/12-tisha-bav-calamities/#. XoqSRdNKhZC.
2. Claudia Kreiman, "Pursue Justice for the Jews of Argentina," *The Blogs*, Times of Israel, July 26, 2016, https://blogs.timesofisrael.com/a-time-of-mourning/.
3. Walter Benjamin, *Illuminations* (London: Collins Fontana Books, 1973), 204.
4. Bessel A. van der Kolk, *The Body Keeps the Score* (New York: Penguin Books, 2014), 97.
5. James Baldwin, *Evidence of Things Not Seen* (New York: Henry Holt, 1985), xv.
6. *Or HaChayim* on Numbers 20:8.
7. Aviva Gottlieb Zornberg, *Bewilderments: Reflections on the Book of Numbers* (New York: Schocken Books, 2015), 213.
8. I follow the interpretation that the staff of Levi is the same staff used by Moses

and Aaron throughout the Torah. Ibn Ezra makes the following comments on the phrase "inscribe Aaron's name on the staff of Levi" in Numbers 17:18: "Some say this proves that 'the staff of Levi' could not be the 'staff of God' that Moses used in Egypt. . . . Others say that it was indeed the 'staff of God,' but that it was just like the other twelve staffs, indistinguishable from them. I think that is correct."

9. According to the sages commenting on Numbers 20:1, this is the fortieth year of their wilderness journey. Nachmanides explains, "Kadesh of our verse in the wilderness of Zin, where they arrived in the fortieth year, and where Miriam died," and Rashbam writes, "This must be 'the first new moon' of the fortieth year."

10. Elizabeth K. Hopper, Ellen Bassuk, and Jeffrey Olivet, "Shelter from the Storm: Trauma-Informed Care in Homeless Service Settings," *Open Health Services and Policy Journal* 3 (2010): 82.

11. Lisa R. Fortuna, Marina Tolou-Shams, Michelle V. Porche, and Barbara Robles-Ramamurthy, "Inequity and the Disproportionate Impact of COVID-19 on Communities of Color in the United States: The Need for a Trauma-Informed Social Justice Response," *Psychological Trauma: Theory, Research, Practice, and Policy* 12, no. 5 (2020): 443–45.

12. Thomas G. McGuire and Jeanne Miranda, "New Evidence Regarding Racial and Ethnic Disparities in Mental Health: Policy Implications," *Health Affairs* 27, no. 2 (March/April 2008).

13. Nadine Burke Harris, *The Deepest Well: Healing the Long-Term Effects of Childhood Adversity* (New York: Houghton Mifflin, 2018).

14. Erika Stallings, "California's 1st Surgeon General Spotlights Health Risks of Childhood Adversity," NPR, July 2, 2019, https://www.npr.org/sections/health-shots/2019/07/02/733896346/californias-first-surgeon-general-spotlights-health-risks-of-childhood-adversity.

Balaam Is Watching: The Jewish Response to Black Lives Matter

RABBI KEN CHASEN

EVERY TIME WE GATHER for morning worship, we are invited to study and restudy *Parashat Balak*, for the portion includes the legendary teaching found at the beginning of our morning prayers: *Mah tovu ohalecha, Yaakov, mishk'notecha, Yisrael* (מַה־טֹּבוּ אֹהָלֶיךָ יַעֲקֹב מִשְׁכְּנֹתֶיךָ יִשְׂרָאֵל), "How fair are your tents, O Jacob, your dwellings, O Israel" (Numbers 24:5). This famous verse is the culmination of a biblical story in which our Israelite ancestors are being watched, observed by a non-Jewish prophet by the name of Balaam, sent by a foreign king to curse them. Balaam is ready to pronounce his curse until he carefully observes the Israelites—their habits, their lived values—after which he opens his mouth to speak and famous words of blessing spontaneously come forth.[1]

Whatever Balaam, an outsider to the Israelite community, sees in our biblical forebears, it possesses the power to transform curse into blessing. Might we possess that same power today? It's a question that every generation of Jews is forced to answer, for Balaam was surely not the first person whose careful watching of our people would determine whether words of curse or blessing would emerge from his lips, and he was certainly not the last. There will always be new observers of the Jews. Ours is a history of being watched by others who stand ready either to curse us or bless us, depending upon what they see—and sometimes we live long enough to see that perception reshaped entirely in the space of just a few decades.

This, sadly, is what has happened to the once friendly Black-Jewish relationship in the United States. Growing up Jewish in the 1970s, as I did, meant being regaled with stories of the inspiring alliance between Black and Jewish leaders during the civil rights movement: Rabbi Joachim Prinz speaking immediately before Dr. Martin Luther King at the 1963 March on Washington; Rabbis Abraham Joshua Heschel and Maurice Eisendrath—the latter with a Torah scroll in his arms—striding side by side with Dr. King and Rev. Ralph Abernathy to oppose the Vietnam War. We wanted the same things and put our bodies on the line for them together. The bond between the two communities was a powerful point of pride and efficacy.

When I reached adulthood in the 1980s, and even more when I was ordained as a rabbi in 1998, I noticed and lamented the decline of that once mighty bond. Why, I wondered, were we Jews still cleaving to those same fading images, still singing a nostalgic refrain of "We Shall Overcome," lacking new photos and new songs and new stances of unity?

The national uprising following George Floyd's death in the spring of 2020 pointed to an answer that makes most American Jews uncomfortable. A key difference between then and now is that today most Jews in the United States have been welcomed as white by the vast majority of our fellow Americans, and we have taken to the invitation with an enthusiasm we aren't itching to relinquish.

Back in the 1950s and 1960s, Jews of European descent still weren't fully accepted as white by white America. Today they and their descendants are generally viewed as white or at least white-passing—except by white supremacists, who continue to see them (like all Jews) as an even greater threat than Black people.[2] This transformation has played an undeniable role in millions of American Jewish family stories like my own, in which the current generation has successfully penetrated so many corners of American life that had not been open or were only beginning to open to our parents and grandparents. They could never have dreamed of the possibilities that would be extended to us—careers, universities, neighborhoods, and country clubs that had been largely or entirely closed to them, back when "No Blacks, No Jews, No Dogs" signs could be found, and not only in the South.

But Balaam is always watching us. In the decades since the heyday of the Black-Jewish relationship, Black people saw European American Jews become white while they remained Black. And of course, being Black was always harder in America than being Jewish was, even when being Jewish was at its most difficult. After all, no Jews arrived in the United States on slave ships. While the biblical narrative of rising from slavery in Egypt once united our two peoples, today it is far more likely to cause a disconnect in the eyes of most Black Americans, for whom white Jews are indistinguishable from white "everybody else." Thus ended the presumption among Black folks that Jews are by default allies. When Balaam looks upon the American Jewish community today, the decades-old words of blessing upon his tongue feel tired and played out, and words of curse begin to form in their place.

Admittedly, the slow fraying of the Black-Jewish relationship cannot be so neatly attributed to a single explanation. Other factors are at work. Some of the most familiar antisemitic tropes have found a home within segments of the Black community, causing understandable hurt and mistrust among Jews.[3] Disagreements about the Israeli-Palestinian conflict throw additional fuel on the fire. And Jews are not so simply defined as white; there is a sizable and growing contingent of Jews of Color, who often run into their own difficulties among the white majority in the Jewish community. All of these components exacerbate the problem, but the more I organize in multiracial and multifaith spaces, the more I see Black folks struggling with a seeming Jewish blindness to the privilege that comes with being white-passing in America.

Large numbers of Jews, including more rabbis than ever, declared without qualification that "Black Lives Matter" during the weeks that followed George Floyd's asphyxiation by a police officer. The difficulty arises when discussing what to do about it. Many Black leaders have, with sadness, concluded that we Jews will be allies, but only until we have to surrender some of the privilege that we are now accustomed to enjoying. They have witnessed, for instance, substantial Jewish resistance to property-tax reforms that might generate the additional revenue necessary to shrink disparities between white and Black neighborhoods in housing, schooling, and community services. When Black self-interest and Jewish self-interest diverge, the Black community observes, the Jewish community will often prioritize its own interests. Today Black leaders see white Jewish partners recoil from the rallying cry "Defund the Police"—calling for reinvesting public funds from law enforcement into other means of increasing safety and opportunity for all—because they know that when we hear a police siren, we, like most white people, worry only about whether we are speeding. They are unmoved by our attempts to explain why their demands for police defunding aren't practical, would have unintended negative consequences, or would benefit tactically from the moderation that we suggest. They know that, deep down, we want something different from what they want in public policy on policing.

The reality of working in multiracial justice spaces is that we Jews are no longer assumed to be allies. Our genteel advice about how Black folks can better achieve their goal of not dying during a routine police stop is seen as the ultimate stamp of white privilege—the belief that we whites know how to work the system better and that everything will end up fine if they just follow our counsel.

Now, though, the rebirth of the Black-Jewish bond could be upon us, but only if white Jews are ready to be true allies, which means wanting for our Black partners what they want for themselves and what we would demand for ourselves. If we Jews were under siege from the police and decided on a particular policy path for addressing our mass endangerment, none of us would be all that interested in a purported "ally" politely explaining to us why our demands aren't the right ones, or the pragmatic ones, or the achievable ones. We would only think, "Easy for you to say . . . they're not killing you."

Being in relationship is hard. The kind of trust that the Jewish and Black communities enjoyed in the middle part of the twentieth century can only be re-earned through full investment in one another's fate. The degree to which today's Jewish community will surrender the impulse to refashion the Black community's aspirations on police reform will play an enormous role in determining the degree to which the break between the two communities will heal. What will Balaam see in us? And what words will he speak?

Remembering that our patriarch Jacob is renamed Israel only when he reaches a more exalted spiritual state, the Baal Shem Tov noticed an important nuance in the words of Balaam's blessing: "How fair are your tents, O *Jacob*, your dwellings, O *Israel*." Our tents—our external appearance, said the Baal Shem Tov—are that of Jacob, a lower level. But our dwelling places—the real content, the interior, the *kishkes*—belong to Israel, and they reflect our highest potential as a Jewish people.[4]

Praying and rallying about systemic racism in policing is all well and good, but our words are just the tents—the outer package, the appearance of our concern. To stop at praying and rallying is to remain merely Jacob. *Acting* in alliance with the Black community to end systemic racism is where our inner determination shows, where we are lifted up to become Israel. We will be reminded every time we gather for morning worship: Balaam is watching, as always. Let us show him Israel, not just Jacob—and inspire blessing, not curse.

Notes

1. For instance, in the Babylonian Talmud, *Bava Batra* 60a, the Gemara explains, "What was it that Balaam saw that so inspired him? He saw that the entrances of their tents were not aligned with each other, ensuring that each family enjoyed a measure of privacy. And he said, 'If this is the case, these people are worthy of having the Divine Presence rest on them.'"
2. This has been documented in the groundbreaking work of Eric K. Ward. For an introduction to Ward's writing on this topic, see "Skin in the Game" in Political Research Associates' online magazine, *The Public Eye*, Summer 2017.
3. Arguably the most influential voice in fomenting antisemitism in the Black community is Nation of Islam leader Louis Farrakhan, who routinely suggests that Jews control Hollywood, banking, and the media, among other powerful industries. See "Farrakhan: In His Own Words," Anti-Defamation League, March 20, 2015, https://www.adl.org/sites/default/

files/documents/assets/pdf/anti-semitism/united-states/farrakhan-in-his-own-words-2015-03-20.pdf.

4. "'How goodly are your tents, O Jacob, and your dwelling places, O Israel' ... 'Your tents'—your external appearance must be that of Jacob, a lower level, while 'your dwelling places'—your interior—must be of the level of Israel" (Ba'al Shem Tov, cited in Aharon Yaakov Greenberg, *Torah Gems*, vol. 3 [Tel Aviv: Y. Orenstein, Yavneh Publishing House, 1998], 128).

A Covenant of Peace for All Who Enter Jewish Spaces

CHRIS HARRISON

JEWISH HISTORIAN Simon Rawidowicz's 1986 essay dubbed the Jews an "ever-dying people."[1] It's often said you can find three opinions among two Jews, but one thing upon which we can nearly all agree is our fear of being the last generation of Jews. This fear isn't without merit; antisemitic terror has threatened the Jewish people since the days of our prophets and remains with us to this day. Religious observance and synagogue membership among Jews seem to be less important to millennials and Generation Z than they were to previous generations. There is a common worry that interfaith marriage and raising children in a multifaith household will lead to a generation of lapsed Jews or, worse, no Jews at all.

This fear of the Jewish people's end, in part due to paranoia regarding interfaith relationships and families, has plagued us since Mount Sinai and is unlikely to disappear. *Parashat Pinchas* is a particularly graphic and blatant testament to this ever-present fear of Jewish demise and the unfortunate lengths zealots have gone to "preserve" Judaism, even at the cost of their souls—and our collective soul.

At the very beginning of this *parashah*, we learn that Pinchas, Aaron's grandson, has committed an act of murder in a story largely told at the end of *Parashat Balak*. A plague is spreading among the Israelites, allegedly due to their intermingling with Midianites. In an act of religious zealotry, Pinchas kills Zimri, an Israelite nobleman, and a Midianite woman named Cozbi, while they are having sex

(Numbers 25:6–9). Because of Pinchas "displaying among them his passion for [God]" (Numbers 25:11), not only is God's wrath settled with Israel, but God also grants Pinchas a "covenant of peace"—a *b'rit shalom* (בְּרִית שָׁלוֹם)—and a pact of priesthood for all of his descendants (Numbers 25:12–13).

This story raises a stark issue of morality for modern progressive Jews. When Pinchas first witnesses Zimri and Cozbi together, he does not break the two apart to prevent them from sinning further. He does not even ask them to stop, so they could have a chance to listen. Fueled by what Rabbi Donniel Hartman aptly refers to as "God intoxication,"[2] Pinchas makes himself judge, jury, and yes, executioner, by stabbing two people to death for the crime of having apparently consensual sex. And the Torah seems to be completely okay with his doing so.

Granted, context is key. The Torah is a work written by an ever-dying people about an ever-dying people. Jews have been endlessly targeted and enslaved and murdered by others simply for the crime of existing. We should not be surprised, then, that some of our stories treat zealotry as heroism. The ends, preserving Jewish continuity and purity, justify the means of murder—even premeditated and cruel murder. In the case of Pinchas, his moment of God intoxication seems to be crucial in saving the Jewish people.

However, while a surface read seems to declare that Pinchas succeeded and earned a pure *b'rit shalom*, our Rabbis tell a more complicated story. According to the Talmud, "Rav Nachman says: The letter *vav* in the word *shalom* is severed. According to tradition, this letter is written with a break in it, and therefore the word can be read as though the *vav* were missing."[3]

According to Jewish mysticism, not only every word but every letter of the Torah tells a story. What does a broken *vav* reveal? A *vav* looks like a hook—and it acts like one, too: one letter that in many contexts means "and," *vav* connects things together. So, this alleged "covenant of peace" that connects generation to generation is in fact a broken covenant. Peace achieved through zealotry, even seen as justified in a surface read, isn't really peace at all.

Not only is Pinchas a zealot and a murderer, he's also a hypocrite. Oddly enough, Pinchas is an Egyptian name,[4] and he is a descendant of non-Jewish priests.[5] And yet, his hypocrisy proves an important point: Judaism is an acculturating religious civilization. Pinchas is a man with an Egyptian name who is the product of an interfaith relationship. Moses, our greatest prophet, also has an Egyptian name.[6] Esther's and Mordechai's names may be said to be based directly on those of Babylonian deities.[7] The names of our Jewish months are also Babylonian.[8] Pinchas, whose name is a living reminder of *Mitzrayim* (Egypt) itself, thought it necessary to murder two people of different tribes for engaging in consensual sex out of a fear of losing Jewish purity. It would be laughable if it weren't devastating.

As a reader of comics, I think back to *Watchmen*, considered the best graphic novel of all time. One of the "heroes," Adrian Veidt, a.k.a. Ozymandias, murders over three million people in the pursuit of world peace.[9] Like Pinchas, he sees his ends as justifying his means: by killing millions, he saves billions, uniting humanity with a common fear so they would no longer be afraid of one another—his very own *b'rit shalom*.

Deep down, though, Ozymandias has his own doubts and even tries to justify his mass genocide to fellow superhero Doctor Manhattan, the graphic novel's stand-in for God. "I did the right thing, didn't I?" asks Veidt. "It all worked out in the end."

"'In the end?' Nothing ends, Adrian," replies Manhattan. "Nothing ever ends."[10] And with no end, there is no justified means. A broken *vav*.

The question then remains: How do we create a real covenant of peace? In short, by not being like Pinchas. If we are to create a Jewish community that is embedded in real peace, we must start by abandoning the self-defeating notion that interfaith relationships are a threat to Judaism and recognize the real threat to Judaism: keeping people out.

We must ask ourselves: Is our Judaism so important that we want to emulate a murderer, a fanatic, just to keep it "pure"? Is our tradition, which commands no fewer than thirty-six times that we protect the stranger, so fragile that including, uplifting, and loving those who seek to be part of our communities who are Jewish adjacent will cause our way of life to crumble? That's not the Judaism I know, nor is it the Judaism I want.

When I imagine a Judaism that is a true covenant of peace, I think back to my own journey as a Jew-by-choice. I remember observing my very first Shabbat in the home of Reform Jews-by-choice, complete with a *zayde* (grandfather) who himself was not Jewish. I was a college student and had not yet gone through conversion. Ever since my mom first told me that some of our ancestors were German Jewish immigrants, though, I knew that I had a Jewish soul that needed to come home. I found that home at a warm, lively dinner table in a house that celebrated and included everyone equally, including a Jewish-adjacent grandpa who loved his Jewish children and grandchildren more than anything in the world.

The Judaism I know involved *Kabbalat Shabbat* services at Miami University Hillel. Not only was there a diversity of Jewish observance in that sacred space, ranging from Conservadox to Reform to Humanist, but there were also attendees who weren't Jewish (yet). When we sang and prayed and had rousing conversation over dinner, it didn't matter where we were on our Jewish journeys—or even if we were on a Jewish journey.

The Judaism I know involved taking an Introduction to Judaism class with other prospective Jews and being embraced for who I was, not shamed for who I wasn't. I was welcomed as a not-quite-Jew with a Jewish soul, as someone in a committed partnership with someone who didn't have any plans to become Jewish herself—a fact, but an irrelevant one.

The Judaism I know involved sitting before a *beit din* with my non-Jewish partner at my side. She wanted so badly to take part in this beautiful and important step with me. I remember her beaming as she spoke about my passion and commitment to living a Jewish life and making our home a Jewish one, about wanting to experience Judaism alongside me, regardless of her plans to become a Jew herself.

When I think of this type of Judaism, I don't think of an "ever-dying people"; I think instead of an ever-living people and an ever-loving people. I think of the countless interfaith and multifaith households that make our Jewish communities vibrant, beautiful places and keep the spirit of Judaism alive. I think of the spouses, partners, and children of Jews who may not be Jewish themselves, yet or ever, but who contribute so much to Jewish life through their presence and their questions and their ideas. I think of all the people who are looking into becoming Jewish, especially people like me whose Jewish lineage may have an asterisk next to it yet whose souls thirst to join *Am Yisrael*.

This Judaism isn't fueled by zealotry, like that of Pinchas, to maintain purity; it's fueled by love rooted in the belief that Judaism is made pure when everyone who wants to be a part of our communities—including those who are Jewish adjacent—get an equal seat at the table.

NOTES

1. Simon Rawidowicz and Benjamin C. I. Ravid, "Israel: The Ever-Dying People" in *Israel: The Ever-Dying People, and Other Essays* (Rutherford, NJ: Fairleigh Dickinson University Press, 1986), 53–63.
2. Donniel Hartman, *Putting God Second* (New York: Penguin USA, 2017), 45–46.
3. Babylonian Talmud, *Kiddushin* 66b.
4. Reuven Chaim Klein, "Appendix B: Egyptian Names in the Bible," in *Lashon Hakodesh: History, Holiness, & Hebrew; A Linguistic Journey from Eden to Israel*, ed. Shira Klein (New York: Mosaica, 2015), 210.
5. Berel Wein, "Pinchas," *Rabbi Wein's Blog*, Rabbi Wein.com, The Voice of Jewish History, accessed January 10, 2021, https://www.rabbiwein.com/blog/pinchas-1050.html.
6. Josephus, *The Antiquities of the Jews* 2:9:6, Sefaria, https://www.sefaria.org/The_Antiquities_of_the_Jews.2.9.6?lang=bi.
7. Irving Greenberg, "Confronting Jewish Destiny: Purim," in *The Jewish Way: Living the Holidays* (New York: Simon & Schuster, 1988), 227.
8. "Festivals and Fasts in the Jewish Calendar," IJS: Israel & Judaism Studies, accessed January 10, 2021, https://www.ijs.org.au/Festivals-and-Fasts-in-the-Jewish-Calendar/.
9. Alan Moore and Dave Gibbons, *Watchmen*, no. 11 (DC Comics, 1987), 18–28.
10. Alan Moore and Dave Gibbons, *Watchmen*, no. 12 (DC Comics, 1987), 27.

MATOT—NUMBERS 30:2–32:42

Human Decency during Warfare

RABBI SAMUEL M. STAHL

PEOPLE PROJECT THEIR HIGHEST IDEALS into their vision of the perfect world of the future. The Norse community did so with Valhalla, which is a wondrous palace. There, war is glorified. Its occupants engage in battle with each other daily.[1] By contrast, peace is the distinguishing feature of our Jewish vision of the future messianic age. Isaiah and Micah awaited that idyllic time, when nations will no longer battle each other and when the destructive implements of warfare will be transformed into productive agricultural tools (Isaiah 2:4; Micah 4:3–4). Peace is the ultimate aim of Jewish yearnings. We greet and bid farewell to each other with the word *shalom*, connoting peace. We address God as *Shehashalom Shelo*, "One whose very nature is peace."

Yet as much as Jews cherish and value peace, pacifism is not part of our normative tradition. In fact, the Rabbis speak about a *milchemet r'shut* (an optional war) and a *milchemet mitzvah* (an obligatory war).[2] The war described in *Parashat Matot* appears to be a *milchemet mitzvah*. Here God commands the Israelites to exterminate the people of Midian to avenge the sin at Baal-peor. They are to retaliate against the Midianites for seducing the Israelites to consort with foreign women and worship Baal, the chief god of the religion of the Canaanites (Numbers 25:1–9, 31:1–3).

The Israelites are savage and callous during this military campaign. They kill all the adult men and capture the Midianite women and children, together with their beasts, herds, and their wealth. They also set fire to the towns and encampments where the Midianites had settled (Numbers 31:7–10). Moses becomes irate that the soldiers spared the females, whereupon he orders them to kill every male child and every woman who was not a virgin (Numbers 31:14–18). Since lineage was determined by patrilineal descent, these virgins did not pose the danger of producing Midianite sons who could grow up to avenge their fathers.[3]

Sadly, this inhumane kind of warfare occurs throughout much of the Hebrew Bible. There are a few restrictions on conduct in war. One is the requirement to give the enemy an opportunity to make peace before engaging in battle (Deuteronomy 20:10). Another is to refrain from destroying fruit trees during a siege (Deuteronomy 20:19). And there is a hint in the Bible that war is morally problematic. David wanted to build the Temple in Jerusalem, but God denied his request. God desired that a man of peace build the Temple, telling David, "You are not to build a house for My name, because you are a warrior and have shed blood" (I Chronicles 28:3).

Centuries later, Maimonides offers this humane provision, together with others: "When we besiege a city that we want to capture, we do not encircle it from all four sides, but only on three. We leave one side open for them to flee. Anyone who wishes to escape with his life may so do, as it says, 'They took the field against Midian, as the Eternal had commanded Moses' (Numbers 31:7)."[4]

But mostly, the morality of warfare seems to be a non-issue. For example, in commenting on the phrase, "and let them fall upon Midian to wreak the Eternal's vengeance on Midian" (Numbers 31:3), Rashi writes that opposing the people of Israel is akin to "opposing God."[5] Thus, holy wars are justified by divine sanction and seemingly limited by few moral restrictions.

In general, slaughter and bloodshed are described throughout our classical literature without any requirement of compassion. We would expect the prophets, who offered searing moral judgments on all kinds of ethical violations, to condemn these inhumane military campaigns. Yet they paid no attention; the horrors of war were just a given. According to an aggadah, Moses, the greatest of all prophets, was happy to go to war against the Midianites. However, the Israelites, knowing that Moses would die after the war had concluded, tried to evade the draft and went into hiding. They were not motivated by any humanitarian objection to this war. Rather, they preferred to sacrifice a victory over the Midianites than lose their leader.[6]

The Rabbinic Sages also seemed oblivious to the savagery of war. Of course, during most of the Rabbinic period, the Jewish people were in exile without national sovereignty. They had no standing army and could not become part of the military of other states. To the Rabbis, any discussion of military matters would have been theoretical, and they tended to shy away from exploring such issues. For example, they did not admit the Books of the Maccabees—replete with vivid descriptions of warfare—into the canon. In discussing the holiday of Chanukah, the Rabbis deemphasized the victory over the Syrian-Greeks. Instead, they focused on the miracle of the cruse of oil found after the Temple was cleansed of its defilement in 165 BCE.[7] Thus, today, the chief religious symbol of Chanukah, a postbiblical holiday, is the *chanukiyah*, a candelabrum, and not a weapon. The haftarah assigned for the Shabbat during Chanukah contains the verse "Not by might, nor by power, but by My spirit—said the God of heaven's hosts" (Zechariah 4:7). Here, the emphasis is on inner strength derived from God and not on military prowess.

It seems that only with the founding of the State of Israel was the issue of morality in warfare finally addressed. At that time, an expression was coined: *tohar haneshek*, "purity of arms."[8] This term was designed to promote high moral conduct in a time of war. To some, this phrase seems like an oxymoron. How are weapons that kill considered pure? It is akin to descriptions like "the cleanliness of dirt" or "the righteousness of the wicked." Yet the Haganah, Israel's pre-state army, included the concept in its charter and employed religious language to describe its mission and goals: "Self-defense is our right and obligation. With all our might, we shall cling to it, as long as the need persists. But we shall also be diligent in preserving its purity and rightness. Any misuse of this right harms this most holy of undertakings and renders our defense defective. Our strength lies in the purity of our aspirations and the rightness of our deeds."[9]

The principles of *tohar haneshek* include the following:

1. Preventing misuse of weapons
2. Using minimum force against combatants
3. Avoiding casualties to civilians
4. Caring appropriately for prisoners
5. Resisting dehumanization and demonization of enemy citizenry.
6. Dealing with criminal orders
7. Equalizing the burden of military service on the entire population[10]

Today, *tohar haneshek* is one major specifically Jewish response—Jewish, in that it is a product of the Jewish national homeland—to preventing savagery and brutality among military forces. It is but one of numerous national and international codes promulgated to advance some humanity in armed conflict, to limit brutality in warfare, to save lives, and to reduce human suffering. The best known and the model for all codes that followed, possibly even *tohar haneshek*, are the Geneva Conventions, first formulated in 1864.[11] Under the Geneva Conventions, harming innocent civilians and destroying what they need to survive are always off-limits. In addition, torturing prisoners of war or withholding food and water is forbidden. Nations are obligated to treat wounded military personnel, even among the enemy. In modern times, the uses of advanced weaponry with its lethal destructive properties also need to be held in check.

Significant violations of the Geneva Accords, such as those at the Guantánamo Bay detention camp, call for severe consequences. This camp was built to house Muslim militants and terrorists, whom the US Armed Forces captured in Iraq, Afghanistan, and elsewhere. At this facility, US authorities were accused of scores of violations of the legal rights of detainees under the Geneva Conventions, such as using waterboarding and other methods of torture during interrogations. Humanitarian organizations—including Amnesty International, Human Rights Watch, and the International Committee of the Red Cross—repeatedly condemned the actions at this detention center.[12]

Unfortunately, US government officials attempted to cover up or rationalize these military abuses. The Bush administration generally defended its actions at Guantánamo Bay, insisting that detainees were well cared for and that none of the enhanced interrogation techniques involved torture.[13]

On January 22, 2009, days after his inauguration, President Barack Obama ordered the closing of the facility at Guantánamo within one year and a review of ways to transfer detainees to the United States for imprisonment or trial. He also required interrogators to use only the gentler methods contained in the US Army's field manual on interrogation.[14] However, he met stiff resistance from Republican and some Democratic members of Congress, who delayed the closure. They feared that transferring the detainees to the United States would pose a security threat.[15] As of this writing, the detention camp remains open.

Thus, when the Geneva Accords are ignored and the government does not assume responsibility for military inhumanity, as occurred at Guantánamo Bay—as well as at My Lai[16] and Abu Ghraib[17]— ruthlessness and barbarism will persist. However, when they are upheld, human decency can be protected and social justice can be advanced.

A notable example is the Rev. Paul Womack, a United Methodist minister who spent many of his years in the military. During Desert Storm and the Iraq wars, he served as a US Army chaplain. In a presentation to the Chautauqua Hebrew Congregation in the summer of 2019, he described the ethical struggles of being in warfare and surrounded by killing. He mentioned that in his presence, he would not permit any derogatory comments about the enemy—he wanted to train his soldiers not to dehumanize them. He recalled the number of times he had, as a military intelligence officer in Vietnam, searched the pockets of the enemy dead to find letters and photos, similar to those of American casualties.[18] Rev. Womack, though not Jewish, expressed the best of Jewish values by affirming humaneness, even during combat.

NOTES

1. Adam Augustyn, "Valhalla," *Encyclopaedia Britannica*, updated March 20, 2020, https://www.britannica.com/topic/Valhalla-Norse-mythology.
2. Babylonian Talmud, *Sotah* 44b.
3. Adele Berlin and Marc Brettler, *The Jewish Study Bible* (Philadelphia: Jewish Publication Society, 1985), 345.
4. Maimonides, *Mishneh Torah, Hilchot M'lachim Umilchamot*, 6:7.
5. Rashi on Numbers 31:3.
6. Louis Ginzberg, *The Legends of the Jews*, vol. 3 (Philadelphia: Jewish Publication Society, 1969), 408.
7. Babylonian Talmud, *Shabbat* 21b.
8. Barry L. Schwartz, "'Tohar Haneshek' ('Purity of Arms'): Reclaiming a Jewish Ethic in War," *Journal of Reform Judaism* 35, no. 3 (Summer 1988): 43.
9. Aharon Meged, *Davar*, May 19, 1978, cited in Schwartz, "'Tohar Haneshek,'" 51.
10. Bonnie Koppell, "Tohar Ha-Neshek/Purity of Arms," azrabbi.com (blog), November 23, 2012.
11. Malcolm Shaw, "Geneva Conventions: 1864–1977," *Encyclopaedia Britannica*, updated March 20, 2020, https://www.britannica.com/event/Geneva-Conventions.
12. Jeannette L. Nolen, "Guantánamo Bay Detention Camp," *Encyclopaedia Britannica*, updated March 13, 2020, https://www.britannica.com/topic/Guantanamo-Bay-detention-camp.
13. Andrew Buncombe, *The Independent*, February 23, 2016, 16:44.
14. *FM 34-52, Intelligence Interrogation*, Headquarters, Department of the Army, Washington, DC, September 28, 1992.
15. Nolen, "Guantánamo Bay Detention Camp."
16. US soldiers were guilty of the mass killing of approximately five hundred unarmed villagers in the hamlet of My Lai on March 16, 1968, during the Vietnam War (Susan Brownmiller, *Against Our Will: Men, Women and Rape* [New York: Simon & Schuster, 1975], 103–5).
17. In the early part of the Iraq War, members of the US Army and the CIA committed a series of human rights abuses against detainees in the Abu Ghraib prison, including physical and sexual abuse (in some cases leading to death). CBS published photographs of these war crimes, which brought them to public attention (*Sixty Minutes*, CBS, April 30, 2004).
18. Betty and Arthur Salz, *Shalom Chautauqua* (Rochester, NY: Mountain Air Books, 2019), 252–53.

Mas'ei—Numbers 33:1–36:13

The Cities of Refuge and Restorative Justice

Rabbi Denise L. Eger

At the end of the Book of Numbers, as the Children of Israel are within sight of the Promised Land, Moses reviews the journey that took them from Egypt to this point. Moses explains in detail the boundaries and territories of the land apportioned to each tribe. Speaking through Moses, God also appoints the leaders of each tribe who will administer their portion of the land. Every tribe will be required to designate a city within its holdings for the Levites, the priestly tribe who will not have a formal share in the division of the land. The priests will dwell among each of the tribes in a designated place, serving that tribe, the people Israel, and God.

Once the tribes set aside the Levitical cities in their midst, they must also set aside six cities of refuge. These cities are special places of sanctuary for those who are guilty of manslaughter, the unintentional or accidental killing of another person. In one of Moses's last acts, he establishes three of the six on the eastern side of the Jordan. The Children of Israel, once they have conquered the Promised Land, will establish three more in Israel proper. There are six of these special cities: two in the south, Hebron and Bezer; two in the central part of the country, Shechem and Ramot; and two in the north, Kadesh and Golan.

The idea of the city of refuge (*ir miklat*, עִיר מִקְלָט) makes its first appearance in *Parashat Mishpatim*: "One who fatally strikes a person shall be put to death. If [a male killer] did not do it by design, but it came about by an act of God, I will assign you a place to which he can flee" (Exodus 21:12–13). But in *Parashat Mas'ei*, in Numbers 35, we gain a fuller understanding of the legal process for those who are accused of murder and seek sanctuary in these cities of refuge. In *Ma'sei*, the Torah is clear that if the murder is intentional, the punishment is death. But unlike in our time, when the state executes the murderer, particularly for murder in the first degree, the Torah describes that the murderer is put to death by an avenging relative, the *go-eil hadam* (גֹּאֵל הַדָּם), or "blood-avenger," after the murderer has been found guilty by the judges. We learn more about these cases and the role of the cities of refuge in Deuteronomy 19:4–6 and Joshua 20:1–6.

The *ir miklat* is a place of asylum. As Maimonides explains it, the murderer would first go to the city of refuge, providing the perpetrator immediate protection from the *go-eil hadam*. The killer would then be taken to trial. If found guilty of premeditated murder, the killer would be put to death by the *go-eil hadam*, the avenging relative. If found innocent, the accused would be set free. But if the court finds the accused to be an accidental killer, they would be returned to the *ir miklat* accompanied by two guards, who would then protect the guilty party from the *go-eil*. The accidental killer must then reside in the city of refuge permanently. If they leave, they may be held accountable and pursued by the blood-avenger. There can be no ransom for the murderer in lieu of residing in the *ir miklat*; the accidental killer must live there permanently unless the High Priest dies, in which case all those who were found guilty of the crime of accidental murder are set free and may return to society without fear of retribution.[1]

These cities of asylum for those convicted of manslaughter and those awaiting trial are an interesting take on the adjudication of justice. The Torah assumes that justice is found in the killing of the perpetrator—not at the hand of the state, but by the avenging relative. *Lex talionis*, the principle of an eye for eye—in this case, a life for a life—is evident.[2]

The cities of refuge circumvent *lex talionis* in the case of manslaughter. The Torah's judicial system recognizes that the perpetrator could become as much of a victim as the person accidentally killed. The cities of refuge allow the pressure to avenge the death to be removed from the blood-avenger, thereby halting the cycle of violence.

Such a process opens the door to a notion of our time: restorative justice. We might envision that the cities of refuge for those who committed manslaughter constitute a first step in the restorative justice process. The *ir miklat*, "sheltering city," could be a place where the victim—in the case of manslaughter, the victim's family—and perpetrator are able to meet without the associated pressures of *lex talionis*.

What if those found guilty of accidental homicide were commanded to sit down with the family of their victim and with tribal leaders to listen to the pain, the loss, the grief, and the sadness of both parties? In the biblical system of justice, the blood-avenger is charged with killing the individual found guilty of murder. What might it look like if the blood-avenger were instead commanded to engage in a process of restorative justice?

Restorative justice, unlike a punitive system, seeks to repair the harm caused by a crime by bringing together victims, perpetrators, and community members. It emphasizes holding perpetrators accountable and allowing for the processing of feelings, harm done, and the very Jewish ideal of *t'shuvah* (repentance). Restorative justice stresses the idea that perpetrators must take responsibility for their actions.

In the Jewish process of *t'shuvah*, the perpetrators of the sin must encounter the individuals they have harmed and seek to make amends. We know that *t'shuvah* only happens when we do not commit the same sin twice, as Rambam makes very clear: "What is repentance? The sinner shall cease sinning, and remove sin from their thoughts, and wholeheartedly conclude not to revert back to it, even as it is said: 'Let the wicked forsake their way'" (Isaiah 55:7).[3]

In the case presented by this Torah portion, restorative justice might include the *go-eil hadam* (blood-avenger), other members of the victim's family, the perpetrator, and the community members of the town where the accident took place. While the victim's life cannot be restored, a restorative justice process seeks to repair the harm caused by the crime. It seeks an encounter *panim el panim*, "face to face"—if possible, between the victim and the perpetrator or between the family of the victim and the perpetrator—and to empower the parties to decide the best procedure for the encounter. Alongside restoration and repair, the third prong of the restorative justice process is transformation, with the hope for fundamental change in the relationships between the victim, the perpetrator, and the community. Ultimately, the goal is that both the perpetrator and the victim—or, in our case, the victim's family—can reintegrate into society.

The restorative justice process gives voice to the pain, trauma, and violence of every party: perpetrator, victim, and society. In North America, we delude ourselves that our criminal justice system seeks and achieves rehabilitation. But in truth, our highly punitive system often retraumatizes both victims and their families without rehabilitating guilty parties.[4] There is little incentive to deal with the physical and emotional violence that happens on both sides of the jail cell. A process of restorative justice seeks redress for victims and their families and recompense for both victims and perpetrators. These acts of accountability also allow the perpetrator to begin their own process of repentance and restoration of human dignity.

In 2011, Jacob Donne killed a man in an unprovoked attack. He was arrested, charged, and sent to prison for his crime. He had had a troubled life as a teen, was expelled from multiple schools, and never graduated from high school. In prison, he felt that he, rather than the man he murdered, was the real victim. He focused on having been "ratted out" by his friends, who were also involved in the altercation. In prison, his anger and rage grew.

Through a process of restorative justice facilitated by his probation officer, Jacob began a journey of accountability and acceptance of his action, and he rebuilt and renewed his humanity. Through mediators, the parents of the murder victim communicated with Jacob through letters, with both sides learning more about each other and what happened on the fateful night. The victim's parents actually became the ones to encourage Jacob, their son's murderer, to complete his education and reenter society. They eventually met face to face. Jacob said, "Opening the door into the room where both David and Joan were waiting was the hardest thing I've ever had to do in my life, but I knew how important it was that I looked them in the eye and told them how sorry I was."[5]

The city of refuge might be seen as a first step in a process of disrupting the cycle of violence encouraged by a blood-avenger. This practice allows the person guilty of an accidental killing to stop running with the worry they are being pursued, themselves becoming another victim of the system. The *ir miklat* was a way our ancestors had to turn revenge seeking on its head. Perhaps restorative justice can replace our society's harsh prison-industrial complex with a more humane way of addressing and redressing victims and those who commit crimes.

Parashat Mas'ei opens by recounting the journey of the Israelites from oppression in Egypt through their years in the wilderness, listing each stop along the way. Using a restorative justice process with crime victims and perpetrators can be a journey toward healing, dignity, responsibility, reintegration into society, and hope for all.

NOTES

1. Maimonides, *Mishneh Torah, Hilchot Rotzei-ach Ushmirat Nefesh* 5.
2. See Exodus 21:23–25.
3. Maimonides, *Mishneh Torah, Hilchot T'shuvah* 2:2.
4. Judith Lewis Herman, "The Mental Health of Crime Victims: Impact of Legal Intervention," *Journal of Traumatic Stress* 16, no. 2 (April 2003): 159.
5. Jacob Dunne, "Restorative Justice: Jacob's Story," *Positive News*, March 7, 2017, https://www.positive.news/society/restorative-justice-jacobs-story/.

DEUTERONOMY

D'varim—Deuteronomy 1:1–3:22

Like God Going before the Israelites: Placing Our Bodies between the Vulnerable and Violence

Rabbi Josh Whinston

On March 15, 2019, a terrorist attacked two mosques in Christchurch, New Zealand. The gunman murdered fifty-one people that day. The outcry across the globe was swift. Communities came together to mourn with the Muslim community. I was invited to offer a prayer at a rally on the University of Michigan campus. The morning of the rally, my wife and I piled our three kids into the car and headed to campus. As my time at the podium approached, I waded to the front of the rally, preparing to climb the speakers' steps. My family remained near the back of the crowd, my kids playing on some benches while my wife watched them and listened to the speakers. I stood there for a few seconds, waving to folks I knew and feeling the nervousness of the moment.

Out of the corner of my eye, almost in slow motion, I could see the mass of people start to move—like a wave, gathering upon itself and building as it crashes onto the shore. A split second later, I heard a police officer yelling, "Run! Run! Run!" His arms were flailing over his head, and he began shouting, "Not that way, not that way." People were screaming; it was complete chaos. I had no idea where my family was. I started running toward the last place I left them and saw my eldest daughter running through the university green. She was all alone. I screamed her name and ran after her. A few seconds later, she heard me and stopped. I caught up to her, and we continued to run together. As we ran, she was saying to me, "We are going to die, we are going to die." With some distance between us and where the rally was held, I pulled my daughter behind a tree, knelt, and said, "We are okay. We are going to be okay. We need to keep moving, and we will find the rest of our family."

Twenty agonizing minutes later, we did finally find the rest of our family. Still not knowing what happened and unable to get to our car, we sat in a local coffee shop for a few hours and waited for more information. Eventually, we found out it was a false alarm—popping balloons sounded like gunshots, and one thing led to another. There was no active shooter, but there wasn't anything false about the terror my family and I experienced that day; no, that was very real.

Eventually, we made it back to our car and were on our way home. I knew I needed to say something to my children sitting in the back seat. They had just lived through the scariest moment of their lives. I shifted the rearview mirror and spoke to them all as we waited at a red light: "I know that was terrifying, but we all found each other, and we're okay. Even though we are all frightened by what just happened, we can't let that stop us from showing up for other people. We always have to show up for other people."

Now, more than at any time in my lifetime, showing up is risky, particularly in light of the rise in mass shootings and the provocations of white nationalists. When America awoke once again to racial injustice in 2020, COVID-19 added a new layer of risk. And yet, showing up with the willingness to place our bodies before those who are vulnerable is how we find our way out of the wilderness.

In *Parashat D'varim*, Moses reminds the Children of Israel, "None other than the Eternal your God, who goes before you, will fight for you, just as [God] did for you in Egypt before your very eyes, and in the wilderness, where you saw how the Eternal your God carried you, as a *parent* carries a child, all the way that you traveled until you came to this place" (Deuteronomy 1:30–31). The use of parental metaphor for God is noteworthy. Similarly, in Exodus 19:4 and later in Deuteronomy 32:11, God's protection is compared to an eagle carrying its young. The imagery of a parent carrying a child is powerful. In picking up the child, a parent communicates so much, implying to the child, "I have you. Whatever burden we approach, I can ensure your safety." As Rashi asserts in his commentary on Deuteronomy 1:31, "This can be compared to a person on a journey with their child in front of them, and robbers come to kidnap [the child]." Rashi emphasizes that the parent figure moves in front of the child to protect the child from harm. The parent places their body between the child and the possible injury. Of significance, Rashi suggests that a human being may play a role analogous to God's in our passage from *Parashat D'varim.*

The Torah's metaphor is beautiful, but it does not describe a relationship in which the vulnerable have agency in their own liberation. Suppose we relieve Deuteronomy of its paternalism and reframe our text in terms of culturally prescribed power. In that case, we find both the Torah text and Rashi's commentary leading us to the assertion that those with more societal power have a responsibility to put themselves between the vulnerable and potential violence. This does not mean that all white people must become martyrs for vulnerable communities. It does not mean that vulnerable communities shouldn't stand up for themselves. However, it does mean that those of us who are less at risk—in the United States, those who are white—are responsible for showing up in body, not only in spirit. We must use our cultural power to advance liberation for the vulnerable and for us all.

In the fall of 2018, in partnership with colleagues and the community organizing group Faith in Action, I helped organize a protest at a tent camp holding undocumented children in Tornillo, Texas. A few weeks before the protest, I went to Tornillo to scout out the site and get a better understanding of the situation on the ground. When I arrived at the desert camp, I met an activist from Brooklyn named Josh Rubin, who had been living outside the camp in protest for a number of weeks. He sat at the entrance holding a black-and-white sign with the words "Free Them." As buses full of kids rolled by, he would stand and wave; as those same buses left the camp empty, he would flag down the drivers and ask them how many kids were on the bus, if they knew what was happening in the camp, or if they knew where the kids were coming from. Josh lived in an RV outside the camp for nearly three months. The Tornillo tent camp was closed in January 2020. Josh did what few of us could: He used his body by placing it in front of the camp for an extended period of time. He showed up day in and day out for kids he never knew and would never meet, but his protest alone would not have shut down the camp. Between the camp opening in spring 2018 and closing in 2020, thousands of protesters stood outside as witnesses to the immoral actions of the United States government.

There are few things as meaningful as showing up for others. When we see or hear of those in power abusing that power, there are many ways to demonstrate our discontent. When we want to make it known that we stand in support of a particular idea or community, there are many ways to show our dedication. Few, though, are as meaningful as showing up. Our bodies—ourselves—represent more than just being physically present in protest and in support. When we show up, we say to others, "I've got skin in this game. I am here, placing my body in a potentially vulnerable place because this is how we change the world; this is how we create the world we need and deserve." In our society, white bodies are less vulnerable to violence than Black or Brown bodies. Those of us with white bodies have a moral obligation to use them to help heal the brokenness of this world.

VA-ET'CHANAN—DEUTERONOMY 3:23–7:11

You Shall Not Murder:
Gun Violence Prevention

RABBI ANDREA C. LONDON

LO TIRTZACH (לֹא תִּרְצָח), "you shall not murder" (Deuteronomy 5:17), is the sixth of the Ten Commandments, reiterated in *Parashat Va-et'chanan*. The first time we learn this commandment is in Exodus 20, when the Israelites stand at the foot of Mount Sinai to receive the Torah. Now, as their forty years of wandering are coming to a close and Moses is preparing to die, Moses delivers a series of speeches recorded in the Book of Deuteronomy to remind the Children of Israel of the laws that God imparted to them during their sojourn in the wilderness and of the consequences of failing to live as God commands.

Thousands of years later, we have yet to heed this admonition. In the United States alone, nearly forty thousand people are killed annually by guns. Of this number, more than thirteen thousand are considered homicides. Americans are twenty-five times more likely to be killed by gun homicide than residents of other high-income countries.[1] The death of even a single person is tragic and unacceptable. The Talmud teaches that every life is precious and every human being, although unique, is equal to every other human being, having descended from the same progenitors—Adam and Eve.[2] But the staggeringly high number of gun murders in our society testifies to the fact that we have an urgent need to curb this rampant violence. The proliferation of shootings in schools, religious institutions, bars, and other gathering places is astounding. We have to ask ourselves: What kind of society do we live in where kids have active shooter drills to try and keep them safe while in school, bulletproof vests are marketed to religious leaders to protect them while they lead worship, and an armed guard at a bar cannot protect people who have gathered to socialize and have a good time?

Although mass shootings are sensational and grab our attention, the vast majority of gun violence deaths don't occur in these incidents. In major cities across the United States, thousands of people die by gun violence annually.

What are we to do about this epidemic? Since countries that have stricter gun laws have fewer gun deaths, controlling access to guns would seem like a logical answer. Some claim, however, that because of the danger of gun violence, they need to own a gun for protection. Jewish tradition does not forbid taking another life in self-defense; we are allowed to protect ourselves.[3] In fact, it's important to note that the Torah forbids not killing, but murder—the sixth commandment is *lo tirtzach*, "you shall not murder," rather than *lo taharog*, "you shall not kill."

In Exodus 22:1–2, we learn that a burglar may be killed if caught while breaking into someone's home if the homeowner is afraid of being killed by the intruder. If it's clear, however, that the burglar is not going to harm the homeowner, then the homeowner may not kill them.[4] Rashi writes that killing the burglar is lawful only when the intruder is "in the very act of forcing the entry."[5] In such a case, there is no bloodguilt for killing the burglar. The intruder, however, should not be killed if the sun shone upon them, meaning they did not come with the intention of killing the owner.[6]

If the purpose of owning a gun is self-defense, then there needs to be some indication that gun ownership keeps one safer. The statistics about gun injuries, however, do not bear this out. In fact, those who have guns in their home are far more likely to be harmed than protected by their weapons. Those who have access to guns are three times more likely to die by suicide; each year there are many more gun deaths from suicide than from homicide. A victim of abuse is five times more likely to die in domestic violence if their abuser has a gun.[7] And those who have firearms in their home are three times more likely to die by accidental shooting than those who do not.[8] The Talmud teaches that one is liable for injury or death caused if one has something in one's possession that is known to harm others.[9]

There are those who try to argue that "guns don't kill people, people kill people," but people who are armed with semi-automatic weapons that can shoot ten rounds per second can kill many people very quickly. High-powered weapons have been used in some of the most notorious mass shootings. In 2016, forty-nine people were murdered in the Pulse Nightclub in Orlando, Florida, and another fifty-three injured. The shooter shot two hundred rounds in less than five minutes. And in 2018, eleven people were killed and another seven injured on Shabbat morning at the Tree of Life synagogue in Pittsburgh. The gunman was armed with an AR-15 semi-automatic rifle and three Glock semi-automatic pistols. Precious lives could have been saved if the shooters didn't have access to such powerful, rapid-fire weapons.

In addition to these mass shooting that make the headlines, the scourge of gun violence is rampant in cities across the United States. The neighborhoods most affected by gun violence are the ones that suffer the most from joblessness, poverty, incarceration, racism, and addiction.[10] If we want to curb gun violence, we must do more than work on gun control; we need to address these systemic issues. Even accounting for mass shootings, the safest communities are the ones that have the greatest resources.

In *Va-et'chanan*, Moses reminds the Israelites numerous times to remember the covenant, observe the laws and rules that God has given them, and uphold the Ten Commandments (Deuteronomy 3:5; 4:13, 23, 6:1, 17–18). The covenant is not just for our ancestors but for all subsequent generations, including our own (Deuteronomy 5:3). Besides the Ten Commandments and a repeated injunction against idolatry, the specific laws to follow are not enumerated in the *parashah*, but it seems clear that Moses is reminding us to adhere to all the precepts of Torah—including those that guide our interactions with other human beings.

Torah instructs us to create a just society and admonishes us to care for the vulnerable (Exodus 22:21–22). While the Torah makes specific mention of society's responsibility to protect the widow and the orphan, later commentators argue that the widow and orphan are stand-ins for the disadvantaged in society. Rashi explains, "This is the law for all people. Here the text speaks to the present reality, for these are not particularly strong, and it is common to find them afflicted. However, it applies to all who are bereft of their human protectors and destitute of the physical force to defend their rights."[11]

Rabbi Samson Raphael Hirsch teaches that God hears the cries of those who are mistreated by society and warns leaders that they are shirking their responsibility if they don't protect those who are in need:

> Woe to you, state leaders, if the state as well ill-treats them and makes them feel the pain of having lost their defenders and supporters. Woe to the state whose widows and orphans suffer among the people, where even the official public representatives do not stand up for them and uphold their rights. . . . Woe to you if their only resort is to cry out to Me; for I will surely hear their cry; I will make the state and the society pay dearly for it, if their weakest members must appeal to Me to find justice.[12]

Hirsch's rebuke warns us of the misfortunes we will suffer if we don't care for the most vulnerable members of our society and strive for justice. Regulating guns is only part of the solution to curbing gun violence; making sure that all communities have the appropriate resources is also critical to making our society safer.

We must adopt a two-pronged approach to decrease the death and injuries caused by guns in our society. One is a public health model that seeks to decrease violence by regulating gun ownership and safety. Regulations on cars and driving—such as seat belt use, air bags, and stricter penalties for drunk driving—made our roads safer. Similarly, ensuring that guns don't fall into the hands of those who are likely to harm themselves or others and making guns safer—by putting locks on them, making them usable only by their owner, and limiting access and providing support to individuals in crisis—would help to decrease gun-related injuries. But this is not sufficient. We also must work on the underlying issues—including poverty, addiction, and racism—that increase the likelihood of violence and that gun possession makes more lethal. *Parashat Va-et'chanan* implores us not to murder and to observe God's laws and commandments that it may go well with us and our children (Deuteronomy 4:40). It's incumbent upon us to pursue these paths to prevent unnecessary deaths and injuries and to make our society safer.

NOTES

1. Giffords: Courage to Fight Gun Violence, accessed January 11, 2021, Giffords.org.
2. Babylonian Talmud, *Sanhedrin* 37a.
3. Babylonian Talmud, *Sanhedrin* 72a: "If someone comes to kill you, rise and kill them first."
4. Exodus 22:1–2: "If the thief is seized while tunneling and beaten to death, there is no bloodguilt in that case. If the sun had already risen, there is bloodguilt in that case."
5. Rashi on Exodus 22:1.
6. Rashi on Exodus 22:1–2.
7. Giffords: Courage to Fight Gun Violence.
8. Children's Hospital of Philadelphia Research Institute, https://injury.research.chop.edu/violence-prevention-initiative/types-violence-involving-youth/gun-violence/gun-violence-facts-and#.X3zpS2hKhPY.
9. Babylonian Talmud, *Bava Kama* 46a: "Rabbi Natan says: From where is it derived that one may not raise a vicious dog in one's house, and that one may not set up an unstable ladder in one's house? As it is stated: 'You shall not bring blood into your house' (Deuteronomy 22:8), which means that one may not allow a hazardous situation to remain in one's house."
10. Nick Cotter, "Black Communities Are Disproportionately Hurt by Gun Violence: We Can't Ignore Them," Public Source, accessed October 30, 2020, https://projects.publicsource.org/pittsburgh-gun-violence-1/.
11. Rashi on Exodus 22:21–22.
12. Samson Raphael Hirsch on Exodus 22:23.

EIKEV—DEUTERONOMY 7:12–11:25

Atoning for Our Broken Covenants: Righting America's Racial Wrongs

RABBI JUDITH SCHINDLER

OUR ACTIONS HAVE CONSEQUENCES. The traces of our past remain. The word *eikev* (עֵקֶב), for which this *parashah* is named, has many meanings. Literally, it can mean "heel" or "footprint"; figuratively, it can mean "trace" or "mark."

As Americans, our footprints speak for themselves. Dr. Gail Christopher, a national expert in racial healing, defines racism as the "false belief in a human hierarchy" based on the color of one's skin.[1] America was built on such a fabricated taxonomy, leading to stolen land, stolen lives, and stolen labor.

America's failure to fulfill the pledge of liberty and justice for all that was articulated in its foundational documents requires atonement. It necessitates facing our past, facing our siblings whose skin color is different from our own, and facing ourselves. Repentance, reparations, restorative justice, and reformed systems are needed.

One can hear the word *eikev* in the name of our patriarch *Yaakov*, Jacob, who held onto his twin brother's heel as they were born. As young adults, after Jacob stole Esau's birthright and blessing, the latter cries, *Vayak'veini* (וַיַּעְקְבֵנִי), "Twice now he [Jacob] has cheated me" (Genesis 27:36). Jacob would spend twenty years wrestling with his past. He returns home following his struggle with an angel ready to reconcile and receives the new name "Israel," meaning "one who struggles with God" (Genesis 32:29).

As a country, we have denigrated and supplanted our siblings of color and are thus called to the task of racial reckoning: for 246 years of slavery, Jim Crow segregation, redlining that prohibited lending to homeowners in Black neighborhoods, urban renewal that demolished Black communities, and mass incarceration. These systems of racism have resulted in radically negative impacts on Black people in virtually every realm. Over 20 percent of Black Americans face soul-killing poverty.[2] Any journey to reconciliation is made by reflecting on our footprints, acknowledging the harm we have caused, making restitution, and committing to change.

Parashat Eikev teaches that living peacefully on our land is conditional: "And if you do obey these rules and observe them carefully, the Eternal your God will maintain faithfully for you the covenant made on oath with your fathers" (Deuteronomy 7:12). Our tranquility and blessings are dependent upon following the *mishpatim* (מִשְׁפָּטִים), the laws that govern relationships. If we safeguard Torah's laws that guide and ground human relations, then God will safeguard us.

Like Moses's first descent from to Sinai with an original set of tablets, America's Declaration of Independence and Constitution amounted to an unfulfilled and incomplete covenant. The July 4, 1776, declaration proclaimed, "We hold these truths to be self-evident, that all men are created equal, that they are endowed by their Creator with certain unalienable Rights, that among these are Life, Liberty and the pursuit of Happiness."

The promise of affirming the equality of "all" Americans did not, however, include "all," and the vision for "We the people" who would have protections was exclusive. Black Americans were denied promises and protections. For far too much of US history, they were viewed as chattel, bodies to be exploited to increase white wealth by any means possible.

Parashat Eikev recognizes the risk that wealth will blind one's eyes: "Beware lest your heart grow haughty and you forget the Eternal your God—who freed you from the land of Egypt, the house of bondage ... and you say to yourselves, 'My own power and the might of my own hand have won this wealth for me.' Remember that it is the Eternal your God who gives you the power to get wealth, in fulfillment of the covenant made on oath with your fathers, as is still the case" (Deuteronomy 8:14, 17–18). It warns us to beware lest our success lead to arrogance and we forget our past. Victims within our own lifetime, too, must remember that pseudoscientific claims regarding race paved the road to the Holocaust. Even in America, white Jews were not seen as white until after World War II, when they received GI Bill and other federal benefits surrounding employment, business, home ownership, and higher education that were largely inaccessible to Blacks.[3]

We cannot forget our past nor fail our siblings of color, both Jewish and otherwise. We need to own the oppressive American soil on which we now stand, which has enabled whites to acquire wealth, privilege, and protections while Americans of color are left economically and physically vulnerable.

In *Parashat Eikev*, Moses knew that the covenant had been broken even before it was delivered. In Deuteronomy's telling, he reflects: "I saw how you had sinned against the Eternal your God . . . . Thereupon I gripped the two tablets and flung them away with both my hands, smashing them before your eyes" (Deuteronomy 9:16–17). Similarly, one must question whether any of the crafters of America's covenantal documents knew that they were incomplete. The majority of those who signed the Declaration and nearly half the delegates to the Constitutional Convention owned slaves themselves.[4] Thurgood Marshall, the first African American Supreme Court justice, claimed the Constitution was "defective from the start."[5]

The shattering of America's metaphorical tablets has echoed through the centuries. The hands that brutally murdered Emmett Till, the billy clubs that bludgeoned peaceful protestors in Selma, the bullet that assassinated the Reverend Dr. Martin Luther King Jr., and the police knee that asphyxiated George Floyd all shattered complacency and brought to light our complicity. Like the broken tablets, which the Talmud teaches were placed in the Ark alongside the whole tablets, these shameful and tragic moments of American history must be remembered and taught.[6]

In Parashat Eikev, God opens the door to Moses for repair: "Thereupon the Eternal One said to me, 'Carve out two tablets of

stone like the first, and come up to Me on the mountain'" (Deuteronomy 10:1). Just as Moses atoned for forty days and nights in order to renew the broken covenant, so must we right historic wrongs
and renew America's covenant. Atonement is a three-step process:
(1) confession and truth telling; (2) reparations and restitution; and
(3) transformative change.

Confession and Truth Telling

Through testimonials, curricula, memorials to the martyred, and a
national truth and reconciliation commission, we can hear the sins
of our society, acknowledge accountability, and offer apology from
personal to organizational to societal to governmental.

Reparations and Restitution

"Two hundred fifty years of slavery. Ninety years of Jim Crow. Sixty
years of separate but equal. Thirty-five years of racist housing policy. Until we reckon with our compounding moral debts, America
will never be whole," Ta-Nehisi Coates writes.[7] Slavery was a crime
against humanity—and, since its abolition, discriminatory system
after system has been created to privilege those who are white, while
harming and even killing Black Americans.

Jews understand the power of reparations. Post-Holocaust reparations had not only material benefits for survivors but also a
restorative impact on Germany. Coates, in his seminal 2014 article on the topic, writes, "Reparations could not make up for the
murder perpetrated by the Nazis. But they did launch Germany's
reckoning with itself, and perhaps provided a road map for how a
great civilization might make itself worthy of the name."[8]

The United States also offers a precedent for reparations. In
1988, the federal government granted $20,000 each to over eighty-
two thousand Japanese Americans who were held in internment
camps during World War II.[9]

Starting in 1989 and for twenty-eight consecutive years, Con-
gressman John Conyers Jr. would introduce H.R. 40—Commission to Study and Develop Reparation Proposals for African-Amer-
icans Act, but not until 2019 was a reparation bill introduced in the

Senate.[10] Proposals from advocates and scholars vary greatly, from direct payments to descendants of slaves to programs that include student loan forgiveness, down payments for housing, and grants for business startups. Reparations, whether issued to individuals or more broadly to eliminate the Black-white wealth gap, will not only uplift African Americans; they will uplift all America.

Transformative Change

New policies, from federal to local, that ensure racial equity must be put in place. A recent example demonstrates the path forward. A Black neighborhood in Charlotte, North Carolina, called Brooklyn was razed in the 1960s when the city received federal urban renewal funding. As a result, 1,007 families and nearly 10,000 residents were displaced; 216 businesses, 12 Black churches, several schools, a library, and a once-thriving Black Wall Street were demolished, most never reopening. Promises of alternative affordable housing were insincere from the start.[11] A courthouse and jail now stand where a Black neighborhood once thrived. The Black community was irreparably harmed.

Restorative justice advocates succeeded in getting an August 2020 apology from the mayor and then sought the same from leaders of key sectors where wounds were caused—from the county to business and philanthropic sectors. They set the goal of establishing the Trust for Black Upward Mobility—a philanthropic fund for restorative justice that would accelerate the accrual of wealth in the Black community through investment in education, business development, mental health services, housing, and more. The objective is to create deep, transformative, systemic change with measurable outcomes regarding upward mobility of Black people. As developers, investors, and businesses find opportunity for themselves, they must be held accountable for creating opportunities for the communities in which they build.

"And now, O Israel, what does the Eternal your God demand of you? . . . Cut away, therefore, the thickening about your hearts and stiffen your necks no more" (Deuteronomy 10:12,16). Rashi calls on us to remove the coverings on our hearts that prevent God's words from gaining entrance.[12] Sforno notes, "It is appropriate that you remove the 'foreskin,' prejudices with which your intelligence is afflicted, so that you will realize the errors you have made in your world outlook based on false premises."[13] Renewing the covenant requires cutting away the callousness—softening our hearts to feel the pain of our neighbors.

As Jacob held onto the heel of his brother Esau, white Americans have held onto the heels of their Black siblings. Commentators teach that the letter *yod*, representing God in Jacob's name, preceded the word *eikev* (heel).[14] The heel, the lowest part of the body, was connected to the *yod*, which kabbalists associate with the brain and wisdom.[15] Rising above our base instincts to see divine unity and the equality of all was within Jacob's grasp at birth, was within reach of the Jewish people at Sinai, and is attainable for America today.

Parashat Eikev is read as the Jewish people prepare for repentance and are immersed in the work of return. Our spiritual work requires addressing not only our personal past but that of our society. Jacob reconciled with his brother not only for Esau's sake, but for his own. In the same way, we must recognize that our redemption is tied up with that of our neighbors.

Now is the time for returning to the pledges made at Sinai and to the promises made and reformed in the Declaration of Independence and Constitution. Now is the season for recognizing our failings and wrestling with our past. Now is the time for repair, reparations, and restoration, so that the blessings of *Parashat Eikev* can unfold and redemption can indeed come.

NOTES

1. Gail Christopher, "A National Day of Racial Healing on January 17 Will Help Americans Overcome Racial Divisions," *PhilanTopic*, January 6, 2017, https://pndblog.typepad.com/pndblog/2017/01/national-day-of-racial-healing-will-help-americans-overcome-racial-divisions.html.
2. "Income, Poverty and Health Insurance Coverage in the United States: 2018," United States Census Bureau, Press Release Number CB19-141,

September 10, 2019, https://www.census.gov/newsroom/press-releases/2019/income-poverty.html.

3. Karen Brodkin, *How Jews Became White Folks and What That Says about Race in America* (New Brunswick, NJ: Rutgers University Press, 1998).

4. Tom Kertscher, "Fact-check: They signed the Declaration of Independence —but nearly three-quarters also owned slaves," *Chicago Sun Times*, September 10, 2019, https://chicago.suntimes.com/2019/9/10/20859458/fact-check-declaration-independence-slaves-trumbull-painting-arlen-parsa; "The Constitution and Slavery," Digital History: University of Houston, accessed August 24, 2020, https://www.digitalhistory.uh.edu/disp_textbook.cfm?smtid=2&psid=3241#:~:text.

5. David Savage, "Marshall on Constitution: 'Defective from Start,'" *Los Angeles Times*, May 7, 1987, https://www.latimes.com/archives/la-xpm-1987-05-07-mn-4540-story.html.

6. Babylonian Talmud, *Bava Batra* 14b.

7. Ta-Nehisi Coates, "The Case for Reparations," *The Atlantic*, June 2014, https://www.theatlantic.com/magazine/archive/2014/06/the-case-for-reparations/361631/?gclid=CjwKCAjwj975BRBUEiwA4whRB89nRQjdInOOUITkPtW7TMIIiZNeexqsgkLvQVRZlRR3Nnk3_RZRCBoCwq8QAvD_BwE.

8. Coates, "The Case for Reparations."

9. "National Archives Commemorates the 25th Anniversary of the Civil Liberties Act," National Archives, Press Release, July 17, 2013, https://www.archives.gov/press/press-releases/2013/nr13-118.html.

10. John Conyers, "My Reparations Bill—HR 40," Institute of the Black World 21st Century, October 3, 2013, https://ibw21.org/commentary/my-reparations-bill-hr-40/; Jamie Ehrlich, "Democratic Lawmakers Call for Vote on Bill to Study Reparations," CNN, June 10, 2020, https://www.cnn.com/2020/06/10/politics/reparations-congress-bill-vote/index.html.

11. Thomas W. Hanchett, *Sorting Out the New South City: Race, Class, and Urban Development in Charlotte, 1875–1975* (Chapel Hill: University of North Carolina Press, 1998), 250; "History," Brooklyn Village CLT, accessed August 22, 2020, https://brooklynvillage-clt.com/history/.

12. Rashi on Deuteronomy 10:16.

13. Sforno on Deuteronomy 10:16.

14. Shaul Yosef Leiter, "Grasping the Heel of Esau," *Kabbalah Online*, Chabad.org, accessed August 22, 2020, https://www.chabad.org/kabbalah/article_cdo/aid/379755/jewish/Grasping-the-Heel-of-Esau.htm.

15. Rabbi Yaakov Yitzchak Horowitz, the "Seer" of Lublin, *Zikhron Zot* 4a, "Something from Nothing," *Kabbalah Online*, Chabad.org, https://www.chabad.org/kabbalah/article_cdo/aid/380558/jewish/Something-from-Nothing.htm; "Basics in Kabbalah: *Chochmah*," *Gal Einai: Revealing the Torah's Inner Dimension*, accessed August 24, 2020, https://www.inner.org/sefirot/sefchoch.htm.

How Do Our Monuments Help or Hurt Our Memories of the Past?

RABBI ARIEL NAVEH

RECENTLY, I FOUND MYSELF in a particularly heated conversation with my father, a veteran diver and paratrooper for the Israeli Defense Forces, regarding the calls for removal of statues of Confederate generals, soldiers, and political leaders. We went back and forth about the purpose of such statues until, voice nearly breaking and face tear-streaked, he exclaimed that because I have never served in battle, I can never fully understand the necessity of honoring sacrifice in war. To him, these statues, though controversial and deeply troubling, are symbols of war's greatest tragedy: the sacrifice of fallen soldiers. This perspective jarred me, partly because it was rare to see my father so visibly overcome with emotion, but also because it got me thinking: What is the purpose of a statue? How does a statue represent the morals, ethics, and values of the society that erected it? Must a statue be responsible for such representation, or can it simply commemorate the historical figure it portrays? As our society slowly begins to reckon with our own structures of racism and bigotry, the question of how and what we choose to remember from our past has taken center stage. In this commentary, I will explore how this question relates to Parashat R'eih, how figures are remembered and honored in Jewish tradition, and the mandate this parashah gives our community to truly honor the multitude of voices and peoples who have shaped our history.

The parashah starts as Moses, speaking on behalf of God, offers the

Israelites two choices as they stand on the precipice of crossing into the land that had been promised to them and toward which they had been journeying for forty years: "See, this day I set before you blessing and curse: blessing, if you obey the commandments of the Eternal your God that I enjoin upon you this day" (Deuteronomy 11:26–27). What follows in the *parashah* are the laws and guidelines enjoined upon the Israelites if they choose to follow the path of blessing and the promise that God's presence will be forever with them, so long as they continue to keep those laws. One of the first laws mentioned is the mandate to "destroy all the sites at which the nations you are to dispossess worshiped their gods, whether on lofty mountains and on hills or under any luxuriant tree" (Deuteronomy 12:2). The text goes on to specify what must be destroyed and the means of destruction, as Moses bellows to the huddled crowd of Israelites: "Tear down their altars, smash their pillars, put their sacred posts to the fire, and cut down the images of their gods, obliterating their name from that site" (Deuteronomy 12:3).

The Rabbis of the Talmud sought to puzzle out the specifications for what this destruction must entail, and exactly which idols and altars warrant such demolition. Rabban Gamliel emphasizes that statues must be destroyed only if they were created or are revered with idolatrous intent:

> Even if people would give you a lot of money, you would not enter before your object of idol worship naked, or as one who experienced a seminal emission who comes to the bathhouse to purify himself, nor would you urinate before it. This statue stands upon the sewage pipe and all the people urinate before it. There is no prohibition in this case, as it is stated in the verse only: "Their gods" (see Deuteronomy 12:2), which indicates that a statue that people treat as a deity is forbidden, but one that people do not treat with the respect that is due to a deity is permitted.[1]

Later in the Talmudic text, Rabbi Akiva posits that Deuteronomy 12:2 doubly emphasizes the demolition of idols and altars—*abeid t'abdun* (אַבֵּד תְּאַבְּדוּן), literally, "destroy, you shall destroy."[2]

The purpose of the destruction, according to the verses that follow, is to establish the land as the sacred and true birthright of the Israelites, but it is also to establish the necessary rites of worship and practice in order for that birthright to be continued. Worshiping idols, statues, and altars like the peoples who inhabited the land prior to the Israelites' arrival would be anathema; a new precedent must be established. And in order for that precedent to hold, all remnants of the previous means of worship must be rooted out, desecrated, and fully destroyed. In the Talmud's *Avodah Zarah*, a tractate about idolatry, Rabbi Eliezer teaches, "From where is it derived that when one deracinates an object of idol worship, he needs to root out all traces of it? The verse states: 'And you shall destroy their name out of that place.'"[3] As the aphorism goes, "history is written by the victors"; and in this instance, the need for communal cohesion under one means of worship, practice, and belief necessitates destruction of even the memory of a culture long past.

As such, the question is raised of what is reflected by a society erecting—or demolishing—a monument, memorial, or altar. When God promises the Israelites "an everlasting name that will endure forever" (Isaiah 56:5), what will that name mean? What will be the impact of removing someone else's name, in order for an Israelite's "everlasting name" to be given full glory? In recent years, these questions have gained prominence in our societal discourse, as we grapple with the elevation of voices once ignored and the lowering of other voices once given full weight of influence. Consider, for example, the voice of Isabella Gibbons. Gibbons was brought to the University of Virginia around 1850 as a slave by Professor William Barton Rogers. She remained enslaved and in service at UVA until emancipation in 1865. Following her emancipation, Isabella received a diploma from the New England Freedmen's Aid Society's Charlottesville Normal School, where she remained to serve as a teacher. In a powerful letter she wrote to the *Freedmen's Record* in 1867, Gibbons posed the question:

> Can we forget the crack of the whip, the cowhide, the whipping post, the auction block, the handcuffs, the spaniels, the iron

collar, the negro-trader tearing the young child from its mother's breast as a whelp from the lioness? Have we forgotten those horrible cruelties, hundreds of our race killed? No, we have not, nor ever will.[4]

These words, once lost to the din of voices and personae whose influence at the time outweighed that of a former slave, now enshrine a new memorial on the campus of UVA. The Memorial to Enslaved Laborers is a testament to the slave labor that quite literally built and operated the university through and beyond its formative years. It replaces a small plaque on the Rotunda that was added in 2007 to honor the slaves and their work, which many staff and students of the University found grossly insufficient in giving the enslaved people who built the institution brick by brick their due.[5] The memorial also stands in stark contrast to the monument to Confederate General Robert E. Lee that adorned a nearby park until its celebrated removal in the summer of 2020.

It is important to note that this statue of General Lee, like many similar statues of Confederate leaders and soldiers, was not erected immediately following the Civil War—but rather many years following, in 1909, by an organization called the United Daughters of the Confederacy. According to its Articles of Incorporation, the UDC's goals are "to honor the memory of those who served and . . . protect and preserve the places made historic by Confederate valor."[6] However, at the celebration of a similar statue known as "Silent Sam," built on the campus of the University of North Carolina at Chapel Hill in 1913 by the UDC, the benefactor of the statue, Julian Carr, laid bare the real purpose of the statue—and, by extension, the UDC:

> This beautiful memorial. The present generation, I am persuaded, scarcely takes note of what the Confederate soldier meant to the welfare of the Anglo Saxon race during the four years immediately succeeding the war, when the facts are, that their courage and steadfastness saved the very life of the Anglo Saxon race in the South—When "the bottom rail was on top" all over the Southern states, and today, as a consequence the purest strain of the Anglo Saxon is to be found in the 13 Southern States—Praise God.[7]

In other words, the statue represented the ultimate sacrifice the Confederate soldiers made to uphold the sanctity of "the Anglo Saxon race." The "Silent Sam" statue remained on the UNC campus until its toppling in 2018 and the removal of its pedestal in 2019.[8] As with the call for desecration and total annihilation of previous societies' idols or altars that we read about in this *parashah*, the context for why is imperative. In that case, it was an attempt to build a new society and with it a new standard of worship and practice. In our modern era, the intent is quite similar: we seek to replace the voices a previous generation once lauded with voices that reflect a society renewed. This society will seek to uplift more and different voices; it will not ignore the ills and sins with which it struggled in generations past, but rather demonstrate our growth and our learning from them. As Rabban Gamliel noted in *Avodah Zarah*, the intention of the statue matters in how we as a society are meant to respond to it. The purpose of these statues was made very clear by Julian Carr: maintaining an everlasting symbol of ongoing white control and superiority. Therefore, merely erecting new slavery memorials is insufficient. We must destroy and annihilate not just the statues of old, but also the despicable mindset they represent. Only then will we as a society hopefully warrant the everlasting name promised to us in generations past.

Notes

1. Babylonian Talmud, *Avodah Zarah* 44b.
2. Babylonian Talmud, *Avodah Zarah* 46a.
3. Babylonian Talmud, *Avodah Zarah* 45b.
4. Kellan Duunnavant, "Behind Her Eyes: The Story of Isabella Gibbons," University of Virginia Office for Diversity, Equity, and Inclusion, accessed January 11, 2021, https://vpdiversity.virginia.edu/isabella-gibbons.
5. Phillip Kenniccott, "A Powerful New Memorial to U-Va.'s Enslaved Workers Reclaims Lost Lives and Forgotten Narratives," *Washington Post*, August 13, 2020, https://www.washingtonpost.com/goingoutguide/museums/a-powerful-new-memorial-to-u-vas-enslaved-workers-reclaims-lost-lives-and-forgotten-narratives/2020/08/12/7be63e66-dc03-11ea-b205-ff838e1-5a9a6_story.html.
6. Articles of Confederation of the United Daughters of the Confederacy,

July 18, 1919, https://archive.org/details/ArticlesOfIncorporationBy-lawsStandingRules/page/n1/mode/2up.

7. Transcript of Julian Carr's Speech at the Dedication of Silent Sam, June 2, 1913, https://hgreen.people.ua.edu/transcription-carr-speech.html.

8. Will Michaels, Elizabeth Baier, and Lisa Philip, "On Her Way Out, UNC Chancellor Orders Removal of 'Silent Sam' Pedestal," NPR, January 15, 2019, https://www.npr.org/2019/01/15/685442684/on-her-way-out-unc-chancellor-authorizes-removal-of-silent-sam-pedestal.

Lynching: Justice and the Idolatrous Tree

Rabbi Thomas M. Alpert

Parashat Shof'tim contains one of the most well-known exhortations in the Torah: *Tzedek, tzedek tirdof* (צֶדֶק צֶדֶק תִּרְדֹּף), "Justice, justice shall you pursue" (Deuteronomy 16:20). It is said that Rabbi Akiva was regarded as a great scholar due to his ability to devise mounds and mounds of meaning from the *tagim*, the ornamental crowns that top some of the letters in the Torah scroll.[1] With his example in mind, we can begin to imagine what a field day the commentators had with the repetition of the word *tzedek* (צֶדֶק), "justice." Why say it twice? If the *tagim* could not have been simply an orthographic flourish, then surely this doubling could not have been simply a rhetorical one.

A midrash suggests that if you have a choice of more than one court—that is, more than one place for *tzedek*—you should go to the one that will be known to administer justice more fairly.[2] The Chasidic commentator Rabbi Simcha Bunim of P'shischa claimed that the repetition meant that not only did one have to administer justice fairly, but you had to *appear* to do so; there could be no question of your probity.[3] Abraham ibn Ezra, the great rationalist of medieval commentators, actually did suggest that the doubling may just have been added for emphasis. But Ibn Ezra was not only a great contrarian; he was also a great grammarian, and he knew that Hebrew often repeats a word as a way of marking continuity. Thus, *sof* is the Hebrew word for "end." When it is repeated—*sof, sof*—it means "finally." So, Ibn Ezra conjectures, perhaps *tzedek, tzedek tirdof* means that you are to pursue justice finally, that is, "as long as you exist."[4]

In any event, this verse fits within the general topic of the beginning of this *parashah*: a set of commandments to appoint judges, *shof'tim*. In the very next verse, however, the Torah appears to introduce an unrelated subject: "You shall not set up a sacred post [*asheirah*, אֲשֵׁרָה]—any kind of pole beside the altar of the Eternal your God that you may make—... for such the Eternal your God detests" (Deuteronomy 16:21–22). According to the best modern scholarship, an *asheirah* was a cultic object, made of wood, for the worship of a Canaanite god—or more likely goddess, such as the goddess Asheirah.[5] Traditional Rabbinic commentary, while agreeing that an *asheirah* was an object for idolatrous worship, preferred to think of it as not a carving but an actual tree.[6] The juxtaposition of these verses—those about justice and those about the idolatrous tree—led the Talmud to suggest that the appointment of an unworthy judge was akin to planting an idolatrous tree.[7] That is to say, a miscarriage of justice is like the planting of a tree that encourages evil and idolatrous practices.

I don't know if Abel Meeropol studied Talmud when he grew up in the Bronx in the early years of the last century. But he knew something about the miscarriage of justice, and he knew something about trees. In 1937, he wrote "Strange Fruit," which was sung by Billie Holliday, among others. It begins:

> Southern trees bear strange fruit
> Blood on the leaves and blood at the root
> Black bodies swinging in the southern breeze
> Strange fruit hanging from the poplar trees

Between the end of Reconstruction in 1877 and 1950, a total of 4,084 terror lynchings took place in twelve Southern states, and 800 more occurred in other states of the Union.[8] Especially in the South, where the vast majority of these actions occurred, whites lynched Blacks to ensure continued racial control after the end of slavery. They were able to do so because the remainder of the country chose to let them.

It is not that the larger population did not know what was going on. In 1882, the pioneering Black journalist Ida B. Wells detailed the situation in her pamphlet *Southern Horrors*.[9] In 1909, she helped found the National Association for the Advancement of Colored People (NAACP), which carried on the work of fighting to end lynching. Starting in 1920, it displayed a banner outside its national headquarters on Fifth Avenue in New York City. In large white letters on a black background, it read, "A MAN WAS LYNCHED YESTERDAY." The banner went up whenever the NAACP leadership heard of a reason to fly it. Someone passing by on one of the great thoroughfares of the largest city in the United States would have been hard put not to see it. The NAACP stopped flying it in 1938. Lynchings hadn't ended; rather, the landlord threatened the organization with legal action if it didn't desist.[10] The NAACP and its allies sought to outlaw lynching at the federal level, but Senate filibusters doomed them.[11] To this day, lynching is not a federal crime.

With members of three congregations, including mine, I visited the National Memorial for Peace and Justice in Montgomery, Alabama, or as it is more popularly known, "the Lynching Memorial." It takes up six acres, and it stands at the site of a former slave pen. Its centerpiece is the pavilion. The pavilion contains stelae—six-foot-tall mini-monuments made of granite. Each one is carved with the name of a county and its state and with the names of African Americans who were lynched there. Many of the stelae are suspended, as if from a tree.[12]

As I walked deeper into the pavilion, I felt as if I were cut off from the safe world I normally inhabit. The counties, one after another, surrounded me, their stelae listing many names, including the name "unknown." LaFourche Parish in Louisiana had 52. Fulton County in Georgia had 35. Phillips County in Arkansas had 245. In 1940, Jesse Thornton was lynched in Luverne, Alabama, for referring to a white police officer by his name without the title of "mister." In 1918, Private Charles Lewis was lynched in Hickman, Kentucky, after he refused to empty his pockets while wearing his army uniform.[13]

As I write this in the summer of 2020, the strange fruit hanging from poplar trees is more than history for museum-goers. In 2006, Black high school students in Jena, Louisiana, sought permission to cool themselves in the shade of what had become known as the "white tree," and not for the color of its wood. School authorities approved. The next day, three nooses were found hanging from the tree. Violence ensued.[14] In the summer of 2020, amid Black Lives Matter protests, nooses were sighted both in real life and on social media.[15]

Tzedek, tzedek tirdof. "Justice, justice you shall pursue." The midrash was right: going in search of a court that will do your bidding degrades a society. That is one thing that lynching did: it set up its own vision of justice, a white people's court, where there was no place for an alternative point of view. And Simcha Bunim was right: the appearance of justice is as vital as the fact of justice. We can't take a noose thrown over a tree lightly, even if someone claims it to be a joke. An idolatrous tree is always calling. But perhaps most of all, Ibn Ezra had it right: we have to pursue justice again and again, for as long as we exist.

The miscarriage of justice is a tree that will bear strange fruit. We must uproot it if we are to endure long in a good and precious land.

NOTES

1. Babylonian Talmud, *M'nachot* 29b.
2. *Sifrei D'varim* 144:14.
3. *Torah Gems*, comp. Aharon Yaakov Greenberg, trans. Shmuel Himelstein (Tel Aviv: Yavneh Publishing House, 1998), 3:257.
4. Abraham ibn Ezra, commentary on *tzedek, tzedek tirdof*, in *The Commentators' Bible: Deuteronomy*, ed. Michael Carasik (Philadelphia: Jewish Publication Society, 2015), 114.
5. W. Gunther Plaut, ed., *The Torah: A Modern Commentary*, rev. ed. (New York: CCAR Press, 2005), 1204, notes on Deuteronomy 5:7.
6. See, e.g., commentators quoted in Carasik, *The Commentators' Bible*.
7. Babylonian Talmud, *Avodah Zarah* 52a.
8. The material about lynching in this commentary comes principally from Equal Justice Initiative, *Lynching in America*, 3rd ed. (Montgomery, AL: Equal Justice Initiative, 2017), https://lynchinginamerica.eji.org/report/.

9. Ida B. Wells, *Southern Horrors: Lynch Law in All Its Phases* (New York: New York Age Print, 1892).

10. Corinne Segal, "This Flag Once Protested Lynching: Now It's an Artist's Response to Police Violence," *News Hour*, PBS, July 10, 2016, https://www.pbs.org/newshour/arts/this-flag-once-protested-lynching-now-its-an-artists-response-to-police-violence.

11. Equal Justice Initiative, *Lynching in America*.

12. See Holland Cotter, "Critic's Notebook: A Memorial to the Lingering Horror of Lynching," *New York Times*, June 1, 2018, https://www.nytimes.com/2018/06/01/arts/design/national-memorial-for-peace-and-justice-montgomery-alabama.html.

13. Equal Justice Initiative, *Lynching in America*.

14. Darryl Fears, "La. Town Fells White Tree but Tensions Run Deep," *Washington Post*, August 4, 2007, https://www.washingtonpost.com/wp-dyn/content/article/2007/08/03/AR2007080302098.html.

15. ArLuther Lee, "Despite False Alarm at NASCAR, Nooses Sighted in at Least 11 Cities across US," *Atlanta Journal-Constitution*, June 24, 2020, https://www.ajc.com/news/nooses-dark-symbols-hate-appear-across-amid-racial-tensions/3XrpC88dfeqz6v5rBp4NdK/.

Reproductive Justice and Levirate Marriage: May I Not Go Out Empty

RABBI LIZ P. G. HIRSCH

PARASHAT KI TEITZEI is replete with challenging situations that do not match our current understanding of a just society, particularly with regard to sexual and reproductive justice. Levirate marriage is a fascinating example of a mitzvah that evolved from its appearance in the biblical text through its understanding in Rabbinic literature. After reviewing this evolution, I offer reproductive justice as a new lens through which to view the practice. Besides giving us a deeper understanding of levirate marriage, employing a reproductive justice framework can expand our perspective on reproductive rights and freedom.

Ki Teitzei offers the complete biblical explication of levirate marriage from a general perspective:

> When brothers dwell together and one of them dies and leaves no offspring, the wife of the deceased shall not be married to a stranger, outside the family. Her husband's brother shall unite with her: he shall take her as his wife and perform the levir's duty. The first child that she bears shall be accounted to the dead brother, that his name may not be blotted out in Israel. But if the man does not want to marry his brother's widow, his brother's widow shall appear before the elders in the gate and declare, "My husband's brother refused to establish a name in Israel for his brother; he will not perform the duty of a levir." The elders of his town shall then summon him and talk to him. If he insists, saying, "I do not want to marry her," his brother's widow shall

go up to him in the presence of the elders, pull the sandal off his foot, spit in his face, and make this declaration: "Thus shall be done to the man who will not build up his brother's house!" And he shall go in Israel by the name of "the family of the unsandaled one." (Deuteronomy 25:5–10)

Levirate marriage is not unique to the biblical text, appearing throughout the ancient world.[1] Rabbi Dr. Dvora Weisberg notes:

> According to Deuteronomy, the primary goal of levirate marriage is to provide the deceased with an heir. Deuteronomy focuses on the needs of the deceased, but levirate marriage may have fulfilled other needs within Israelite society. [One] beneficiary . . . would be the widow. While women could inherit their husband's estate in many parts of the ancient Near East, this was not the case in ancient Israel. A widow with children could expect her children to provide for her. If a man died childless, his estate reverted to his brother or other male kin; in these circumstances, a widow would be left with no source of support. Levirate marriage would ensure a childless widow a home and the possibility of children.[2]

The motivations of a widow with the status of a *y'vamah*, one awaiting a levirate marriage, are less apparent in Deuteronomy's legal text than in another narrative example from the Bible. The story of Tamar brings to life Deuteronomy's account of levirate marriage. Through Tamar's experiences, we see further evidence that this practice of levirate marriage is both beneficial to the widow and, in part, motivated by the widow's desire to bear children.

Genesis 38 recounts the story of Tamar. Originally married to Judah's eldest son, Er, until his death, she is remarried to his second son, Onan, through levirate marriage. Onan, wary of this arrangement because the children born would be accounted to Er, instead "wastes [his seed]" (Genesis 38:9). When he, too, dies, Judah withholds his third son, Shelah, from Tamar, thinking she is the common link between his first two sons' demise. "Stay as a widow in your father's house until my son Shelah grows up" (Genesis 38:11), Judah tells Tamar. As Tikvah Frymer-Kensky explains, rather than await a marriage and opportunity for childbirth that will never come, Tamar takes control of the situation: "Once Tamar realizes that Judah will not give her Shelah, she knows that she herself must act to protect her future. She must trick Judah into performing the levirate himself. Tamar ceases to be a victim and takes her destiny into her own hands."[3]

The midrash *B'reishit Rabbah* imagines a prayer that Tamar offers prior to her action, hinting at her priorities and desires: "May it be Your will, Eternal my God, that I will not go out from this house empty."[4] She prays that she will parent a child.

Posing as a prostitute, Tamar invites Judah, saying, "Pray let me couple with you," and she secures his "signet seal, [his] cord, and the staff in [his] hand" as a pledge (Genesis 38:16, 38:18). Several months later, after finding her pregnant, he threatens to kill her for her infidelity to his family; only after she presents his seal, cord, and staff does he realize what has occurred (Genesis 38:25–26). Tamar gives birth to sons Perez and Zerah, ancestors of King David, emphasizing the significance of her parenthood and her place in Jewish history.

Weisberg notes that levirate marriage, as portrayed in the Bible, particularly preferences the widow and the deceased brother, while later Rabbinic law transforms it into a ritual that preferences the living brother. As she explains:

> While acknowledging the possibility that a man might see levirate as a burden, the Bible insinuates that childless widows saw levirate as a beneficial institution. In Deuteronomy 25, the widow's appearance before and declaration to the elders suggests that she desires the union. . . . [Overall,] the widow has less to lose. Levirate allows her to remain in her husband's family, a family to which she may have grown accustomed and in which she may have found support and comfort. A childless widow was a vulnerable member of society, and levirate ensured a woman a home and the possibility of children.[5]

Rabbinic sources prefer the *chalitzah* (release) ritual over fulfilling levirate marriage. They privilege the rights of the levir, the living brother, over those of the dead brother and the widow by opting to assign the child to the living brother as his heir alone. The desires of the widow, whether regarding childbearing or remaining in the deceased husband's family unit, are deemphasized.[6]

The practice of levirate marriage may initially strike moderns as morally offensive. However, we can at least understand the biblical formulation, which privileges the *y'vamah*, enabling her to parent children and protecting her social and economic security.

Reproductive justice offers another opportunity to reexamine preconceived notions about reproductive freedom and sexual autonomy. As Loretta Ross and Rickie Solinger outline, "Reproductive justice is a contemporary framework for activism . . . [that] goes beyond the pro-choice/pro-life debate and has three primary principles: (1) the right to *not* have a child; (2) the right to *have* a child; and (3) the right to *parent* children in safe and healthy environments. In addition, reproductive justice demands sexual autonomy and gender freedom for every human being."[7]

Levirate marriage offers a unique look at the second principle of reproductive justice. A movement founded by Black women in the 1990s, reproductive justice grew out of the lived experiences of women who were deemed unfit to parent due to their race, socioeconomic status, or both. Ross and Solinger elaborate:

> Reproductive justice has lofty goals requiring the reconstruction of all unjust institutions and practices that affect reproductive decision making. The needs and the voices of poor women, disabled women, women of color, immigrant women, and other vulnerable individuals must be at the center of debates about reproduction. Each of these populations can trace attacks on their reproductive capacity back to the eugenics movement's insistence that only "fit" people should reproduce.[8]

Such a sentiment goes far beyond the priorities of the largely white, upper-middle-class reproductive rights movement, which focuses solely on legal access to the first prong of the reproductive justice framework, the right to *not* have a child. Keeping abortion legal has long been a crucial priority of the Reform Movement, with the Women of Reform Judaism, Central Conference of American Rabbis, and Union for Reform Judaism all on record with resolutions supporting *Roe v. Wade*.[9] However, maintaining a narrow focus on the right to *not* have a child denies the experiences of Black, Indigenous, and people of color (BIPOC) who have been systematically excluded from the right to *have* a child for centuries.

The reproductive justice framework adds depth and nuance to our understanding of levirate marriage. On the one hand, reproductive justice argues for sexual autonomy, which is inherently restricted in this system by preferencing either the deceased brother in the biblical text or the levir, the living brother, in the Rabbinic text. However, just as reproductive justice can expand a narrower framework of a reproductive rights, we can look beyond our initial distaste for archaic marital practices to understand levirate marriage's intended benefits for the widow. She may need access to her deceased husband's estate. She may even desire the right to have a child, as midrash imagines Tamar did. With a reproductive justice mindset, we can honor and elevate the prayers of biblical women—from our matriarchs Sarah and Rebekah to Tamar and Hannah—who sought divine intervention to enable them to bear children.

We have much to learn from the Black women who articulated the reproductive justice paradigm applicable to both our modern justice work and our interpretation of the experiences of our biblical ancestors. We pray with Tamar, "May it be Your will, Eternal my God, that I will not go out from this house empty."[10]

NOTES

1. Dvora E. Weisberg, *Levirate Marriage and the Family in Ancient Judaism* (Waltham, MA: Brandeis University Press, 2009), 5.
2. Weisberg, *Levirate Marriage*, 26.
3. Tikvah Frymer-Kensky, *Reading the Women of the Bible* (New York: Schocken Books, 2002), 269.
4. *B'reishit Rabbah* 85:7.
5. Weisberg, *Levirate Marriage*, 198.
6. Weisberg, *Levirate Marriage*, 105.
7. Loretta J. Ross and Rickie Solinger, *Reproductive Justice: An Introduction* (Oakland: University of California Press, 2017), 9.

8. Ross and Solinger, *Reproductive Justice*, 191.
9. "Jewish Values and Position of the Reform Movement: Reproductive Rights," Religious Action Center, accessed January 15, 2021, https://rac.org/jewish-values-and-position-reform-movement-reproductive-rights.
10. *B'reishit Rabbah* 85:7.

Ki Tavo—Deuteronomy 26:1–29:8

Jewish Supremacy: The Danger of Chosenness

Rabbi Noa Sattath

And the Eternal has affirmed this day that you are, as promised, God's treasured people who shall observe all the divine commandments, and that [God] will set you in fame and renown and glory, high above all the nations that [God] has made, and that you shall be, as promised, a holy people to the Eternal your God.

—*Deuteronomy 26:18–19*

THE MEANING of the term *s'gulah* (סְגֻלָּה), "treasure"—and of the concept of being chosen—was interpreted differently throughout history. Rashi viewed *s'gulah* as demonstrating that the Israelites are treasured in the eyes of God, in comparison to all other peoples.[1] The sixteenth-century commentator Sforno had a different, more egalitarian, take: "Even though I [God] value all people ... you will be special to Me above others because you will act as a kingdom of priests, instructing all of humankind to worship God together."[2]

These frameworks of thinking about the Jews/Israelites and other peoples—specifically, the ideas of Jewish supremacy and being chosen by God—take on explicit political significance in contemporary Israeli politics.

Much of the discourse on racism in recent years has been focused on how our society is racist without acknowledging it: systemic racism, discrimination and profiling, or in perceptions and opinions that translate into discriminatory policies. In this time of antidemocratic norms and practices, it is crucial to pay attention to two points on the racist spectrum—both covert racism and overt, blatantly racist speech that is often on the margins of the political scene. Democracies become weaker and even face critical danger when extreme right-wing ideologies take over the center-right. Civil society must react to blatant racism, drawing clear lines and making clear what is unacceptable.

White supremacist doctrines were prominent as a political ideology and accepted as a scientific truth between the nineteenth and the mid-twentieth centuries in Europe and North America. This ideological base supported policies of slavery, violence, discrimination, and exclusion around the world. In the 1960s, overtly supremacist ideologies were sidelined, giving way to other forms of governmental racism. Although supremacist groups since the '60s have had few public adherents, their influence on the mainstream right wing continues to be significant.[3]

Even though white supremacist ideologies around the world target Jews as enemies of the superior race, an analogous ideology has existed in Israel since the 1970s: the Kahanist movement, which advocates Jewish supremacy. Rabbi Meir Kahane immigrated to Israel from New York in 1971, following several convictions for acts related to domestic terrorism in the United States. Once in Israel, Kahane developed his racist theories, essentially targeting Arabs both within Israel and in the occupied territories. Underlying his theories was the dissemination of the idea that Jews are the chosen, superior people who must therefore separate themselves from others: "The people of Israel were chosen to continue the first human, and they are called *adam*, human, since they have the souls of humans, the wonderful special creation in the world. Gentiles, while they are physically equal to Israel, aren't 'human' in the spiritual sense."[4]

Kahane perceived the mere presence of non-Jews, specifically Arabs, in the Land of Israel to be "blasphemy," or *chilul HaShem*. He added a new concept of *eretz s'gulah*, a "treasured land" for the treasured people, Jews, where Jews would be separate from all other peoples.[5]

Once the Jews are in the Land of Israel, Kahane taught, all the non-Jews living there are subject to the law from Deuteronomy about the peoples who lived in Canaan during the time of Joshua: "In the towns of the latter [non-Israelite] peoples, however, which the Eternal your God is giving you as a heritage, you shall let not a soul remain alive" (Deuteronomy 20:16). According to his theory, Arabs should be either killed, deported, or enslaved and humiliated. He preached that the duty to uphold the commandment to either kill or expel Arabs from Israel rests both on the State of Israel and on all individuals.[6]

While Kahane had a minuscule base of support, with his Shabbat classes being attended by ten to twenty students, he had a profound impact. His radical views were influential on the settlement movement, particularly in the Hebron area.[7] Kahane established a political party, Kach, in 1972 and ran for the Knesset in 1973, 1977, and 1981. Despite gaining only a few thousand votes on each of these occasions, he did better in 1984, managing to win a seat in the Knesset. The reaction to his election was unanimous across the Israeli political spectrum: all members of Knesset would leave the plenary when he spoke from the podium. In 1985, the Knesset passed a law banning parties and candidates who incite racism from running for the body.[8] In 1988, the right-wing Likud party appealed to the central elections commission to disqualify the Kach party and succeeded, thus blocking Kahane's path as an elected official. Kahane followers have been trying to run for the Knesset since 1992. In most elections, they do not get enough votes to gain a seat.

In 1987, Kahane established the HaRaayon HaYehudi (the Jewish idea) yeshiva, where he focused on indoctrinating a small group of committed followers. Kahane was assassinated in New York in 1990, but his followers continued to uphold his extreme and violent teachings. Following the Cave of the Patriarchs massacre in Hebron, committed in 1994 by one of Kahane's students, the Knesset outlawed the Kach movement. In 1997, the US State Department added Kach and other Kahane-related organizations to the list of foreign terrorist organizations,[9] as Kahane's disciples created new organizations to advance their ideas and legitimacy.

The Israel Religious Action Center (IRAC)—the social justice arm of the Reform Movement in Israel, of which I am the director—has been keeping track of Kahane's followers since 2009. One of Kahane's most prominent students, Bentzi Gopstein, continues to manipulate the Jewish language for purposes of hatred, adopting Kahane's methods and ideology. Under the guise of working against "assimilation," he established a hate group focused on hyper-sexualizing Arab men, inciting against them, and advocating against their employment. Their goal is to deter Arabs from visiting or working in mixed areas in central Jerusalem, purportedly to deter Arab-Jewish intermarriage. Gopstein regularly incites hatred against Arabs and Christians on his Twitter account—his handle is "Kahane_zadak," "Kahane was right"—and operates a "Kahane a day" app that sends daily Kahane teachings to teenagers. After years of monitoring, ninety complaints placed by IRAC, and three appeals to the Supreme Court, Gopstein was charged in 2019 and is set to face trial.

IRAC has been working to disqualify Kahanist candidates from running for Knesset since 2012. During the tight 2019 election campaigns, Likud, which had led the efforts to disqualify Kahanists in 1988, made intense and concerted attempts to include Kahane followers in the mainstream right-wing parties, giving those extremists a much better chance of entering the Knesset than in previous years. Prime Minister Benjamin Netanyahu made multiple promises, including guaranteeing spots for Orthodox right-wing parties inside Likud, in exchange for the integration of Kahanist candidates into the Orthodox party, among the most alarming pieces of evidence that far-right politics have become increasingly mainstream.

We at IRAC have been monitoring, collecting evidence, and perfecting our legal strategies for years. In both 2019 elections, we were able to disqualify Kahanist candidates from running. One of them would have been elected if we had failed in our disqualification efforts. Even more important, we managed to raise public awareness about the dangers of this movement and to delegitimize it. As a result, for the third election cycle, all right-wing parties rejected Kahane followers, preventing them from collaborating with any of the mainstream parties. IRAC thus protected Israeli democracy from racist extremists while representing the Sforno interpretation of *s'gulah*, that we were chosen for the duty and commitment to uphold justice for all the people in the world.

Notes

1. Rashi to Deuteronomy 26:17.

2. Sforno to Deuteronomy 26:18.

3. Chip Berlet and Matthew N. Lyons, *Right-Wing Populism in America: Too Close for Comfort* (New York: Guilford, 2018).

4. Meir Kahane, *Or Hara'ayon: The Jewish Idea* (Jersalem: Institute for Publication of the Writings of Rabbi Meir Kahane, 1996).

5. Ehud Sprinzak, *Political Violence in Israel* [in Hebrew] (Jerusalem: Jerusalem Institute for the Study of Israel, 1995), 215–21.

6. Kahane, *Or Hara'ayon*, 262–63.

7. M. Uriel, "The Thought and Work of Rabbi Meir Kahana as a Source of Inspiration for the Settlers of Kiryat Arba and Hebron in the Years 1969–1984," *Studies in Judea and Samaria* 27, no. 2 (2018), 249–68.

8. Dan Gordon, "Limits on Extremist Political Parties: A Comparison of Israeli Jurisprudence with that of the United States and West Germany," *Hastings International and Comparative Law Review* 10, no. 2 (winter 1987), 349.

9. Office of the Coordinator for Counterterrorism, "Chapter 6—Terrorist Organizations," in *Country Reports on Terrorism* (Washington DC: US Department of State, April 30, 2007), https://2009-2017.state.gov/j/ct/rls/crt/2006/82738.htm.

NITZAVIM—DEUTERONOMY 29:9–30:20

Voting Rights:
A Constitutional Covenant

RABBI ERICA SEAGER ASCH

PARASHAT NITZAVIM brings us to the end of the ceremony sealing the covenant between God and the people of Israel. Throughout the previous chapters of Deuteronomy, we have seen the treaty stipulations and sanctions to be implemented if the people do not follow through on their promises. Now, we come to the ceremony of imprecation, where the community accepts that if they do not follow through with their part in the covenant, there will be serious consequences.[1] At the moment the people are about to enter the land, they are bound in relationship to God. But who is there? Who is part of this promise between God and the people Israel? The text is clear: everyone.

The first lines of the *parashah* emphasize that the entire community is part of this covenant. "You stand this day, all of you, before the Eternal your God" (Deuteronomy 29:9). In case "all of you" is not clear enough, the text elaborates: "your tribal heads, your elders, and your officials, all the men of Israel, your children, your women, even the stranger within your camp, from woodchopper to water drawer" (Deuteronomy 29:9–10). Unlike other sections of the Torah text, where the second-person masculine plural pronoun is ambiguous— it could mean both males and females or exclusively males—here the text explicitly includes women and children. Moreover, it lists those who are specifically marginalized. The stranger—a person who is not an Israelite but still subject to civil law and religious prohibitions—must be a part of this ceremony.[2] The woodchopper and water drawer, representing menial laborers, are specifically included. The message is unequivocal: everyone is a part of the covenantal community. Indeed, it is impossible for there to be a true and complete relationship between God and Israel without everyone participating.

The text continues to discuss the dire consequences that will befall the people if they do not hold up their end of the covenant and instead follow other gods. God will "single [them] out . . . for misfortune" (Deuteronomy 29:20), and their land will be devastated and cursed. While other nations will recognize Israel's wisdom if they obey God, those nations will see the punishment if they disobey God.

Today, our lives are very different from those of our ancient ancestors. We do not live in a mostly Israelite society where we are all bound to follow God's laws. As Jews, we are bound by a covenant with God. As citizens, we are bound by the laws of the country in which we live. Those laws are written in the Constitution, expanded in the amendments, enacted in statutes, and interpreted by the courts. Some, including James Madison, have viewed the Constitution as the focal point of America's "civil religion." Much like the Torah, it is a document to be revered.[3] As Americans, we the people, the governed, are bound in relationship with our government. We agree to abide by the laws or suffer the consequences if we do not. We also agree to take an active part in this relationship. In a democracy, we manifest and reaffirm our commitment to our government through voting. Just as the Jewish people stand and hear the Ten Commandments read every Shavuot, thus reenacting and reaffirming the covenant, the act of voting reaffirms the relationship between the government and the governed.

No analogy is perfect. The Israelite covenant is more expansive than American democracy. The covenant described in *Nitzavim* includes children and noncitizens. Our American democracy is not that expansive, but we have been gradually expanding the definition of who is able to participate in our elections.

When our nation was founded, only free white males, a fraction of the population, were granted the right to vote.[4] Over time, we extended voting rights: to Black men in 1870, although they were disenfranchised in large parts of the country after Reconstruction ended; to women in 1920; to Native Americans in 1924; and to those aged eighteen to twenty in 1971.

Although laws permitting voting were on the books, the courts often kept minorities, particularly Black southerners, from voting. This de facto disenfranchisement took the form of poll taxes, literacy tests, and grandfather clauses applied only to Black men and women. The Voting Rights Act, adopted in 1965, addressed many of these tactics and helped to enfranchise Black southerners. The act outlawed literacy tests and gave the federal government the power to enforce voting rights. This led to a large increase in voter turnout in the Black community.[5] However, those with felony convictions, often men of color, remain disenfranchised in a number of states.[6] Our Torah text goes out of its way to include those people most likely to be vulnerable—women, those who are poor, those who are strangers, those who are often marginalized. The text recognizes a harsh reality we also know from American history: members of certain groups are more likely to be excluded from the community. In modern times, our text is warning us that we must grant all citizens the right to vote. While some see voting as a privilege that must be earned, our text says being a part of the community is a right that is universally granted.

While the expansion of voting rights has not been linear, the general trend was toward allowing more people to vote. That changed with the 2013 Supreme Court decision in *Shelby v. Holder*. This ruling struck down a key provision of the Voting Rights Act, allowing states with a history of discrimination to change their voting laws without pre-authorization from the federal Department of Justice.[7] States including Texas, Mississippi, North Carolina, and Alabama moved quickly to make voting more difficult for Black citizens by instituting stringent photo identification requirements, which disproportionately impact Black voters, and by eliminating same-day voter registration.[8] States also closed polling places in Black and Latino neighborhoods and shortened voting hours, causing much longer wait times for communities of color, further eroding the right of all citizens to vote.[9]

The Torah warns us of consequences if we do not follow God's laws. Similarly, there will be consequences if not all of us participate in the constitutional covenant. Today in America, people are intentionally left out of our democracy, when barriers are erected denying them the fundamental right to vote. And we are suffering consequences. In 1958, 73 percent of Americans expressed trust in the federal government to do what is right; in 2020, only 17 percent did.[10] Part of that erosion of trust likely results from lack of confidence in our elections. In 2020, nearly half of US voters expected to have difficulties voting.[11] We are seeing an erosion of confidence in our covenant between the governed and the government.

The situation seems dire, but the Torah portion reassures us that repair is not impossible: "Surely, this Instruction which I enjoin upon you this day is not too baffling for you, nor is it beyond reach" (Deuteronomy 30:11). Expanding voting rights is within our grasp. While the Reform Movement has called for expanding access to the ballot box and voter registration, and ending policies such as "voter purges . . . strict ID requirements . . . and closing polling locations, particularly in communities of color," we can go further.[12] Making voting easier means more people will vote. To start, we should automatically register all eligible voters. Automatic registration increases both registration and turnout in minority communities.[13] In 2018, only 67 percent of eligible US voters were registered to vote, trailing voter registration in most developed countries.[14] However, registration is not enough—people need to be able to vote. In 2018, the number one reason people did not vote (27 percent) was that they were too busy or had a conflict in their schedule.[15] Allowing no-excuse mail-in voting and early voting means people do not have to wait in line or vote on a specific day. These options should be available in all states. Additionally, Election Day should become a national holiday, with nonessential businesses required to close on that day. We should ensure that essential workers are given paid time off during the workday to go to the polls, increasing access and showing younger generations the importance of voting.

We read *Nitzavim* on Yom Kippur, reminding us that we are all part of the covenant. Our community is complete only if all people, regardless of their job or gender, are present. Similarly, each time we vote, we know that our democracy is not complete unless everyone can participate. Ensuring that every citizen is able to exercise their right to vote is the foundation of our democracy.

Notes

1. Adele Berlin and Marc Zvi Brettler, eds., *The Jewish Study Bible* (Oxford: Oxford University Press, 2004), 435.
2. David L. Lieber, ed., *Etz Hayim: Torah and Commentary* (New York: Jewish Publication Society, 2004), 1165.
3. James Madison, *The Writings of James Madison*, vol. 6, *1790–1802*, ed. Gaillard Hunt, Online Library of Liberty, accessed August 17, 2020, https://oll. libertyfund.org/titles/madison-the-writings-vol-6-1790-1802.
4. Daniel Ratcliff, "The Right to Vote and the Rise of Democracy 1787–1828," *Journal of the Early Republic* 33 (Summer 2013): 219, https://jer.pennpress. org/media/26167/sampleArt22.pdf. In the article, Ratcliff argues that voting was less restrictive in the colonial United States than in England and that 60–90 percent of free white males could vote by 1790. Regardless of the number of free white men who could vote, it took years for the United States to enfranchise other groups of people.
5. "Voting Rights Act of 1965," History.com, accessed August 25, 2020, https:// www.history.com/topics/black-history/voting-rights-act.
6. "Felon Voting Rights," National Conference of State Legislatures, accessed July 28, 2020, https://www.ncsl.org/research/elections-and-campaigns/ felon-voting-rights.aspx.
7. "Shelby County vs. Holder," Oyez, accessed August 17, 2020, https://www. oyez.org/cases/2012/12-96.
8. "The Effects of Shelby County v. Holder," Brennan Center for Justice, August 6, 2018, https://www.brennancenter.org/our-work/policy-solutions/effects-shelby-county-v-holder.
9. Hannah Klein, Kevin Morris, Max Feldman and Rebecca Ayala, "Waiting to Vote," Brennan Center for Justice, June 3, 2020, https://www. brennancenter.org/our-work/research-reports/waiting-vote.
10. Michael Dimock, "How Americans View Trust, Facts, and Democracy Today," *Trust*, Pew, February 19, 2020, https://www.pewtrusts.org/ en/trust/archive/winter-2020/how-americans-view-trust-facts-and-democracy-today.
11. "Election 2020: Voters Are Highly Engaged, but Nearly Half Expect to Have Difficulties Voting," Pew Research Center, August 13, 2020, https://www. pewresearch.org/politics/2020/08/13/election-2020-voters-are-highly-engaged-but-nearly-half-expect-to-have-difficulties-voting/.
12. "Union for Reform Judaism Resolution on Free and Accessible Elections,"

Union for Reform Judaism, 2020, https://urj.org/what-we-believe/resolutions/urj-resolution-free-and-accessible-elections.

13. Caitlin Oprysko, "Oregon Governor Calls Automatic Voter Registration a 'Phenomenal Success,'" Politico, February 22, 2019, https://www.politico.com/story/2019/02/22/automatic-voter-registration-oregon-1181199.

14. Drew Desilver, "U.S. Trails Most Developed Countries in Voter Turnout," Pew Research Center, November 3, 2020, https://www.pewresearch.org/fact-tank/2018/05/21/u-s-voter-turnout-trails-most-developed-countries/; "Table 4a. Reported Voting and Registration, for States: November 2018," US Census Bureau, accessed August 17, 2020, https://www2.census.gov/programs-surveys/cps/tables/p20/583/table04a.xlsx.

15. "Table 10. Reasons for Not Voting, by Selected Characteristics: November 2018," US Census Bureau, accessed August 17, 2020, https://www2.census.gov/programs-surveys/cps/tables/p20/583/table10.xlsx.

Vayeilech—Deuteronomy 31:1–30
The Courage To Be Different

Rabbi Jeffrey K. Salkin

IT IS THE LAST DAY of Moses's life. Once you know that, you'll understand the fevered urgency—his sense of mortality, his need to address the people of Israel one more time; the mere fact that *Vayeilech*, "Moses went"—personally, out to his people. We can imagine him saying to himself, "Here I am—going out to my people—just like the first time, back in Egypt, before I even knew who I was."

It is not as if Moses is leaving his people "like sheep that have no shepherd" (Numbers 27:17). At God's direction, Moses has appointed Joshua to fill his role. But nowhere does the Torah tell us why Joshua is particularly qualified to be Moses's successor. God says that Joshua is "an inspired individual" (Numbers 27:18), yet is that enough?

What special life skill does Joshua possess that will make him the leader for that crucial moment? The answer comes to us from the story of the spies (Numbers 14). Recall that Moses sent spies into the Land of Israel to see what the Land was like—whether the inhabitants were strong or weak, whether the cities were fortified or open. Ten of the spies, representing ten of the tribes, brought back negative reports: the Land was simply unconquerable. Two spies, however—Joshua and Caleb—brought back a minority opinion. Yes, the project of conquering the Land would be daunting, but the people of Israel would be up to the task.

Joshua is fit to be the next leader of the people of Israel because he is willing to be part of a minority—a radical one. This experience of being in the minority would be repeated for much of Jewish history.

There is an old joke about two Jews walking in a dangerous

neighborhood late at night. They hear footsteps behind them and turn around to see who is there. "We had better be careful," says one Jew to the other. "There are two of them, and we are alone." That has been the paradigm of Jewish history—a sense of radical aloneness, of being a minority. Leo Baeck put it this way in *The Essence of Judaism*: "A minority is compelled to think; that is the blessing of its fate. It must always persist in a mental struggle for that consciousness of truth which success and power comfortingly assure to rulers and their supporting multitudes. The conviction of the many is based on the weight of possession; the conviction of the few is expressed through the energy of constant searching and finding."[1]

Joshua is the archetype of the dissenting minority.

According to the ADL, antisemitism in the United States is at a four-decade high.[2] Physical attacks on Jews have increased both in number and intensity. "Why do they hate us so much?" a Jewish teenager asked me.

Another kid offered the following answer: "Because they're jealous of us."

"Whatever for?" someone else retorted.

"Because we believe good stuff."

But what is the "good stuff" that Jews believe? That question haunted one of the most prolific, original, and controversial thinkers of the contemporary cultural landscape, the late George Steiner, a scholar of comparative literature and novelist. According to Steiner, the role of the Jews is to be a royal pain in the neck. A dissenting minority.

Back in the "good old days," humanity had many gods. This allowed for a diversity of human belief and ethics, a kind of sacred relativism. And then the Jews came and invented monotheism. They taught about the God who was all demanding and judgmental. That is how the Jews became a "moral irritant and insomniac among men," a role Steiner calls an "honor beyond honors." The Jew represents the uncompromising demand for universal morality, the intoxicating idea that human beings can overcome their selfish impulses.[3]

Judaism's great contribution to humanity is the establishment of an inescapable divine conscience, of an uncompromising demand for moral elevation, unconditional love, and total altruism. This is the legacy of the Jewish people, through which it has irrevocably changed the moral face of humankind.

But this legacy came with a price: Jew-hatred and Judaism-hatred. I prefer those terms to the seemingly scientific yet inaccurate "antisemitism." Steiner suggests that the Jews' invention of the ethical idea caused the rest of the world to hate them. The ancient Rabbis loved to make a wonderful pun: Sinai, the moment of revelation, led to *sinah,* "hatred."

The best way to understand this is to read Steiner's 1981 novel *The Portage to San Cristobal of A.H.* Steiner imagines Hitler still alive in the jungles of South America. Israeli agents find him, arrest him, and bring him to trial. In the last two pages of the novel, the ninety-year-old Hitler takes the stand in his own defense. Hitler says that he had to do what he did because the Jews invented not only conscience but God: "Was there ever a crueler invention, a contrivance more calculated to harrow human existence, than that of an omnipotent, all-seeing, yet invisible, inconceivable God? . . . The Jew invented conscience and left man a guilty serf."[4]

Steiner was on to something. Consider the words of the historian Paul Johnson, in his book *A History of the Jews:*

> The Jews believed themselves created and commanded to be a light to the gentiles and they have obeyed to the best of their considerable powers. The results, whether considered in religious or in secular terms, have been remarkable. The Jews gave to the world ethical monotheism, which might be described as the application of reason to divinity. In a more secular age, they applied the principles of rationality to the whole range of human activities, often in advance of the rest of mankind. The light they thus shed disturbed as well as illuminated, for it revealed painful truths about the human spirit as well as the means to uplift it. The Jews have been great truth-tellers, and that is one reason they have been so much hated.[5]

So, WWJD? What would Joshua do? Consider that our one-chapter, thirty-verse Torah portion contains three repetitions of the admonition "Be strong and resolute" (Deuteronomy 31:6–7, 23) and similarly, "Fear not and be not dismayed" (Deuteronomy 31:8). Those words encapsulate what Jews must do in order to fight antisemitism.

First: Make antisemitism socially unacceptable. Call it out wherever and whenever it crawls out of the muck.

Stigmatize it like tobacco. Once upon a time, it seemed that everyone smoked cigarettes. Just watch mid-twentieth-century movies. Revisit news programs and you will see the famous talking heads of the time smoking cigarettes. It was ubiquitous. And then what happened? In 1964, the US surgeon general released a famous report linking tobacco use to lung cancer and heart disease. A year later, the federal government mandated that cigarette packaging include warnings that smoking could be hazardous to one's health. By 1971, tobacco advertising on television and radio became illegal. We also realized the harmful effects of secondhand smoke on nonsmokers. No amount of legislation or social engineering could fully end smoking. However, through a concerted effort over decades, our culture relegated tobacco to the sidelines of polite society.

Today, we face a similar, though less lethal, public health crisis: the explosion of antisemitic acts. It is time for America to do for antisemitism what it did for cigarette smoking—make it taboo.

Second: Reject all forms of hatred. While not every kind of hatred is the same, they all feel the same to those who have been their target.

Third: Don't make antisemitism the center of your Jewish identity. As the Torah portion demonstrates, the eternal struggles of the Jewish people will tempt them to say, "Surely it is because our God is not in our midst that these evils have befallen us" (Deuteronomy 31:17). But God has always been in our midst, even though it might seem that God has hidden the divine face from us. We do not reveal the face of God through fighting hatred. Rather, that act of revelation comes from mitzvot, study, prayer, celebration, song, poetry—the vital aspects of life that make Judaism worth living.

As Bari Weiss said at a rally against antisemitism:[6]

I am not a Jew because people hate my religion, my people, and my civilization.

I am a Jew because of the audacity and the iconoclasm of Abraham,[7] the first Jew of all. The whole world was awash in idols and he stood alone to proclaim the truth: There is one God.

I am a Jew because my ancestors were slaves. And I am a Jew because the story of their Exodus from Egypt, their liberation from slavery, is a story that changed human consciousness forever.

The Jewish people were not put on earth to be anti-antisemites. We were put on Earth to be Jews.

We are the people whose God never slumbers or sleeps, and so neither can we.

We are the lamp-lighters.

We are the ever-dying people that refuses to die.

NOTES

1. Leo Baeck, *The Essence of Judaism* (1936; repr., Pygmalion Press, 2018), chap. 1.
2. "Antisemitic Incidents Hit All-Time High in 2019," ADL, May 12, 2020, https://www.adl.org/news/press-releases/antisemitic-incidents-hit-all-time-high-in-2019.
3. George Steiner, *Errata: An Examined Life* (London: Weidenfeld and Nicolson, 1997), 57, quoted in Assaf Sagiv, "George Steiner's Jewish Problem," *Azure*, Summer 2003, 131, http://www.azure.org.il/download/magazine/1147az15_Sagiv.pdf.
4. George Steiner, *The Portage to San Cristobal of A. H.: A Novel* (Chicago: University of Chicago Press, 1999), 164.
5. Paul Johnson, *A History of the Jews* (New York: Harper Perennial, 1987), 583.
6. "The Full Text of Bari Weiss's Address to the 'No Hate, No Fear' March," Jewish Insider, January 5, 2020, https://jewishinsider.com/2020/01/the-full-text-of-bari-weiss-address-to-the-no-hate-no-fear-march/.
7. To this, Reform Jews would add "and Sarah."

One Person, One Vote:
A Biblical Precedent

RABBI NOAM KATZ

ON THE FIRST DAY of my Homiletics course, I was let in on a little secret—every rabbi has but one sermon. Rabbis may revise, reinvent, and repurpose that one sermon throughout their career, but a careful listener can discern a single thesis serving as spiritual undercurrent every time they preach from the pulpit. This is the lens through which the rabbi sees the world, the reflective mirror they deem essential to hold up before their congregation.

Politicians must have their own version of this too, as they bend the ears of their constituents toward a particular framing of history—and, more importantly, a blueprint for future progress. Even if their stance on a certain issue changes over the course of their career, the convictions that propelled them into public service, be they noble or self-aggrandizing, remain at the core of their message, their one true stump speech.

And for Moses, a prophet and political visionary all rolled into one, *Parashat Haazinu* affords an opportunity to deliver one last great sermon. As this penultimate Torah portion unfolds, the prose of Deuteronomy transforms into two pillar-like columns of poetry. The stark contrast in genre and textual format beckons the reader to take notice, in much the same way that Moses rouses the heavens to "give ear" and jolts his earthbound audience to heed every word that escapes his lips: "Give ear, O heavens, let me speak; / Let the earth hear the words I utter!" (Deuteronomy 32:1). This will be the final speech of Moses's illustrious career, his swan song, and he wants to ensure that his message is neither misheard nor misconstrued. Experienced orator and skilled politician that he is, Moses addresses the Israelites with a soliloquy that is at once a recollection of their past and a vision for the future.

From the outset of his lyrical offering, Moses warns his audience to avoid becoming a "dull and witless people" (Deuteronomy 32:6), not to repeat the same mistakes of "that crooked, perverse genera-tion" (32:5), who continually showed themselves to be disloyal and dismissive of God's laws. Rather, he beseeches them to "remember the days of old" (32:7), when God divided the land equitably among *B'nei Yisrael* (the Children of Israel) and their neighbors:

> When the Most High gave nations their homes
> And set the divisions of the human race,
> [God] fixed the boundaries of peoples
> In relation to Israel's numbers. (Deuteronomy 32:8)

Here Moses recounts two of God's initial gifts to humanity: the distribution of inhabitable land to disparate communities and the establishment of set boundaries for nations relative to their, and Israel's, populations. The first hearkens back to the aftermath of Babel, wherein God confounds the speech of humans and disperses them across the earth (Genesis 11:1–9). This moment in biblical his-tory foretells the creation of tribes, ethnic groups, and local as well as national entities, who are ideally united by a shared set of social standards, language, and government.

In order to build a society in which these splintered nations are not constantly at war, God bestows a second gift: borders, prescribed boundaries that delineate where one's people will reside and how they will self-govern therein. Tribal and national lines will be divinely decided and lands apportioned, God promises, "in relation to Israel's numbers." And while this proclamation speaks to the apportionment of all the world's lands in relation to Israel, logic follows that a similar distribution of land should occur *within* Israel's borders as well—that the twelve tribes shall inherit territories commensurate with their population, resulting in an equitable, though not necessarily equal, distribution of land.

Sforno, an early sixteenth-century commentator from Italy, contextualizes these divine allotments as a limitation imposed on local or regional power:

> After the Tower of Babel episode, when humankind had lived in a single community, God separated them, dividing them up, and established territorial boundaries for the various new nations. Instead of destroying the people who had engaged in building the tower as a challenge to God, God did not destroy them as God had the generation of the flood, but limited their future scope of influence, by assigning only clearly marked territories within which they could be sovereign.[1]

According to Sforno, self-governance requires an acknowledgment of the limits to one's land and authority. The opportunity to govern does not grant a nation or its leadership carte blanche to attack its neighbors, conquer more territory, or abuse its own citizens. While the concept of basic and inalienable human rights did not emerge until the dawn of the Enlightenment, this passage from *Haazinu* depicts an ancient ethic of equitable land distribution—and, implicitly, equitable treatment of the individuals who make up each sovereign nation.

Today, our democracy depends on such civilized treatment of its population, on its citizens having the freedom to speak, to express, to assemble, to hold property, and to *vote*. This last freedom, above all, ensures that our leaders are fairly elected according to the will of the majority, *in relation to our numbers*. By putting the power into the hands of the individual voter holding a ballot, those serving in government come to recognize the limits of their own authority, so that tyrants cannot arise, officials cannot overstay their welcome, and presidents cannot claim to be infallible.

But in the five and a half decades following the landmark passage of the Voting Rights Act of 1965, which finally enacted the Fifteenth Amendment at its centennial by prohibiting racial discrimination in voting in the United States, that basic right to vote for one's local and

national leaders has been threatened for so many segments of the
population, primarily minority groups. Voter suppression has taken
on a number of insidious forms. We have seen the removal of polling
stations, the imposition of voter identification laws, and purging of
voter registration lists, for example—all primarily impacting poor,
low-income, elderly, disabled, and young voters.[2] But it was the controversial *Rucho v. Common Cause* decision by the Supreme Court in
June 2019,[3] adopted by a slim 5–4 majority, that legitimized one of
the cornerstone elements of voter suppression in the United States:
partisan gerrymandering.

Partisan gerrymandering—the practice of redrawing boundaries
of electoral districts to favor specific political interests and parties,
often resulting in districts with convoluted, winding boundaries—is
possibly the most widespread tool of voter suppression in the United
States today. In twenty-five states, district boundaries are determined by state legislatures and confirmed by the governor's signa-
ture. When one political party controls the state's legislative bodies
as well as the executive branch, it can wield its power to gerrymander
district boundaries, benefiting its candidates and heavily disadvan-
taging political opponents. The practice of "packing votes"—that
is, concentrating like-minded voters who generally oppose the party
in charge of redistricting into one district—can significantly reduce
one party's congressional representation and lead to corrupted elections. And while the Supreme Court has deemed extreme cases of gerrymandering that disadvantage a minority ethnic or racial group to
be unconstitutional, it has struggled to determine when such an
extreme case applies. Moreover, *Rucho v. Common Cause* rendered partisan gerrymandering a nonjusticiable political question that cannot
be addressed by the federal court system. That decision left it to state
legislatures and Congress to develop remedies for challenging and
preventing partisan gerrymandering *if* those bodies choose to make
it a priority. Not surprisingly, in many states, gerrymandering is still
a viable way for those in power to retain their position.

In 1965, the authors of the Voting Rights Act celebrated a landmark victory, but they might not have foreseen the myriad ways that

state legislators, governors, and special interest groups would try to undo its protections in the ensuing decades. What good is the right to vote when others work tirelessly to suppress, silence, or seize this basic tenet of democracy? What value does an election hold if its victors do not represent the will of the people?

Haazinu might well hold the answer—or, at the very least, the prophetic stump speech that is just as pertinent today as it was in biblical times. Moses's exhortation to the Israelites shows an awareness of the inherent duplicity of the body politic. His subtle reference to the generation of Babel—victims of their own self-importance—and his subsequent recall of God's delineation of borders for each tribe provide a blueprint for how societies should behave in any age.

We might imagine Moses exhorting Americans: *Do not* deify yourself so as to showcase your superiority; it will surely be your downfall. *Do not* artificially redraw the borders, both within and beyond your allotted territory, in order to guarantee your continued dominance over the land and its people. Those boundaries, says Sforno, are there to remind you of your own limitations—which is very much a good thing, a healthy mindset to keep you humble and human. Instead, *do* distribute the land, as well as the voices and votes of its citizens, in a fair and equitable manner corresponding to the people's numbers. Construct a community that adheres to the principle of "one person, one vote," so that the citizenry will always enjoy equitable and proportional representation.

Haazinu isn't merely Moses's final speech. It's his first one, too, and each one in between. It is a version of what he has consistently preached to the Israelites since accepting the mantle of leadership, from their redemption out of Egypt to their rebirth in the wilderness. Regardless of the literary genre or rhetoric he employs, Moses's one sermon, the sermon of his life, is a vision of the world in which justice prevails, hope looms in the heavens above, and the earth listens intently to the needs of its inhabitants, providing for them a bedrock of equity and equality.

NOTES

1. Sforno on Deuteronomy 32:8.
2. *Suppressed 2020: The Right to Vote* (film), directed by Robert Greenwald (Brave New Films, 2020).
3. Rucho v. Common Cause, 18-422, 588 U.S. (2019).

Time to Say Goodbye: Reforming Cash Bail

Rabbi Joshua Stanton

KNOWING HOW TO SAY GOODBYE is challenging. Knowing when to do so is rare enough that it befits the greatest of our prophets, Moses. His poignant farewell illustrates the immense power and privilege that go with knowledge of how long you will be with the people you love—and when you might no longer be.

For Moses, in life as in death, timing is everything. He is a bestower of justice, and he also receives just treatment, permitted to continue on until his death at an understood place and time. Moses first learns of his fate in Numbers 20, when he defies God and strikes a rock in anger, rather than bringing forth water from it with words alone. God swiftly delivers a painful verdict: "Because you did not trust Me enough to affirm My sanctity in the sight of the Israelite people, therefore you shall not lead this congregation into the land that I have given them" (Numbers 20:12). Yet Moses continues living and leading until the very last moment.

Our Sages suggest that Moses leads until the moment before his death. In *Parashat V'zot Hab'rachah*, we read of Moses's death itself: "So Moses the servant of the Eternal died there, in the land of Moab, at the command of the Eternal" (Deuteronomy 34:5). The Talmud relates a teaching in which Joshua writes the final eight verses of the Torah, picking up where Moses left off and eulogizing his predecessor as leader of the Israelites.[1] Because Moses's punishment has been anticipated so far in advance, his transition has been eased, and the continuity of our sacred text ensured.

We look to Moses as the exemplar in saying farewell, but we should also look to the example of divine justice that God metes out to him. God does not tarry. God does not surprise Moses. God does not confine Moses or limit his ability to be with family, friends, or all of the Israelites until the last possible moment.

Today, such examples are few and far between in the American justice system. Cash bail was initially intended to ensure that defendants show up for their trial, but now it has become a mechanism of unequal treatment. If you have money, you readily post bail pending trial in most criminal cases. If you do not, you likely cannot afford bail and may face jail time before having your case tried. Our system of cash bail ensures an immediate injustice for many defendants awaiting trial.

According to the Prison Policy Initiative, "99 percent of the rise in incarceration between 1999 and 2014 involved the pre-trial population,"[2] with more than half of all people in jail waiting to post bail or unable to do so for financial reasons.[3] This injustice is staggering, especially given the known rates of mistreatment, violence, and even murder in America's jails.[4] The 450,000 people held behind bars awaiting trial are treated as guilty until proven innocent.[5] A disproportionate number of them are people of color.[6]

Beyond the indefensible pain and suffering that we inflict upon many awaiting trial—and the usurious bond industry that has arisen to lend money for cash bail for fees of 10 percent and penalties for tardiness several times as high[7]—one can only imagine lost time and potential among those hundreds of thousands of souls who are incarcerated each year because of their inability to pay cash bail. Think of the relationships lost, professional strides reversed, and broken course along their life's path. If Moses is able to continue serving after having committed a public offense so grievous as to cost him the chance to enter the Promised Land, surely other nonviolent offenders today deserve to live, give, and learn in the presence of family and community.

This very Torah portion represents the chance that Moses has enjoyed from the time of his sin at Meribah until the ultimate Judge sealed his fate. The valedictory address in *V'zot Hab'rachah* lives on long after Moses, providing spiritual and social sustenance to the Israelites as well as legitimacy to his successor, Joshua. It is so significant that Abraham ibn Ezra compares it to the words that Jacob bestows upon each of his children before his death.[8] The blessing expressed within the ultimate chapters of the Torah is the realization of the promises that God has made to Israel—and which Israel (Jacob's acquired name) made to each of his sons.

Each one would be uniquely blessed, the descendants of Abraham would be as numerous as the stars in the sky, and Israel would enter the Promised Land. They would be "a people delivered by the Eternal, your protecting Shield, your Sword triumphant" (Deuteronomy 33:29). The Israelites now have a story of origin, a story of liberation, and now a path to self-actualization. They have received laws and guidance, inspired leadership, and a vision of the society of which all would be a part. They have become free in the fullest of senses.

With Moses's words of blessing, they could live on as a people even after his death. In their absence, the Israelites might have resorted to further infighting, sought to overthrow Joshua, or missed the chance to self-actualize altogether. Imagine the hundreds of thousands of people in our jails today who were incarcerated before even preparing for trial. Imagine the blessings that they might have uttered and succor that they might have given to family and friends.

While the name of this Torah portion, *V'zot Hab'rachah*—"and this is the blessing"—refers to Moses's words, so too does it refer to the final blessing that God has given Moses: time. God blesses Moses with time to bless others, as well as time to see the Promised Land to whose border he has finally returned them.

Contemporary notions of justice have progressed significantly since the Torah, both within Rabbinic tradition and in our secular system of justice in the United States. Yet we could still stand to learn from our holy text that until convicted of a crime, most defendants should be set free.[9]

Notes

1. Babylonian Talmud, *Bava Batra* 15a.
2. Kayla James, "How the Bail Bond Industry Became a \$2 Billion Business," Global Citizen, January 31, 2019, https://www.globalcitizen.org/en/content/bail-bond-industry-2-billion-poverty/.
3. Peter Wagner, "Jails Matter: But Who Is Listening?," *Prison Policy Initiative* (blog), August 14, 2015, https://www.prisonpolicy.org/blog/2015/08/14/jailsmatter/.
4. E. Ann Carson and Mary P. Cowhig, "Mortality in State and Federal Prisons, 2001–2016—Statistical Tables," Bureau of Justice Statistics of the US Department of Justice, February 2020, https://www.bjs.gov/content/pub/pdf/msfp0116st.pdf.
5. Alysia Santo, "No Bail, Less Hope: The Death of Kalief Browder," The Marshall Project, June 9, 2015, https://www.themarshallproject.org/2015/06/09/no-bail-less-hope-the-death-of-kalief-browder.
6. Maggie Germano, "How Cash Bail Disenfranchises People of Color and Makes Our Criminal Justice System Inherently Unjust," *Forbes*, June 26, 2020, https://www.forbes.com/sites/maggiegermano/2020/06/26/how-cash-bail-disenfranchises-people-of-color-and-makes-our-criminal-justice-system-inherently-unjust/#dcdcaec3b54d.
7. Jessica Silver-Greenberg and Shaila Dewan, "When Bail Feels Less Like Freedom, More Like Extortion, *New York Times*, March 31, 2018, https://www.nytimes.com/2018/03/31/us/bail-bonds-extortion.html.
8. Ibn Ezra to Deuteronomy 33:1.
9. A clear exception to this is in the event that the person being held pending trial is found to be at risk of committing an act of violence against themself or others.

Afterword

Rabbi Jonah Dov Pesner

THE TORAH is a call to action.

The prophet Micah famously said, "It has been told to you, O human, what is good, and what the Eternal requires of you: only to do justice, love mercy, and walk humbly with your God" (Micah 6:8).

The Jewish people collectively understand what "has been told" to us as the covenantal moment at Sinai when God called and we responded. The Torah—the record of that encounter, the telling of our story, and the obligations of our people—is a blueprint for the doing of justice, the loving of mercy, and thus walking humbly with God.

This seminal new commentary to the Torah joins centuries of interpretation, from the prophets to the rabbis, who, like Micah before us, understood the essence of the Torah as a call to action.

So many biblical passages exemplify the justice imperative central to Torah. Countless are contained in this volume, so I will simply mention my favorite. The Torah repeats a version of the injunction to love the stranger because we were slaves in Egypt in thirty-six different ways. For the Torah, love is realized not as a feeling, but in deeds. Over and over, the Torah calls us to take concrete action to protect the most vulnerable—the widow, the stranger, the orphan, and the poor.

Indeed, it seems redundant to call this volume *The Social Justice Torah Commentary*, since the Torah is inherently a call to action for a just and fair society. As the early Reform rabbis stated, and Rabbi Block rightly quotes in his introduction, "In full accordance with the spirit of Mosaic legislation, [*namely Torah*,] which strives to regulate

the relations between rich and poor, we deem it our duty to participate in the great task of modern times, to solve, on the basis of justice
and righteousness, the problems presented by the contrasts and evils
of the present organization of society."[1] This Torah commentary
represents the contemporary generation of Reform Rabbis who are
following in the tradition of our founders. They understood that
Torah is in and of itself a charge to all who study the text, to all who
take the covenant seriously, to help "solve . . . the evils of the present
organization of society."

How radical and simple at the same time. As the diverse and creative commentators represented in this volume prove, the challenges
of the present day are no less urgent than those that confronted earlier generations who read the Torah text as a demand to "do justice"
in response.

What have we witnessed during the time that the authors and edi-
tors have collaborated on this commentary?

- Violent, murderous acts of hate that have targeted Jews,
  Muslims, and people of color (most often Black people)
- A racial reckoning exposing the radical inequalities in
  policing, criminal justice, health care, income, and more,
  grown out of hundreds of years of systemic racism in the
  United States and abroad
- An assault on democracy, voting rights, and democratic
  norms
- A pandemic that has not only taken the lives of millions
  and affected many more, but that has also disproportionately devastated low-income families, low-wage workers,
  Native Americans, and communities of color
- Mass shootings and gun violence disproportionately
  plaguing low-income Americans and Black and Brown
  people in the United States
- Catastrophic wildfires, weather "events," and ecological
  devastation, as humans continue to warm and poison the
  planet through emissions and pollutants

- Massive global dislocation of tens of millions of souls fleeing poverty, political violence, and climate change, who have become a mass of migrants, refugees, and today's "strangers"
- Continued assaults on truth, facts, and science, as social media and other outlets are employed to spread disinformation and fuel demagogues and autocrats
- Dangerously widening income and wealth gaps that cause enormous suffering and threaten democracy
- A failure to bring Israelis and Palestinians back to true negotiations, allowing the continued occupation to become a cancerous source of profound suffering

And, I write this afterword days after a mob of antisemitic, racist white supremacists took over the United States Capitol for four hours—sedition, enabled by the president of the United States and other elected officials. It seems the world is literally on fire.

During a convening of Reform rabbis committed to social justice, we studied a classic midrash that helped me make sense of times like these, clarifying our role as Jews. According to the Rabbinic legend, Abraham was journeying and came across a palace on fire. He asked, "Is it possible that this palace has no master?" Whereupon God comes out of the palace and says, "I am the owner."[2]

The midrash teaches that Abraham—who famously argues with God to demand protection for the innocent and justice for the people of Sodom and Gomorrah—discovers God in the burning palace, a metaphor for the world itself. Abraham's call to follow the one God comes in the context of the universe on fire and his commitment to respond. The Rabbis then say that God called Abraham the one who "loves justice and hates evil."[3]

The world is on fire, and like Abraham before us, we are called to protect the innocent and demand justice.

We can. And we must.

Reform rabbis and cantors, professionals and lay leaders, have proved time and again for more than a century that when we organize our congregations and communities, as we reach across lines of difference and build collective power with others who care about equity and justice for all, we can overcome. Like Shiphrah and Puah, the ancient Hebrew midwives who refuse to carry out Pharaoh's edict of genocide, we have proved that resistance to injustice is always possible.

When the United States government began to tear migrant families apart and place children in cages, violating the core Jewish principle of "loving the stranger," Reform Jews mobilized, protested, and helped create enough public pressure to shut down at least one detention facility, if not more.

When George Floyd was brutally murdered by law enforcement, as he cried out for his mother and begged to breathe, Reform Jews decried the injustice that disproportionately claims the lives of Black people at the hands of law enforcement, stating clearly and unequivocally that Black Lives Matter. They joined in protests across the United States, demanding criminal justice reform on a local and state level. Amid the racial reckoning, Reform Jews have increasingly centered Jews of Color and begun the hard work of addressing racism within the Jewish community itself.

When the Trump White House rolled back protections for trans students in schools, Reform Jews mobilized and demanded accountability and commitments from local school boards to protect their students.

When elected officials tried to remain in power through voter suppression, Reform Jews mobilized in a nonpartisan effort to ensure all eligible voters had access to the ballot. During the 2020 United States election, fifteen thousand Reform Jewish leaders engaged more than 875,000 voters, many in communities targeted for voter suppression, to ensure they knew their rights and that they voted. And when Georgia's Senate races went to a run-off, sixteen hundred Reform Jewish activists continued their efforts and reached 125,000 voters, who in turn elected the state's first-ever Jewish senator and first-ever Black senator.

From gun violence to reproductive rights and the campaign to address the climate crisis, Reform Jews joined with allies to demand action from local, state, and national policymakers. And where we lacked the power to influence elected officials, our leaders mobilized to offer direct support to the vulnerable people most impacted by systems of inequality and bigoted policies.

It is worthy to note that many of the contributors to this very Torah commentary were the same leaders who organized our community to rise up and act. They spoke truth to power; they engaged their communities in the work; they reached across lines of difference and created deep, enduring relationships and coalitions. Through it all, they grounded the work in enduring Jewish values. They taught biblical and rabbinic texts addressing the issues of our time and offered Jewish prayer and song to both nurture our people and agitate them to act.

What have we learned?

First, *leadership matters*. Our rabbis, cantors, and lay leaders can effectively speak truth to power. They can interpret our tradition in ways that help the Jewish people and the wider community understand the persistent Jewish concern for justice and constant call to protect the most vulnerable. Too often, our leaders are constrained by the limiting realities of fundraising, job security, and more. But when they are able to articulate the core values of our texts and meet the people where they live, they can lead them with courage and faith into struggles for the common good.

Second, *relationships matter*. Clergy who have cared for their congregants can take risks and raise their prophetic voices. Synagogues that have stood with other communities in their neighborhoods and beyond—from Black churches to Muslim mosques—find their protection when Jews are threatened. We have found safety in our solidarity. And most important, we have built broad, trusting coalitions, centering the voices of those most often marginalized in society. Through those reciprocal relationships of listening, trust, and solidarity, we have built political power to hold elected officials accountable, make systemic changes in public policy, and enhance democracy. And even as we advocate for systems and policies, we cannot neglect direct support for the most vulnerable.

One last point, perhaps the most important of all: *Torah matters.* The Rabbis taught that of all the mitzvot—all our sacred obligations—the most important is serious Jewish learning. They said, "The study of Torah is equal to them all, because it leads to them all."[4] So study. "Turn it and turn it."[5] Let every action for justice we take be rooted first and foremost in our understanding of the Torah, as refracted through millennia of interpretation, commentary, and application. This volume reflects the very best of our generation's attempt to apply enduring Jewish values to the most vexing problems confronting contemporary life. What makes us unique, what makes us compelling and powerful, is not just our ability to organize and mobilize our people to make change, though we celebrate that power. Our authenticity is grounded in the voices of those who came before us and our students who will come after us, calling upon us to fulfill our obligations as Jews, to live the covenant we made at Sinai, and to apply the Torah's teachings in our lives. Torah is the ultimate call to action for justice and mercy, those deeds in the world whose rewards are beyond measure—"For the study of Torah leads to them all."

NOTES

1. "Declaration of Principles," more commonly known as the "Pittsburgh Platform," Central Conference of American Rabbis, 1885.
2. *B'reishit Rabbah* 39:1.
3. *B'reishit Rabbah* 39:7.
4. Babylonian Talmud, *Shabbat* 127a.
5. *Pirkei Avot* 5:22.

Glossary

aggadah: A Rabbinic narrative or category of classic Jewish text that does not relate to law.

ahavah: "Love."

Akeidah: The biblical story of the Binding of Isaac (Genesis 22), which is read in the morning of the second day of Rosh HaShanah.

Am Yisrael: "The people of Israel"; Jews.

asham: The ancient "reparation" offering in the Jerusalem Temple (see, for example, Leviticus 5).

avadim: "Slaves."

Azazel: An unknown desert deity; commonly understood as the devil, to whom the scapegoat is sent in the framework of the cleansing ritual of Yom Kippur (see Leviticus 16).

bal tashchit: "Do not destroy"; "don't waste"; principle of Jewish law that forbids wastefulness (see, for example, Babylonian Talmud, *Shabbat* 67b; *Chulin* 7b; *Kiddushin* 32a).

bamakom: "In this place"; "in the same place"; "instead of."

beit din: Rabbinic court consisting of at least three rabbis.

beit midrash: "House of study."

ben soreir umoreh: "The rebellious son" (based on Deuteronomy 21:8).

bi'ah: "Sexual intercourse"; "the act of taking ownership."

bimah: Platform in the synagogue from which services are led and sacred text is chanted.

Birkat Eirusin: Betrothal blessing; first of two parts of the Jewish wedding ceremony.

B'midbar: "In the wilderness"; the Hebrew name for the Book of Numbers, which comes from a word in the first verse.

B'reishit: "In the beginning"; the Hebrew name for the Book of Genesis, which comes the first word in the book.

b'rit shalom: "Covenant of peace"; often refers to the covenant between God and Abraham (Genesis 12).

b'tzelem Elohim: "In the image of God" (Genesis 1:27); the idea that all humanity was created equally and deserves equal respect and dignity.

chai: The numerical value of eighteen; the word for "life."

chalitzah: The ritual of "taking off one's shoe"; part of the ancient ritual of freeing someone from their obligation to levirate marriage (see **levirate marriage**).

chanukiyah: Candelabra used to light the eight candles for Chanukah.

chatat: A sacrificial offering made to atone for a sin.

chazak: "Strong."

chesed: "Loving-kindness."

cheshbon hanefesh: "Self-assessment."

cheit: One of the Hebrew terms for "sin"; traditionally translated as "missing the mark."

chilul HaShem: "Profanation of God's name."

chizuk: "Strengthening."

chochmah: "Wisdom."

choshen mishpat: "Breastpiece of judgment" worn by the High Priest (based on Exodus 28:30).

D'varim: "Words"; "things"; the Hebrew name for the Book of Deuteronomy, which comes from a word in the first verse.

eid: "[Male] witness."

eidah: "Community."

emunah: "Faith, trust."

Eretz Yisrael: "The Land of Israel."

ezrach: "Citizen."

ger (pl. *gerim*): Biblical term for "stranger in your midst"; Rabbinic term for "convert."

go-eil hadam: "Blood-avenger;" the relative of a murder victim who is responsible for putting the murderer to death

(Deuteronomy 19:4–6, Joshua 20:1–6).

halachah: Jewish law, as opposed to aggadah (see **aggadah**). Halachah and aggadah make up the corpus of classic Rabbinic literature.

havlagah: "Restraint"; strategic restraint of the Israeli underground forces during the time of the British Mandate.

ir miklat: Biblical term for one of six "cities of refuge" (Numbers 35).

Kahanist: Supporter of Rabbi Meir Kahane, a right-wing American-born Israeli rabbi (1932–90).

kareit: "One cut off [from the community]"; excommunicated person.

kashrut: Jewish laws concerning food and eating, ranging from which kinds of animals can be eaten to which kinds of dishes may be used for different kinds of food.

k'dushah: "Holiness."

ketubah: "That which is written"; Jewish marriage contract.

kilkul hadin: "The degradation of the court"; causing a court to lack in care.

kishkes: Yiddish term for "gut" (for example, "I can feel it in my *kishkes*"); stuffed food item.

k'lalot (sing. *k'lalah*): "Curses."

kofer: "Heretic; unbeliever."

levirate marriage: Biblical principle according to which a widow had to be married to her deceased husband's brother (based on Deuteronomy 25:5–10).

lex talionis: Law of retaliation.

l'shem shamayim: "For the sake of heaven."

makom: "Place"; also one of the biblical names of God.

Mi Chamochah: "Who Is Like You?"; name of a liturgical section of the third blessing of the *Sh'ma*.

midrash (pl. midrashim): Rabbinic exegesis on or expansion of Torah. Midrashim are documented in Talmud as well as other rabbinic books of Jewish teachings and interpretations.

mikveh: Ritual bath.

milchemet mitzvah: "Obligatory war"; war that is commanded by the Torah.

milchemet r'shut: "Optional war" or "just war"; war that is permitted by a Jewish authority.

minchah: The ancient "meal" offering in the Jerusalem Temple (see, for example, Leviticus 2); the afternoon prayer service.

Mishkan: The Tabernacle that the Israelites built in order to worship God in the wilderness.

Mishnah: A second-century work of Jewish law, which is the basis for the majority of the Jewish legal tradition.

mitzvot (sing. mitzvah): "Commandments"; refers to the prescriptions and prohibitions in the Torah, Mishnah, and later Jewish legal works.

motzi shem ra: Halachic term for "slanderer"; "hurtful lie."

Mussar: Medieval school and body of literature of Jewish ethical practice(s).

naaseh v'nishma: "We will do and we will listen" (Exodus 24:7).

nefesh: One of three biblical words for "soul"; often translated as "life-force."

parashah (pl. *parashiyot*): Torah portion.

parshanut: Rabbinic term for "hermeneutics; biblical interpretation."

pasuk (pl. *p'sukim*): "Verse."

pei-ah: "Corner"; Rabbinic term for the law to leave a section of each field of crop to the poor to harvest (based on Leviticus 19:9 and 23:22).

Pesach Sheini: "Second Passover" for those who had to miss the exact date of Passover; observed one Hebrew month after Passover on the fourteenth of Iyar.

p'shat: The simple, literal sense of a biblical word or verse.

ruach hakodesh: "The spirit of the Eternal;" one of the biblical names for God.

sar hamashkim: "Butler; minister of the markets"; one of the two ministers imprisoned with Joseph (Genesis 40).

s'gulah: "Chosenness"; often used in the constructed term *am s'gulah*, "the chosen people."

shaleim: "Whole, complete."

shalom: "Peace"; "wholeness, completeness"; hello."

Shechinah: "Dwelling"; the female name and aspect of God, associated with exile, as this is the aspect of God that dwells with the Israelite people also outside the Land of Israel; the lowest of the ten *s'firot*, the mystical layers of God's emanation, also called *Malchut* (kingdom).

shekel: Name both of a biblical and a modern Israeli coin.

Sheva B'rachot: The "Seven Blessings" recited as part of the Jewish wedding ceremony.

shirah: "Song"; "singing"; "poetry."

Shirat HaYam: "The Song at the Sea," the biblical poem in Exodus 15:1–18; part of the traditional morning liturgy.

Sh'mot: "Names"; the Hebrew name for the Book of Exodus, which comes from a word in the first verse.

shof'tim (**sing.** *shofet*): "Judges."

shoresh: "Root"; grammatical term used for the three letters making up the basis of most Hebrew words.

sh'tar: "Document," e.g. a bill of divorce.

sidrah: (Aram.) Torah portion.

Sifrei: Collections of Rabbinic interpretations and laws of the Books of Numbers and Deuteronomy.

sinah: "Hatred."

sipurim (**sing.** *sipur*): "Stories."

sof: "End."

sotah: "Whore"; "adulteress"; Rabbinic term for the ritual attempting to determine the infidelity of a wife (based on Numbers 5:11–31).

Tabor: The name of a mountain in Israel, close to the Sea of Galilee, mentioned in the biblical books of Joshua and Judges.

tagim: Decorative elements of the letters in handwritten biblical words and verses.

tahorah: "Purification, cleaning, cleansing"; Rabbinic term for the ritual of washing a Jewish corpse before burial.

Talmud: A work of Jewish law from late antiquity based on Rabbinic discussions of the behaviors prescribed and prohibited in the Mishnah, a compendium of Jewish law compiled in the second century. The Babylonian Talmud has for centuries been the core legal source of Rabbinic Judaism.

tamei: "Unclean"; "full"; "mixed-up"; the opposite of *tahor* ("pure"; "empty"; "dry").

Tanach: The Jewish canonical Bible, comprising Torah (lit. "Law," the Five Books of Moses), *N'vi-im* (Prophets), and *K'tuvim* (Writings).

tikkun olam: "Repairing the world"; often refers to the Jewish call to social justice. In traditionally Orthodox spaces, *tikkun olam* refers to Jews doing mitzvot to bring about the Messiah and the messianic redemption; in liberal Jewish spaces, *tikkun olam* can mean anything from social action to the performance of mitzvot.

Tishah B'Av: "The Ninth of Av"; Jewish fast day in the summer commemorating the destruction of both Temples in Jerusalem and a number of other historical catastrophes.

tocheichah: "Rebuke."

tohar haneshek: "The purity of arms"; value part of the code of ethics of the IDF.

Torah: "Teaching"; refers to the first five books of the Hebrew Bible (Genesis, Exodus, Leviticus, Numbers, Deuteronomy), also called the Five Books of Moses; depending on context, may refer to the larger compilation of text, the full Hebrew Bible, or a Jewish teaching in general.

T'ruah (organization): A rabbinic organization that advocates for human rights (see www.truah.org).

t'rumah: The ancient "gift" offering in the ancient *Mishkan* and Jerusalem Temple (see Exodus 25:2–3, 29:27; and Numbers 15:18–19).

tzara'at: Biblical skin disease, Rabbinically interpreted as the result of unethical behavior (based on Leviticus 13–14).

tzedakah: "Charity"; comes from the Hebrew root for "justice."

tzedek: "Justice."

t'shuvah: "Repentance" or "return"; one of the guiding themes of the High Holy Days.

t'shuvah g'murah: "Full and lasting repentance"; a term coined by Maimonides (twelfth century) in his *Mishneh Torah, Hilchot T'shuvah.*

Vayikra: "And God called"; the Hebrew name for the Book of Leviticus, which comes from the first word in the book.

v'chai bahem: "And live by them"; Rabbinic term for "sustainability" (Leviticus 18:5)—God's laws should support life and livability and not bring death.

v'nahafoch hu: Rabbinic principle for the festival of Purim, advocating to "turn the world upside down" (dress up, get drunk, reverse social hierarchies, etc.), from Esther 9:1.

v'nitchazeik: Form of the Hebrew word *chazak*, "we will strengthen [each other]."

yetzer hara: The evil inclination.

yetzer hatov: The inclination to do good.

yirat HaShem: "The fear/love of God"; Rabbinic theological concept for the human relationship to the Divine.

zachar un'keivah: Hebrew terms for "male and female," often used in the context of the story of Creation: "male and female God created them" (Genesis 1:28).

zayde: Yiddish term for "grandfather."

Zohar: Kabbalistic interpretation of the Torah, academically dated back to the thirteenth century, Spain; tradition dates its authorship back to Rabbi Shimon bar Yochai (first century, Israel).

Contributors

Rabbi Thomas M. Alpert is the rabbi at Temple Etz Chaim in Franklin, Massachusetts. In addition to his rabbinic ordination from Hebrew Union College–Jewish Institute of Religion, he holds a master's degree in American history from Harvard University and a law degree from Harvard Law School.

Rabbi Erica Seager Asch is the rabbi of Temple Beth El in Augusta, Maine, and the assistant director of the Center for Small Town Jewish Life. She serves on the Commission on Social Action of Reform Judaism and is the president elect of the Central Conference of American Rabbis.

Rabbi Ethan Bair grew up in the Jewish Renewal movement in Boston and was ordained by Hebrew Union College–Jewish Institute of Religion, Los Angeles, in 2011. He served in congregations for eight years and is now college rabbi and Hillel director at Hamilton College in Clinton, New York.

Rabbi Jeremy Barras currently serves as the senior rabbi of Temple Beth Am in Miami, Florida, and is a member of the CCAR Board of Directors.

Rabbi Deana Sussman Berezin, MAJE, is the associate rabbi of Temple Israel in Omaha, Nebraska. Prior to her arrival in Omaha, she served as the rabbi educator at Central Reform Congregation in St. Louis, Missouri. She was ordained by Hebrew Union College–Jewish Institute of Religion in Los Angeles in 2014 and received her master's in Jewish education from the Rhea Hirsch School of Education in 2012.

Rabbi Barry H. Block serves Congregation B'nai Israel in Little Rock, Arkansas. A Houston native and graduate of Amherst College, Rabbi Block was ordained by Hebrew Union College–Jewish Institute of Religion in New York in 1991, and he received his DD, *honoris causa*, in 2016. A member of the CCAR Board of Trustees, currently serving as vice president of organizational relationships, Block is the editor of *The Mussar Torah Commentary* (CCAR Press, 2020), a finalist for the National Jewish Book Award. He also contributed to several earlier CCAR anthologies, including *Inscribed: Encounters with the Ten Commandments, The Sacred Exchange, The Sacred Encounter, Navigating the Journey,* and *A Life of Meaning: Embracing Reform Judaism's Sacred Path,* and he is a regular contributor to the *CCAR Journal.* Rabbi Block currently serves as faculty dean at URJ Henry S. Jacobs Camp, similar to a role he previously held for twenty-one years at URJ Greene Family Camp. He is a past board chair of Planned Parenthood of South Texas. He is the proud father of Robert and Daniel.

Imani Romney-Rosa Chapman, founder of imani strategies, LLC, has more than twenty-five years of experience developing curriculum, organizing, and educating for social justice. She works for an equitable world in which her children and the young people in your lives can live wholly and safely into their full humanity and where race is not a major determinant in health, wealth, legal, and educational outcomes.

Rabbi Ken Chasen is the senior rabbi of Leo Baeck Temple in Los Angeles, California. He is a leading activist and prolific author on a wide variety of social justice matters in the United States and Israel, with writings appearing in numerous books and print and digital media publications. In addition, he is a nationally recognized composer, whose original liturgical and educational works are regularly heard in synagogues, religious schools, Jewish camps, and sanctuaries across North America, Israel, and Europe.

Rabbi Mari Chernow is senior rabbi at Temple Israel of Hollywood, a synagogue with a long history of prioritizing social justice as a primary message of the Torah. She loves hiking, skiing, and above all, spending time with her ridiculous and perfect children.

Rabbi Shoshanah Conover is the senior rabbi of Temple Sholom of Chicago. Her poems and essays have been published in numerous CCAR Press collections, including *A Life of Meaning: Embracing Reform Judaism's Sacred Path*; *Seven Days, Many Voices: Insights into the Biblical Story of Creation*; and *Moral Resistance and Spiritual Authority*.

Rabbi Denise L. Eger is the founding rabbi of Congregation Kol Ami in West Hollywood, California, and a past president of the CCAR. A longtime social justice advocate for women's rights and LGBTQ rights, she is the editor of *Mishkan Ga'avah: Where Pride Dwells* (CCAR Press, 2020).

Rabbi Marla J. Feldman is the executive director of Women of Reform Judaism and former director of the Commission on Social Action of Reform Judaism. She co-leads the Reform Pay Equity Initiative and was the co-guest editor of the *CCAR Journal* symposium on pay equity.

Rabbi Joshua R. S. Fixler serves as the associate rabbi at Congregation Emanu El in Houston, Texas. He is a member of the steering committee for the Texas Religious Action Center of Reform Judaism (RAC-TX).

Kristine Henriksen Garroway, PhD, was appointed the visiting assistant professor of Hebrew Bible at the Los Angeles campus of Hebrew Union College–Jewish Institute of Religion in 2011. She is the author of numerous articles and books, including *Children in the Ancient Near East*, *Growing Up in Ancient Israel*, and coauthor with John Martens of *Children and Methods*.

Rabbi Rachel Greengrass, MAHL, MARE, RJE, is a rabbi of Temple Beth Am in Pinecrest, Florida. Rabbi Greengrass serves as chair of the CCAR Resolutions Committee and is a RAC Balfour-Brickner Fellow, a Clal Rabbis Without Borders Fellow, a Hartman Rabbinic

Fellow, and a member of the fifth cohort of the Clergy Leadership Incubator for Clal. She was honored in 2021 with T'ruah's Rabbinic Human Rights Hero Award, largely for her work as a founding member of RAC-Florida. Rabbi Greengrass is currently president of the Rabbinical Association of Greater Miami.

Chris Harrison is a marketing and communications professional and a former writer/editor at the Union for Reform Judaism (URJ). A two-time "36 Under 36" award recipient, Chris has been featured in *None Shall Make Them Afraid: A Rabbis Against Gun Violence Anthology* and online publications such as ReformJudaism.org, the URJ's *Inside Leadership* blog, and eJewish Philanthropy.

Rabbi Liz P. G. Hirsch serves Temple Anshe Amunim in Pittsfield, Massachusetts. She has been published in the *Boston Globe* and the *CCAR Journal* and is a contributor to the CCAR Press commentary *Prophetic Voices: Renewing and Reimagining Haftarah.*

Rabbi Jill Jacobs is the CEO of T'ruah: The Rabbinic Call for Human Rights, which trains and mobilizes its more than two thousand rabbi and cantor members to bring a moral voice to human rights in North America, Israel, and the occupied Palestinian territories. She is the author of *Where Justice Dwells: A Hands-On Guide to Doing Social Justice in Your Jewish Community* and *There Shall Be No Needy: Pursuing Social Justice through Jewish Law and Tradition.*

Rabbi Rachel Kahn-Troster is the executive vice president of the Interfaith Center on Corporate Responsibility, working with faith- and values-based investors to catalyze their assets to make a difference for both people and planet. She previously served as the deputy director of T'ruah: The Rabbinic Call for Human Rights, where she was the lead strategist on T'ruah's human rights campaigns and headed the organizing and training of more than two thousand rabbis and cantors.

Rabbi Noam Katz, MAJE, is the dean of Jewish living at the Leo Baeck Day School in Toronto, Canada. In addition to his work in progressive Jewish education and worship, Rabbi Katz is a touring musician and composer of original Jewish music, whose melodies are sung around the world and have been published in the *Noam Katz Anthology* (Transcontinental Music Publications). His website is noamkatz.com.

Ilana Kaufman, executive director of the Jews of Color Initiative, is an educator and social scientist by training who previously worked with the Jewish Community Relations Council. Pairing her passion for social justice, Jewish community, and racial justice with her philanthropy know-how, she has transformed the Jewish ecosystem by centering the voices and leadership of Jews of Color.

Rabbi Naamah Kelman was born and raised in New York City and moved to Israel in 1976. She became the first woman ordained in Israel when she completed Hebrew Union College–Jewish Institute of Religion's Israel Rabbinical Program in 1992. She currently serves there as dean.

Rabbi Sharon Kleinbaum serves as spiritual leader of Congregation Beit Simchat Torah in New York City. She was installed as CBST's first rabbi in 1992, arriving at the height of the AIDS crisis, when the synagogue was in desperate need of pastoral care and spiritual leadership. She guided the congregation through a period of loss and change, while addressing social issues of the day and building a strong and deeply spiritual community.

Rabbi Asher Gottesfeld Knight is the senior rabbi of Temple Beth El in Charlotte, North Carolina, and serves as the vice chair of the Commission on Social Action of Reform Judaism and chair of the CCAR's Committee on Peace, Justice and Civil Liberties. He was formerly board chair of the Human Rights Initiative and has held several leadership positions with the CCAR.

Rabbi Emily Langowitz currently serves as program manager for Jewish learning and engagement at the Union for Reform Judaism. She was ordained by Hebrew Union College–Jewish Institute of Religion in 2017, and her rabbinic thesis "In Our Bodies to Do It: A Feminist Theology of Reproductive Choice" informs her contribution to this book.

Rabbi Sandra Lawson serves as the inaugural director of racial diversity and inclusion for Reconstructing Judaism. She works with senior staff, lay leaders, clergy, rabbinical students, and Reconstructionist communities to help Reconstructing Judaism realize its deeply held aspiration of becoming an anti-racist organization and movement.

Rabbi Esther L. Lederman is the director of congregational innovation at the Union for Reform Judaism. She received her rabbinic ordination from Hebrew Union College–Jewish Institute of Religion in 2008.

Rabbi Craig Lewis serves the historic Mizpah Congregation in Chattanooga, Tennessee. Before receiving ordination from Hebrew Union College–Jewish Institute of Religion in Cincinnati, he studied at the University of Kansas and at L'École Supérieure de Commerce in Clermont-Ferrand, France.

Rabbi Seth M. Limmer, DHL, serves as senior rabbi of Chicago Sinai Congregation. He has served as chair of the CCAR's Committee on Justice, Peace and Civil Liberties, vice chair of the Commission on Social Action of Reform Judaism, dean of faculty for Eisner and Crane Lake Camps, and adjunct professor at Hebrew Union College–Jewish Institute of Religion; he currently serves as the CCAR vice president of leadership.

Rabbi Ellen Lippmann is rabbi emerita at Kolot Chayeinu/Voices of Our Lives, the progressive Jewish congregation in Brooklyn she and others founded in 1993. She serves on the boards of Jews for Racial and Economic Justice and IntegrateNYC, and she mentors rabbis and social justice activists.

Rabbi Andrea C. London is the senior rabbi of Beth Emet The Free Synagogue in Evanston, Illinois. She is engaged in social justice causes, including racial justice, reparations, Palestinian rights, and the Poor People's Campaign.

Rabbi Rachel Grant Meyer is a social justice advocate, community organizer, rabbi, and educator, who hopes to help all Jews—particularly those on the margins—live their most authentic life using Judaism as a guide. A graduate of Columbia University, Rabbi Meyer was ordained by Hebrew Union College–Jewish Institute of Religion in New York City and currently lives and works in Brooklyn.

Rabbi Joel Mosbacher, DMin, serves as the senior rabbi of Temple Shaaray Tefila in New York City. He serves on the strategy team of the Metro Industrial Areas Foundation (Metro IAF) and is a national co-chair of Metro IAF's campaign to reduce gun violence, entitled Do Not Stand Idly By. He is also a contributor to CCAR publications such as *The Sacred Table*, *The Sacred Exchange*, and *Moral Resistance and Spiritual Authority*.

Rabbi Mike Moskowitz is the scholar-in-residence for Trans and Queer Jewish Studies at Congregation Beit Simchat Torah, the world's largest LGBT synagogue. He is a David Hartman Center Fellow and the author of *Textual Activism*; his writings can be found at rabbimikemoskowitz.com.

Rabbi Ariel Naveh is a rabbi, educator, and organizer in the New York area. This is his first contribution to a book that has not been spiral bound and sent home in his backpack for the sole readership of his parents and grandparents.

Rabbi Jonah Dov Pesner is the director of the Religious Action Center of Reform Judaism and the senior vice president of the Union for Reform Judaism. Called one of the most influential rabbis in America, Rabbi Pesner has devoted his career to building interfaith and multiracial coalitions in successful campaigns for civil rights and social justice.

Maharat Rori Picker Neiss serves as the executive director of the Jewish Community Relations Council of St. Louis. She is one of the first graduates of Yeshivat Maharat, a pioneering institution training Orthodox Jewish women to be spiritual leaders and halachic (Jewish legal) authorities.

Rabbi Ruti Regan is an associate at the Harvard Law School Project on disability, where she researches Jewish ritual innovation. She is a practical and theoretical educator on disability issues and works with individuals and communities to build capacity to embody inclusive values.

Rabbi Mackenzie Zev Reynolds is a palliative care chaplain at the Hertzberg Palliative Care Institute at the Icahn School of Medicine at Mount Sinai in New York City. His writing appears in *Mishkan Ga'avah: Where Pride Dwells* (CCAR Press, 2020); *Evolve: Groundbreaking Jewish Conversations*; and *Trans Bodies, Trans Selves: A Resource for the Transgender Community*. Rabbi Reynolds was ordained at the Reconstructionist Rabbinical College and holds an MA in philosophy of religion from Union Theological Seminary.

Rabbi Jeffrey K. Salkin serves as the interim rabbi at Temple Israel in West Palm Beach, Florida. He is a noted author of ten books, and his award-winning column for Religion News Service, "Martini Judaism: For those who want to be shaken and stirred," appears regularly at religionnews.com.

Rabbi Noa Sattath is the director of the Israel Religious Action Center, the social justice arm of the Reform Movement in Israel, and a member of Kehilat Kol HaNeshama in Jerusalem.

Rabbi Julie Saxe-Taller, ordained by Hebrew Union College–Jewish Institute of Religion in New York in 2004, served as a rabbi of Congregation Sherith Israel in San Francisco, California, from 2004 to 2017. She is now the lead organizer for RAC-California, the Religious Action Center's network of Reform congregations working together to implement Jewish values through advocacy and community organizing.

Rabbi Judith Schindler is the Sklut Professor of Jewish Studies and director of the Stan Greenspon Center for Peace and Social Justice at Queens University of Charlotte and rabbi emerita of Temple Beth El in Charlotte, North Carolina. She coauthored *Recharging Judaism: How Civic Engagement Is Good for Synagogues, Jews, and America* (CCAR Press, 2018) and was a consulting editor for *Deepening the Dialogue: Jewish-Americans and Israelis Envisioning the Jewish-Democratic State* (CCAR Press, 2019).

Rabbi David Segal is a member of the *CCAR Journal* Editorial Board and, starting in the fall of 2021, a law student at the University of Houston Law Center. From 2017 to 2021, he was the Texas lead organizer of the Religious Action Center of Reform Judaism (RAC-TX), where he worked with Reform Jews across Texas to pursue justice in multi-faith and multiracial coalitions at the local and state level.

Rabbi David Spinrad lives with his family and is the senior rabbi at Beth El Hebrew Congregation in Alexandria, Virginia, thus fulfilling a dream of serving as a rabbi, being parent in his children's schools, and contributing as a citizen in the city in which he lives. In his free time, Rabbi Spinrad collects sports trading cards. He shares his collection and their stories on Instagram: @ratedrabbi.

Rabbi Samuel M. Stahl is the rabbi emeritus of Temple Beth-El, San Antonio, Texas, where he served as senior rabbi for twenty-six years. He is the author of *Making the Timeless Timely* and *Boundaries, Not Barriers*, as well as numerous articles.

Rabbi Joshua Stanton is spiritual co-leader of East End Temple and senior fellow at Clal—The National Jewish Center for Learning and Leadership.

Rabbi Ronald Stern directs the Center for Tikkun Olam at Stephen Wise Temple and leads temple efforts to establish *tikkun olam* as a central spiritual practice and mode of engagement for the community. Allied with major social justice organizations in the city, state, and country, Wise, under Rabbi Stern's leadership, is determined to be a force for good in our world.

Rabbi A. Brian Stoller is the senior rabbi of Temple Israel in Omaha, Nebraska. He is a member of the editorial board of the *CCAR Journal: The Reform Jewish Quarterly* and a doctoral candidate in Jewish law at Hebrew Union College–Jewish Institute of Religion.

Rabbi Susan Talve is the founding rabbi of Central Reform Congregation in the City of St. Louis, Missouri. She and her husband, Rabbi James Stone Goodman, are the proud parents of three adult children and two grandchildren. Everything they do today is to honor the life of their beloved youngest daughter, Adina, who continues to teach them in death as she did every day in life.

Evan Traylor is a rabbinical student at Hebrew Union College–Jewish Institute of Religion, where he is a Wexner Graduate Fellow and a Ko'ach Fellow.

Rabbi Lauren Tuchman, ordained by the Jewish Theological Seminary in 2018, is a Maryland-based Jewish educator and consultant. She teaches Jewish contemplative practice and speaks widely on the need for Jewish communities to become maximally inclusive and open to individuals living with disability and chronic illness.

Cantor Seth Warner was ordained by the Debbie Friedman School of Sacred Music at Hebrew Union College–Jewish Institute of Religion. He proudly serves as cantor for Congregation Shaare Emeth in St. Louis, Missouri, and as vice president of the American Conference of Cantors.

Rabbi Andrea L. Weiss, PhD, is Jack, Joseph and Morton Mandel Provost and associate professor of Bible at the Hebrew Union College–Jewish Institute of Religion. She organized the 2017 and 2021 "American Values, Religious Voices" campaigns and coedited *American Values, Religious Voices: 100 Days, 100 Letters*. She served as the associate editor of *The Torah: A Women's Commentary* (CCAR Press, 2008), is the author of *Figurative Language in Biblical Prose Narrative: Metaphor in the Book of Samuel*, and has written many articles on metaphor, biblical poetry, and biblical conceptions of God.

Ruhama Weiss, PhD, lives in Jerusalem and is a writer and poet. She is associate professor of Talmud and spiritual care at Hebrew Union College–Jewish Institute of Religion in Jerusalem.

Rabbi Josh Whinston has served congregations in Washington, California, and Connecticut and is currently the rabbi at Temple Beth Emeth in Ann Arbor, Michigan.

Rabbi Dr. Shmuly Yanklowitz is president and dean of the Valley Beit Midrash, a national Jewish pluralistic adult learning and leadership center; founder and president of Uri L'Tzedek, a Jewish social justice organization; founder and CEO of Shamayim, a Jewish animal advocacy movement; founder and president of YATOM, the Jewish foster and adoption network; and the author of twenty-one books on Jewish ethics. *Newsweek* named Rav Shmuly one of the top fifty rabbis in America, and the *Forward* named him one of the fifty most influential Jews.

Rabbi Marina Yergin is the associate rabbi at Temple Beth-El in San Antonio, Texas, where she has been serving since ordination from Hebrew Union College–Jewish Institute of Religion in Cincinnati in 2015. She never saw herself as a "social justice rabbi" and is enjoying learning about community organizing, balancing the views from every side of justice issues, and connecting Jewish values and texts to all of it.

Rabbi Mary L. Zamore is the executive director of the Women's Rabbinic Network, which works to narrow the wage gap, create safer, respectful Jewish communities, and promote equity for all. She is the editor of *The Sacred Exchange: Creating a Jewish Money Ethic* (CCAR Press, 2019) and *The Sacred Table: Creating a Jewish Food Ethic* (CCAR Press, 2011), designated a finalist by the National Jewish Book Awards.

Rabbi Reuben Zellman is a rabbi, music educator, and professional countertenor, who lives in San Francisco with his family. He is fortunate to teach and sing at many of the city's great homes for music and Jewish culture, and he speaks and writes about the intersection of transgender experience and Judaism.